D1360966

About This Book

Why is this topic important?

Improving organizational effectiveness requires modifying heads *and* hearts. People change only because a profoundly joyful, tragic, or otherwise emotional experience has encouraged them to see themselves in a new light. eLearning needs to become as potent as the other emotionally rich media people seek out in their free time if it is to bring about long-term, profound change. *Renaissance eLearning* looks at how popular culture narratives—movies, books, television, music, theater, and so on—can be emulated to make a more satisfying and effective learning experience that will add to an organization's bottom line in the long run.

What can you achieve with this book?

Renaissance eLearning is one type of learning system design (LSD) for the learning and training world. Every element of this book—from the text to the interviews to the quotes to the graphic design—is intended to encourage conceptual blending, to encourage you to expand your mind in a way that both stretches beyond the ordinary and realizes new connections between concepts that previously seemed unrelated. Sure, along the way you'll pick up some practical stuff about how to use narrative to make eLearning more effective and emotionally compelling. But, hopefully, you'll come away with something much more valuable, although you may not realize it for many years hence. You'll come away with a new voice speaking in your head—one that will pop up at unexpected moments, giving you the courage and reassurance to know that a crazy new idea or stupid question may actually be far more important than any "serious" thought or already established concept.

How is this book organized?

To get the most value from this book, envision it as a catalogue. There are lots and lots of individual ideas. Some you will "buy" in their entirety. Others you will dismiss and wonder how on earth anyone could buy them. Some you will replicate step by step. Others will be sources of inspiration—springboards providing a frame on which to hang your own unique ideas and implementations.

Because we see this book as a collection of ideas, we have designed it to be useful to all types of people:

Those who want to absorb all we have to say can read it in linear order.

Those who just want to cut to the chase should use the visual table of contents to find topics of interest as entry points.

Those who are into the whole theoretical thing should start with Chapters One, Two, and Three.

Those who really wanted to be a director should start with Part Two.

Those who think our ideas are completely unfeasible should start with Part Three.

And those who are just looking for something to read while eating breakfast can just randomly open to any page.

About Pfeiffer

Pfeiffer serves the professional development and hands-on resource needs of training and human resource practitioners and gives them products to do their jobs better. We deliver proven ideas and solutions from experts in HR development and HR management, and we offer effective and customizable tools to improve workplace performance. From novice to seasoned professional, Pfeiffer is the source you can trust to make yourself and your organization more successful.

Essential Knowledge Pfeiffer produces insightful, practical, and comprehensive materials on topics that matter the most to training and HR professionals. Our Essential Knowledge resources translate the expertise of seasoned professionals into practical, how-to guidance on critical workplace issues and problems. These resources are supported by case studies, worksheets, and job aids and are frequently supplemented with CD-ROMs, Web sites, and other means of making the content easier to read, understand, and use.

Essential Tools Pfeiffer's Essential Tools resources save time and expense by offering proven, ready-to-use materials—including exercises, activities, games, instruments, and assessments—for use during a training or team-learning event. These resources are frequently offered in looseleaf or CD-ROM format to facilitate copying and customization of the material.

Pfeiffer also recognizes the remarkable power of new technologies in expanding the reach and effectiveness of training. While e-hype has often created whizbang solutions in search of a problem, we are dedicated to bringing convenience and enhancements to proven training solutions. All our e-tools comply with rigorous functionality standards. The most appropriate technology wrapped around essential content yields the perfect solution for today's on-the-go trainers and human resource professionals.

www.pfeiffer.com

Essential resources for training and HR professionals

RENAISSANCE eLEARNING
Creating Dramatic and Unconventional Learning Experiences

Samantha Chapnick and Jimm Meloy

Pfeiffer
A Wiley Imprint
www.pfeiffer.com

Published by Pfeiffer
An Imprint of Wiley
989 Market Street, San Francisco, CA 94103-1741
www.pfeiffer.com

Readers should be aware that Internet Web sites offered as citations and/or sources for further information may have changed or disappeared between the time this was written and when it is read.

For additional copies/bulk purchases of this book in the U.S. please contact 800-274-4434.

Pfeiffer books and products are available through most bookstores. To contact Pfeiffer directly call our Customer Care Department within the U.S. at 800-274-4434, outside the U.S. at 317-572-3985, fax 317-572-4002, or visit www.pfeiffer.com.

Pfeiffer also publishes its books in a variety of electronic formats. Some content that appears in print may not be available in electronic books.

ISBN: 0-7879-7147-2

All the screenshots in *Renaissance eLearning* were used through the generosity of their respective copyright owners. We thank them: BrainPOP, LLC; eCornel; Enspire Learning, Inc.; Junction-18; Kodak; Yuri Makino, University of Arizona; www.online-learning.com; PiCircle, Inc.; QCA Enterprises Limited; Real Creative Learning; Root Learning; *The Sacramento Bee*; Trilogia; Thompson NetG; PBS; and *Web Style Guide*

Library of Congress Cataloging-in-Publication Data

Chapnick, Samantha
    Renaissance elearning : creating dramatic and unconventional learning experiences / Samantha Chapnick and Jimm Meloy.
        p. cm.
    Includes bibliographical references and index.
    ISBN 0-7879-7147-2 (alk. paper)
    1. Employees—Training of—Computer-assisted instruction. 2. Internet in education. 3. Instructional systems—Design. I. Meloy, Jimm II. Title.
    HF5549.5.T7C537 2005
    658.3'124'0285—dc22   2004014358

Acquiring Editor: Lisa Shannon
Director of Development: Kathleen Dolan Davies
Production Editor: Nina Kreiden
Editor: Elspeth MacHattie
Manufacturing Supervisor: Bill Matherly
Editorial Assistant: Laura Reizman
Interior Design: Yvo Riezebos Design
Illustrations: Sussana Johanssan

Printed in the United States of America

Printing   10   9   8   7   6   5   4   3   2   1

TO SIERRA

*If no one out there
understands, you start your
own revolution and cut out
the middle man.*
—BILLY BRAGG

CONTENTS

ACKNOWLEDGMENTS

TRYING TO WRITE a book while nursing an infant, a marriage, a start-up business, and an elderly dog; renovating an apartment; moving cross country; and attempting to keep some semblance of sanity and health can be a challenge. This simply would not be in your hands right now were it not for the myriad of people who touched our lives in both small and profound ways.

Mom, Dad, and Marianne, thanks for the food, shelter, and clothing—but mostly for the bottomless cup of respect, admiration, and encouragement you give us. Maureen, David, DJ, and the rest of the Cluckie clan, our lives are richer with you in it. Alex, Claire, and Veronica, thanks for being there at a moment's notice and giving Sierra as much love and attention as we do ourselves—sometimes even more! Without you we would not have had the peace of mind to sit and write. But mostly thank you for being who you are: you prove that trustworthy, caring, and loving child-care providers are truly the most important and wonderful people in the world.

Thanks to Hope, Fillip, Jan, Thule, Ema, and Nestle for being the kind of friends and adopted family you can drop in on at any time. To our dear friends and eLearning colleagues Leni Silberman and Lew Jamison for saying all the right things at the right moments. To Roxi Spiegel, the consummate screenplay writer, without whose perspective and conversation many of the ideas in this book would have remained beyond our scope and reach. To April Sutherland, who infuses color in every gray moment; John Elvidge and Maureen McGinn, Jeanne Freeman and Susan Stewart, who constantly open our eyes to new possibilities. To Captain Stan, Sandee, Ruffin, Jeff F.,

Jan, Scott (Foss), the Johns (F. and I.), Kendall, Meryl, and Steve S. for being there. And to Sheila and Dana—the coffee was great!

To our mentors: Mr. Castleman, who first opened Samantha's eyes to metaphor and show don't tell; Louis Joylon West, one of those rare people who goes far out on a limb for others without expecting anything in return; Marc Mishkind, Trudy Kehret Ward, Regina Touhey, Lew Jameson, and others who saw talents and gifts within us that we didn't know existed and then nurtured them; and Joe Vose, Diego Zuchetti, Sally Jo Schreivogel, and Paul Schreivogel.

To all the great creative people who threw open the doors to their organizations and gave generously of their time: Sol Adler and Cathy Marto, who fearless and tirelessly lead the 92nd Street Y; Daniel Bernardi, Tom Crawford, and Jim Haudan of Root Learning; Yves Saada of BrainPOP; Doug Talbott of Online-learning.com; Yvonne Brown, Frank Pignatelli, and Kirk Ramsey of learndirect scotland; Eilif Trondsen of SRIC; and everyone else who makes imaginative outstanding eLearning.

To the Scottish people who have unquestionably the most creative minds we have run into in a long time: the Lighthouse's Stuart Macdonald (the embodiment of "leap and the net will appear") and Dawne McGehy (the flame behind the fire and the spark for this project); Wendy Alexander, who dared to make a reality what others couldn't even see; Junction-18's stars; the people at Scottish enterprise: Jonathan and Charlie Watt; the always irreverent Kevin O'Doyle; and Susan Stewart.

To work colleagues and friends Vijay Patel, Peter Ostowski, Marcia Conner, Alex Gray, Eilif Trondsen, Jane Massey, Steve Inch, Rich Wagner, and Pat Kane.

A special thank you to the editor who took a great chance on this project, Lisa Shannon. To editors Leslie Stephen and Nina Kreiden and to the director of development who eagerly coaxed it beyond the boundaries, Kathleen Dolan Davies. To Sussana Johanssan for her great and tireless illustration work.

We owe a pint to each of you: Stuart MacDonald (the other one), Laura Chant, Frank Pignatelli, Yvonne Brown, Laurie O'Donnell, Daniel Bernardi, Stuart Macdonald (Lighthouse), PBS, La Leche League, and people who have the courage to do what we don't: Michael Moore, Ralph Nader, and Kate Turlington.

Fuzz, you were our guardian angel for thirteen and a half years. There never lived a more constant, true, faithful, loving, happy, intelligent, creative, kind, gentle, and generous soul. We know wherever you have gone you are running around with your tail circling wildly, bringing boundless love and joy to those around you. We love you and only wish we could have another thirteen and a half years together with you.

Chvatsky—this book was written much the way my life has been lived. I derived enthusiasm, perseverance, and wisdom by anticipating the pride lighting up your face when at last the bound, signed copy would be unwrapped on your birthday. "Good work, L.J.!" you'd beam. How am I to muster the stamina to win the rest of life's races without knowing you'll be ready with a huge hug at the finish line? For all you've ever done, and all you've been to me, I offer up this tribute, my twenty-one gun salute.

Samantha Chapnick
Jimm Meloy
www.itours.org/renaissanceelearning.htm

MEET OUR CASE STUDIES AND INTERVIEWEES

THE BEST WAY to get to know our case study organizations is to visit their Web sites and see their actual work. Actions speak far louder than words. For people who don't have immediate Web access, we have included the summary descriptions the organizations themselves use to explain who they are.

We selected these case studies from a pool of over 400 organizations, large and small, public and private. The two requirements were that the organization had to create eLearning and the eLearning (at a minimum, demos of the real programs) had to be publicly accessible to all our readers. We want to make sure you can quickly and easily come to your own conclusions about the eLearning's quality or lack thereof.

Beyond these requirements, we picked organizations that best demonstrated the following:

- Uniqueness
- Creativity
- eLearning program efficacy
- Impact and evidence of results
- Use of drama, narrative, and storytelling
- Obscurity

In order to avoid inaccurately representing the organizations, we decided to let their words speak for themselves. Most of the following descriptions are taken directly from the organizations' Web sites.

92nd Street YM/WHA
http://www.92ndsty.org
Interview with Sol Adler page 191

The 92nd Street Y is about people. The people of New York City and the surrounding area. The people of the United States and of the world. It's about people who entertain and challenge, inform and educate. It's about people who learn and discover, observe and participate.

The 92nd Street Y operates in the context of a history that spans over 130 years. Founded in 1874 as the Young Men's Hebrew Association where Jewish men could find harmony and good fellowship, the 92nd Street Y today has evolved into a world-renowned community and cultural center, an organization of exhilarating vitality and remarkable diversity, a proudly Jewish institution that reaches out to people of every race, ethnicity, religion, age and economic class.

At once a lecture hall, a performance space, a school, a health center and a community organization, the Y remains focused on its mission of enriching the lives of the people who pass through its doors—women and men, young families and senior citizens, accomplished artists and aspiring beginners, master instructors and enthusiastic students, world leaders and concerned citizens.

Real Glasgow
http://www.intoreal.com

Real is a brand name for learning in Glasgow. It covers a wide variety of online learning activities, ranging from short fun bites of learning to accredited full-time courses.

Real makes it extremely easy for everyone to access high quality learning. A network of Real Learning Centres has been set up throughout the city, in libraries, businesses, universities, and colleges. These provide support, information, and a huge range of learning resources. Real helps you to achieve anything you want.

Junction-18
http://www.junction-18.com

Junction-18 is an interactive digital solutions provider with extensive experience of online and offline learning and application development. Utilizing the latest technologies, Junction-18 has excelled in the areas of eLearning, interactive 3D, multimedia, and business-focus applications.

Enspire Learning
http://www.enspire.com/index.html

Enspire Learning develops eLearning courses that motivate learners with interactive multimedia, simulations, and engaging scenarios. Our scenario-based courses are relevant, immersive, and fun—driving real business results.

learndirect scotland
http://www.lds4partners.com/about_us/role.cfm
Interview with Kirk Ramsey on page 41

Learndirect scotland's overriding goal is to champion the needs of Scotland's learners and potential learners, creating a framework in which people from all walks of life can and do access learning at the place, time, pace, and style which best suits their needs.

In practice this means that we will:

- act to stimulate demand for learning, increasing overall participation and encouraging a client-focused approach to meeting learners' needs

- act to ensure that learners and potential learners are offered comprehensive, impartial, and current information and advice on all aspects of learning

- act to facilitate ease of access to learning by encouraging community and work-based provision of learning and flexible and innovative delivery of learning

- act to encourage client-centred learning, characterized by a welcoming and nonthreatening environment and effective, personalized learner support

- work as a broker with our many partners across the education, community, business, and voluntary sectors to offer an accessible, effective, and impartial national gateway to learning

Working with Partners
Learndirect scotland is not a provider of learning but a broker, seeking to engage people and businesses in learning and to connect them with the learning that best suits their needs. We are committed to achieving this in partnership with key stakeholders across the community, business, education and training, and voluntary sectors.

PiCircle
http://www.picircle.com

We specialize in designing, developing, and delivering creative custom blended learning experiences to meet the needs of global organizations and individuals. We are known for designing our student engagement through digital storytelling, games, simulations, and effective virtual classroom and online collaboration design.

P.O.V. (PBS)
http://www.pbs.org/pov/utils/aboutpov.html

P.O.V. (a cinema term for 'point of view') is public television's annual award-winning showcase for independent nonfiction films. Passionate, powerful, and poignant, P.O.V. films—regardless of their subjects—are ultimately personal and unvarnished reportage on our lives.

Root Learning
http://www.rootlearning.com
Interview with Jim Haudan and Tom Crawford on page 255

Root Learning delivers innovative learning, communications, and change management solutions to help clients engage their employees and achieve their goals. We accomplish this by helping our clients:

- Define strategic content,
- Develop an understanding of the strategic content, and
- Deploy the content effectively within their organizations.

By linking learning and communication to the business, organizations can achieve their goals quickly and sustainably.

BrainPOP
http://www.brainpop.com
Interview with Yves Saada on page 219

BrainPOP is the leading producer of educational animated movies for K–12. The company creates original animated movies to explain concepts in a voice and visual style that is accessible, educational, and entertaining for both children and adults.

Daniel Bernardi, University of Arizona
web.cfa.arizona.edu/people/bio.php?bio=15
Interview with Daniel Bernardi on page 73

Dr. Bernardi teaches courses on critical/cultural theory, new media, interactive storytelling, and race & whiteness studies. He is published in *The Encyclopedia of Knowledge*; *The Encyclopedia of Television, Film & History*; *Science Fiction Studies*; *Stanford Humanities Review*; and in collected works. He is the editor of *The Birth of Whiteness: Race & the Emergence of U.S. Cinema* (Rutgers University Press) and *Classic Hollywood/Classic Whiteness* (Minnesota University Press), and the author of *Star Trek & History: Race-ing Toward a White Future* (Rutgers University Press).

He is currently working on a book titled *Signs of Aliens*, which investigates the multifaceted, shifting meaning of "aliens" in American popular culture.

Dr. Bernardi is Director of Graduate Studies in the Department of Media Arts [at the University of Arizona].

Think Map
http://www.plumbdesign.com/index.html

Think Map creates online experiences that facilitate exchanges of ideas and the interplay of ideas.

Merrill Lynch Global Philanthropy
philanthropy.ml.com/ipo/
Interview with Eddy Bayardelle on page 27

From optimism comes action. At Merrill Lynch we're working to make a difference through innovative giving and volunteering in communities where we live and work. As a global company built on local relationships, we believe Responsible Citizenship is essential to good business— and to who we are.

FROM "HOW TO?" TO "HOW ABOUT . . . ?"

Open Your Mind to New eLearning Possibilities

RENAISSANCE eLEARNING is an alternative toolbox for people seeking additional ways to develop themselves and others. We use nontraditional methods to communicate a wide range of ideas, some foreign, some unconventional. We offer a wealth of case studies and ideas spotlighting people and programs typically upstaged by more established theories and more conventional corporate initiatives. We weave all these elements together to create an idea book or catalogue highlighting numerous ways for you to accomplish a particular goal.

This book does for people involved in learning and training, learners themselves, and results-driven managers what a good guidebook does for travelers. For new visitors, it familiarizes them with the territory, provides context, and allows more meaningful exploration of different areas. For natives and those who are practically so, it encourages journeying into less familiar territory and getting to know familiar areas on a deeper level.

> *We cannot become what we need to be by remaining what we are.*
> **MAX DE PREE**

WEARING TWO HATS

Writing a book from an expert's perspective limits authors to areas in which they are well versed. Writing a book from a journalist's perspective is also limiting because readers expect and deserve objectivity.

To make this book the best it could possibly be, we decided to wear both hats.

There are times when we rely on our thirty-plus years' experience to support our advice and opinions. Then there are times when we provide information from other sources who know much more about a topic than we do. This enables us to provide an introduction to areas outside our expertise within the context of a topic we know well. The ". . . And Even More Reading!" section at the end of the book is laden with information to provide a deeper treatment of the topics that we are able only to skim. We suggest you consult it when you wish to gain a deeper understanding of any topic covered in this book.

The three main goals of this book: (1) to stimulate thought (2) to increase new solutions and approaches and (3) to provoke dialogue

OUR MAIN ASSUMPTIONS

We are working from four assumptions that underlie our belief systems and underscore the content in this book:

1. We have moved into an economic era where implemented creativity is a widely acknowledged success factor.

2. Better business results are achieved when learning opportunities and leisure activities are barely distinguishable.

3. Creative thinkers in domains outside human resources can significantly enhance the effectiveness of eLearning.

4. To be effective, *Renaissance eLearning* must employ many of the principles and methods we suggest readers consider using.

Assumption 1

Creativity and innovation have always been critical to success. What we see changing is the increasing recognition of the contribution made by traditionally less valued forms of creativity and creative people. Specifically, we see signs that (1) political and financial power holders are expanding their circle of viable sources of economic growth to encompass previously dismissed intangibles such as the arts, design, and popular culture and (2) the people who make a living from creativity are starting to see themselves as a unified force to be reckoned with.

Feelings and understanding may sleep under the same roof but they run completely different households in the human soul.

ARTHUR SCHNITZLER

Data for numbers types: the Creative Economy contributes US$2.2 trillion to the world economy and is growing at 5 percent annually worldwide (14 percent and 12 percent, respectively, in the United States and Britain).[1] Contrast this with the $2.2 trillion education industry, which is growing at a much slower rate, less than 5 percent per year in the United States and United Kingdom. These trends and statistics (among others) have inspired thought leaders Richard Florida, John Howkins, Tom Bentley, and Charles Landry to claim the Information Economy, or Knowledge Economy, is evolving into the Creative Economy.

This shift is having a profound impact on the business world, which means that in the near future eLearning must be aligned with this shift to lead to direct business results.[2] The overview and documentary support we provide in the first section of this book are presented to persuade you the methods, ideas, and examples encountered thereafter—many of which may at first be unfamiliar or uncomfortable—are worth at least a moment's consideration or inclusion in the eLearning dialogue.

Assumption 2

Heutagogy, an ideological form of education in which learners are truly the owners of their own process, may be too utopian for today's typical organization to swallow or adopt wholesale. However, some valuable gems to borrow for creating effective eLearning are heutagogy's principles of organic and informal learning.

Much of the opportunity for informal or organic learning has decreased with the increasing adoption of technology. This is particularly true when learning management systems are used to plan, direct, track, and coordinate learner activities. Even when the content is valuable, the artificial aspects of the learner's experience can lead to difficulty in applying lessons learned in real-world situations. Additionally, much of what has been characterized as eLearning requires context switches and intentionality—in other words the experiences are so disconnected from everyday work and leisure activities that overcoming significant mental and physical inertia becomes a major barrier to widespread and voluntary use.

In contrast the eLearning programs that have been the most effective—simulations—have typically been modified versions of leisure activities that became popular through a groundswell of grassroots support. These leisure activities have been successful (even though many contain significant learning opportunities) primarily because they grow organically: users are able to control *and* modify almost all elements.

Much of the simulation movement grew out of the immense popularity of game forms involving role playing (for example, Dungeons & Dragons, Final Fantasy), game show formats (You Don't Know Jack), multiple-player games (Doom), virtual worlds (Myst), strategizing (Alpha Centauri), reflex and eye coordination (Ping, Atari), artificial intelligence (Grand Theft Auto), and construct and control activities (SimCity).

Part Two of this book, containing content directly related to the design of eLearning, was carefully crafted to provide assistance and encouragement to those wishing to create programs resembling leisure activities and therefore

> *I can't stand to sing the same song the same way two nights in succession. If you can, then it ain't music, it's close order drill, or exercise or yodeling or something, not music.*
> **BILLIE HOLIDAY**

more effective. Additionally, Chapter Three, focusing on the theory and practice of heutagogy, directly addresses this assumption.

Assumption 3

Effective eLearning design has to rest on solid theoretical underpinnings and also take advantage of the wealth of disciplines beyond the realm of education. This book begins the task of closing the current gap between these sources. We have culled architecture, city and regional planning, design, screen arts, physics, philosophy, journalism, graphic design, business management, information architecture, politics, academia, and screenwriting—to name a few—to find pivotal ideas and relevant pointers that can greatly enhance eLearning design.

Most of the people and ideas discussed are prominent in their field because of their track record of success, despite being unknown to many human resource or business managers. We consider this anthology element of our book akin to grazing: space constraints allow only a nibble of each idea, which we hope will lead to your further investigation of the flavors that could please your taste buds.

Assumption 4

We could not in good conscience write a book that encourages readers to take risks by venturing down less popular or more daring avenues and then play it safe ourselves. For example, we suggest readers consider applying exogenous ideas and methods to their design. And we also do that ourselves by, for example, using mind mapping and information design techniques to structure some of the traditional elements of this book (such as the table of contents) to make them more engaging and creative.

EXPECT THE UNEXPECTED

Because all these assumptions lead many of this book's features to deviate from the typical eLearning book formula, a brief review of what we have done and why will make the book more effective for some readers—and save forty hard-earned dollars for others.

In *Renaissance eLearning* you will find

- A *conversational tone*. You'll notice almost immediately our writing is friendly and casual. Our goal is to enter into a dialogue with you—to make reading this book the print equivalent of having a heated discussion at the local café or across a dinner table after a few bottles of wine. A formal or impersonal tone would only get in the way and

There are several instructional design books available to people who want a solid foundation in learning design principles. Our favorite first set is the Mager Six Pack, a collection of six books by Robert Mager.

It is only with the heart one can see rightly what is essential is invisible to the eye.

ANTOINE DE SAINT-EXUPÉRY

create distance between you and us. History has shown that the communicators who establish an intimate connection with each audience member have greater impact than those who use a professional tone.

- *Heavy use of anecdotes and metaphors from outside the training and business worlds.* Many of the most significant advances in society, science, and business were made while the discoverers were engaged in anything but trying to make the discovery. Archimedes discovered displacement while taking a bath. The anesthetic properties of nitrous oxide (also called laughing gas) were discovered in 1844 by a dentist who noticed that a person who injured himself at a laughing gas exhibition didn't feel any pain until after the gas wore off. The Rosetta stone (which unlocked the door to Egyptology) was discovered by army officers during Napoleon's campaign to capture a trade route to the east.[3]

We want to encourage you to look to your day-to-day life for inspiration and ideas that will lead to new combinations of elements and connections. Leading by example, we have decided to use primarily examples or metaphors that constantly draw attention away from eLearning, training, and human resource concerns, often away from the business world itself. As you expand the mental domains you are referencing simultaneously with your reading, new insights and creative "aha" moments will enter your mind. They may well be ideas you would not have had if examples had been restricted to the topic at hand. That's our version of journalistic LSD.

- *Newer theories and ideas from people outside the training domain or mainstream and citation of a wide variety of sources.* Just as Andy Warhol brought the supermarket soup can into the art world, we are applying well-established ideas from well-respected thought leaders and putting them into a new context. Ideas from architecture, psychology, journalism, physics, business management, screen arts, writing, politics, and more are applied to eLearning situations. This is our way of introducing a wide survey of ideas you may have had limited exposure to in an attempt to provide you with a springboard for innovation and learning.

Some might object to our intentional avoidance of rigorous research procedure: namely, that we favor "unsubstantiated" ideas and sources outside the confines of academia. No one, and we do mean no one—regardless of how much experience she has had or how many letters are after her name or how high her salary is—has a monopoly on

Conform and be dull.
J. FRANK DOBLE

I have not failed. I've found 10,000 ways that won't work.
THOMAS EDISON

common sense, creativity, or ideas about how to help people learn. Implying that one idea or another is more valid because it has been blessed by one institution or another also implies that one's own ideas—which may not be accepted, published, cited, or even known by anyone else—are less valid. In order to give you the greatest possible value, we created this anthology, portfolio, idea book, catalogue—call it what you will—following the principle of inclusion instead of exclusion.

- *Publicly accessible case studies from individuals, small private businesses, and government organizations.* The vast majority of case studies and best practices in standard material on eLearning typically focus on the internal eLearning programs of large U.S.-based corporations. For example, Hall and LeCavalier's study of best practices "includes Cisco Systems, IBM, Dell Computers, GTE, Shell, Unipart, Rockwell Collins and the U.S. Navy."[4] Roger Schank's *Designing World Class e-Learning* looks at "how IBM, GE, Harvard Business School, and Columbia University are succeeding at e-Learning."[5] The majority of conferences embrace speakers from these same large corporations and universities. For example, ASTD Techknowledge, an international conference of the American Society for Training and Development, is filled with representatives from Bank One, Ford Motor Company, Wells Fargo, T-Mobile, Oracle—the list goes on. The same is true of the majority of publications available from research organizations and on the Web.

  Simply put, the person who is looking to find the best practices of nonmultinational or private organizations has few options. We know, because we have been there. *Renaissance eLearning* provides a glimpse behind a curtain that has too rarely been pulled back. Until there are more people focusing on the micro eLearning economy, we felt it important to provide at least a small clip from a much larger movie.

- *Independent chapters.* We expect that most readers are using eLearning as a means to an end. They need to glean valuable information quickly without referring to prior or later material. *Renaissance eLearning* can be viewed as a collection of freestanding nuggets, each of which has the potential to make eLearning more effective, with extra value provided through an easy in–easy out interface. Although it is easy to see how the independent chapters connect, especially in Part Two, in most instances we intentionally avoid building one upon another. We encourage you to make the

> *Conformity is the jailer of freedom and the enemy of growth.*
>
> **JOHN F. KENNEDY**

most of this structure by offering multiple pointers for moving around in the book: for example, lots of cross-references, invitations to skip around, graphical and topical guides, and tables of contents.

THE BOTTOM LINE

Renaissance eLearning offers the maximum benefit to those seeking to journey beyond the mainstream to gather new ideas, methods, and examples. We invite you on a tour of areas you may be unfamiliar with in order to gain insights and inspiration for more creative eLearning solutions leading to better business results. Some of the areas are just slightly off the main highway, others—at the fringes of the fringes—will require taking the road less traveled.

At the end of the day, we hope that makes all the difference.

NOTES

1. John Howkins, *The Creative Economy* (New York: Penguin Books, 2002).

2. Due to time and space constraints, *Renaissance eLearning* is focused exclusively on learning that directly affects business results.

3. For more examples see one of these two great books: Royston Roberts, *Serendipity: Accidental Discoveries in Science* (Hoboken, N.J.: Wiley, 1989), or Royston Roberts and Jeanie Roberts, *Lucky Science: Accidental Discoveries from Gravity to Velcro* (Hoboken, N.J.: Wiley, 1995). Or simply do a Web search for "accidental discoveries."

4. Brandon Hall and Jacques LeCavalier, *E-Learning Across the Enterprise: The Benchmarking Study of Best Practices*, Jan. 2001, http://www.brandon-hall.com.

5. Roger Schank, *Designing World Class e-Learning* (New York: McGraw-Hill, 2002).

THE CREATIVE ECONOMY IS COMING!

Why a New eLearning Paradigm Is Needed

A DECADE AGO Peter Drucker held a mirror up to society. He showed government, education, and industry that they were operating under a new economic paradigm. The rock they had built their castle on, tangible things, was no longer what was supporting the fortress. The new foundation was intellectual capital, intangibles such as technology and information that were growing the economy and underpinning society's health.

Almost immediately leaders started asking the same questions about knowledge they had asked about durable goods for hundreds of years before:

- How do we transform knowledge into profit?
- How do we acquire knowledge?
- What do we need to do to manage knowledge?
- Where do we store knowledge? How do we move it?

Given the intangible nature of knowledge, a few questions were being asked that hadn't been asked on the same scale before:

- What exactly is knowledge?
- Which elements of knowledge are most valuable?
- How do we capture, absorb, transmit, increase, and communicate knowledge?
- How do we prevent knowledge loss?
- What changes do we need to make to shift from a manufacturing-based economy to a knowledge-based one?

Movements grew in response to the first two questions about what knowledge is and which aspects of it are most valuable. Many people focused

> If you have built castles in the air, your work need not be lost; that is where they should be. Now put the foundations under them.
>
> **HENRY DAVID THOREAU**

BOOKSHELF BEST BETS

The Act of Creation, Arthur Koestler

Creativity, Mihaly Csikszentmihalyi

The Rise of the Creative Class, Richard Florida

The Creative Economy, John Howkins

Understanding Organizations, Charles Handy

9

on facts and data (*metrics*) as being the most critical aspects of knowledge. They built knowledge management systems and processes to capture and transmit those bits and bytes.

A separate movement sprang up that not only recognized the importance of this type of knowledge but also saw a critical ingredient of the economic pie being left out of the recipe: creativity.

Where knowledge came to be about learning and applying newly learned information to familiar situations or learned situations, proponents of this new paradigm saw economic growth resting in the hands of those who apply information they have learned in new and novel ways.

A metaphor for the difference between knowledge and creativity is the contrast between classical painting and modern art. Classical painters learned techniques for painting portraits, still lifes, or landscapes in a realistic style. Modernists (Picasso is a particularly well known example) learned this exact same curriculum but decided to apply their learning in radically new and novel ways.

Visiting the Reina Sophia Museum in Madrid to see Picasso's *Guernica* demonstrates the process of transforming knowledge into creativity. The visitor must first pass through a hall with many sketches showing objects, animals, and people represented traditionally, in a realistic style with much detail. Children could easily identify almost all the items in the sketches. It is only when the visitor encounters the actual *Guernica* that the new application of traditional knowledge appears. The contrast between the artist's studies for the painting and his final masterpiece clearly demonstrates how Picasso was well aware of classical painting and drawing styles and consciously chose to break out of that knowledge and art paradigm.

THE CREATIVE ECONOMY

Many now advocate for the use of the term *Creative Economy* to describe the current economic era. The phrase underscores that the Knowledge Economy is ongoing but gives heightened recognition to creativity's significant and quantifiable contribution to the economy.

Richard Florida, a Carnegie Mellon professor, the author of one of amazon.com's best-selling books (*The Rise of the Creative Class*), and an in-demand consultant, describes this subtle distinction between the Knowledge Economy and Creative Economy:

> I certainly agree with those who say that the advanced nations are shifting to information-based, knowledge-driven economies. Peter Drucker, who outlined the rise of the "knowledge economy," has been the most noted exponent of this view: "The basic economic resources—'the means

of production' to use the economists' term—is no longer capital, nor natural resources . . . nor 'labor.' It is and will be knowledge.". . . Yet I see creativity—the creation of useful new forms out of that knowledge—as the key driver. In my formulation, "knowledge" and "information" are the tools and materials of creativity. "Innovation" whether in the form of a new technological artifact or a new business model or method, is its product.[1]

This Creative Economy is one in which much economic and societal success rests on the shoulders of those creative individuals and organizations whose ideas are implemented and economically valued.

We believe, as do thought leaders such as Richard Florida, Tom Bentley, John Howkins, and hundreds of business and civic leaders, that modern societies are at the dawn of this creative age. Organizations that leverage creativity and its derivates will gain the competitive edge. "The most successful economies and societies in the twenty-first century will be creative ones," says UK Secretary of State for Culture, Media and Sport Chris Smith. "Creativity will make the difference—to businesses seeking a competitive edge, to societies looking for new ways to tackle issues and improve the quality of life. I want all businesses to think creatively, to realize creativity is not an add-on but an essential ingredient for success."[2]

There will be exponential benefits available to businesses that learn to leverage the Creative Economy, and certain extinction for those that cannot. "Now the Industrial Economy is giving way to the Creative Economy, and corporations are at another crossroads," observes Peter Coy.

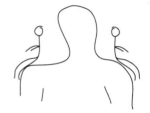

The empires of the future are the empires of the mind.
WINSTON CHURCHILL

> Attributes that made them ideal for the 20th century could cripple them in the 21st. So they will have to change, dramatically. The Darwinian struggle of daily business will be won by the people—and the organizations—that adapt most successfully to the new world that is unfolding. . . .
>
> In an economy based on ideas rather than physical capital, the potential for breakaway successes . . . is far greater. That's because ideas, like germs, are infectious. They can spread to a huge population seemingly overnight. And once the idea—say, a computer program—has been developed, the cost of making copies is close to zero and the potential profits enormous.[3]

Learning and training professionals are experiencing an almost unprecedented increase in esteem as business leaders look to them to find ways to thrive in the knowledge economy. The person wishing to use eLearning to drive business results can turn to any of hundreds of resources to enhance the type of knowledge that involves facts, figures, technical skills, and so on.

Where are they to turn when they want to enhance not only those skills but also the innovation of their people? When they want to increase the amount of economic or societal gain achieved through new ways of approaching problems? Questions such as those are what prompted us to write this book, and they are why we are introducing the Creative Economy paradigm.

CREATIVITY AS AN ECONOMIC DRIVER

> *I skate to where the puck is going to be, not where it's been.*
> **WAYNE GRETZKY**

We are *not* implying that creativity is a recent discovery nor are we saying there wasn't any recognition of the economic importance of creativity before now. Creativity has been around since the first creature found a clever way to emerge from the primordial soup and breathe air. Since before Archimedes was rewarded for discovering that the crown the king received as a gift was not made of pure gold, organizations have made all sorts of investment to increase innovation.

Rather, we simply observe that we are entering an economic era in which the pendulum is swinging towards the application of knowledge in new and novel ways and thus is directly responsible for positive social and economic outcomes.

Aren't quite convinced society is moving toward the Creative Economy? Want hard evidence to pass on to others? See "More on the Creative Economy," at the end of this book, for a gathering of hard and soft data.

We are speaking specifically of economic creativity. Some of the benefits of this economic creativity are

- Increased new job creation
- Increased amount and value of exports
- Increased stock value and market capitalization
- Increased gross domestic and gross national products
- Increased business revenues
- Increased brand recognition and valuation

So far this discussion has addressed the mile-high level. Now let's take a telescope and zoom in on some of the elements that make up the whole. First we will define creativity and then, using our definition, discuss who is creative.

DAILY DOSE OF CREATIVITY

We have discussed creativity on a macro economic level. Now we turn to a day-to-day definition that can be acted on and used to guide organizations.

As with knowledge, there is no one correct definition of creativity. We have selected Mihaly Csikszentmihalyi's definition because of his systems approach. Rather than seeing creativity as an individual trait, he approaches it as residing in a larger context.

On the first page of his seminal book *Creativity: Flow and the Psychology of Discovery and Invention*, Csikszentmihalyi, one of the world's leading authorities on the psychology of creativity,[4] emphasizes this distinction:

> An idea or product that deserves the label "creative" arises from the synergy of many sources and not only from the mind of a single person. *It is easier to enhance creativity by changing conditions in the environment than by trying to make people think more creatively* [emphasis added].[5]

Csikszentmihalyi defines *creativity* as

> any act, idea or product that changes an existing domain, or that transforms an existing domain into a new one. . . . A creative person is someone whose thoughts or actions change a domain, or establish a new domain.

Before this definition can be completely understood some of its unfamiliar elements must be addressed. First, we present a more detailed treatment of the difference between individual creativity and societal creativity, and then we elaborate on what is meant by *domain* and how an idea comes to warrant the label *creative*.[6]

Individual Versus Societal Creativity

Most of us think of creativity as an intangible characteristic of an individual. We remark, "How creative!" when we watch our children's impromptu skits, eat a tantalizing new dish at a restaurant, or hear how someone got the attention of a busy corporate recruiter. Everyone, including Csikszentmihalyi, labels this creativity.

He values this "creativity with a small c," which resides completely within the individual and does not involve any external value system. It is "important for everyday life . . . [something] we definitely should try to enhance."

CREATIVITY WITH A CAPITAL C

The creativity Csikszentmihalyi has spent his life investigating—the creativity meant in the term Creative Economy,[7] and what we are referring to when we use the word in this book—consists of the novel ideas that have a significant impact beyond the individual or small group. This form of creativity "does not happen inside people's heads, but in the interaction

Creativity is the ability to see relationships where none exist.
THOMAS DISCH

between a person's thoughts and the sociocultural context. It is a systemic rather an individual phenomenon."

The major difference between personal creativity and big "C" creativity is impact. Does the idea change society or the economy? Does it increase the profits or revenues of an organization? Does it decrease poverty or hunger or joblessness? Does it earn the respect of industry leaders and members? Does it add to the canon of literature or knowledge in a field?

VALUE AND THE MEASURE OF CREATIVITY

The next logical question is, how do we measure this larger creativity? Csikszentmihalyi has done an outstanding job of analyzing the process and systems that make or break an idea's dream of being called creative.

To be considered creative according to Csikszentmihalyi's scheme of things, an idea must

- be couched in terms that are understandable to others
- pass muster with the experts in the field
- be included in the cultural domain to which it belongs

And what does he mean by *domain?* The *domain* is what is commonly referred to as an *area*—as in a subject area (for example, psychology), a physical or political area (for example, France), an economic area (for example, an industry such as education), a workplace area, and so forth, or a subset of any of these. The official definition: "the set of symbolic rules and procedures."

The *field* is "all the individuals who act as gatekeepers to the domain." In other words the people with the clout to give the idea respect and consideration or to nix it (whether overtly or through passive lack of recognition).

Because this is confusing jargon, let's use a tangible example. Suppose you create a phenomenal, personally creative eLearning program. It is graphically gorgeous and well written, and every learner who sits down to do it achieves unprecedented business results.

Now let's consider two alternate scenarios:

Scenario 1:

The eLearning program catches the eye of the president of ASTD who passes it on to Tom Kelly at Cisco and the head of eLearning at Motorola, and nominates it for a Webby (which it wins). As a result a new trend appears in which hundreds of eLearning programs are made reflecting the innovations in your trailblazing program. You are constantly in demand as a speaker, consultant, and adviser. Ten years from now people still see your influence in the eLearning being developed.

Scenario 2:

The president of ASTD and others see your program and remark that it is interesting. It continues to be used until better ones replace it.

The program itself in each scenario is exactly the same, but how it is received is not. In the first instance the field (those people who determine the worth of an idea in a particular domain, in this case training) give it the extra attention and seal of approval it needs to have a long-lasting impact on the domain.

In the second scenario, it is the same good program, but for whatever reason it doesn't catch the eye of the field (again, the gatekeepers who determine the worth of a creative idea) and so does not have a long-lasting impact on the domain.

Now that we have covered *domain* and *field*, Csikszentmihalyi's definitions will make more sense:

> Creativity is any act, idea or product that changes an existing domain, or that transforms an existing domain into a new one.

> A creative person is someone whose thoughts or actions change a domain, or establish a new domain.

> *In the modern world of business, it is useless to be a creative, original thinker unless you can also sell what you create.*
> **DAVID OGILVY**

Lowering the Bar

We are using Csikszentmihalyi's take on creativity because it elucidates a nebulous concept well, it is one of the most widely respected analyses, and we agree with its fundamental premise. However, we diverge when it comes time to select the appropriate hurdle size. Many ideas can have a smaller impact than that Csikszentmihalyi requires and still be creative, still be a critical part of the Creative Economy.

To continue the example cited earlier, suppose your new eLearning program gives several learners new ideas about how to make more sales and causes managers to seek and nurse more budding ideas. It is realistic to expect this might result in increased revenue, a rising stock price, and maybe a spot on *Fortune* magazine's list of the 100 best companies to work for. Your program may not alter the course of history but it is having a significant impact in its own little universe (which is larger than just you and a few friends or family members).

In this book, when we talk about creativity we are referring to Csikszentmihalyi's concept but with the modification that the standards of acceptance and impact must be more than having a positive effect on the immediate circle of the individual but not necessarily as monumental as fundamentally altering the domain and society.

CREATIVITY CONFIDENCE-BUILDING CORNER

Countless creations have lost the race before they even leave the gate. Well-intentioned skeptics who share their discouraging words are one of the many potholes standing between creators and finished products.

We all need some encouragement sometimes. When you need some encouragement, glance at some of the statements that follow. All were made by people who predicted the demise or limitations of an inventor's product. In the end the invention prevailed, demonstrating how important it is to stay true to your vision even in the face of the most stalwart opposition.

Famous Last Words

"Everything that can be invented has already been invented." *Charles H. Duell, director of the U.S. Patent Office, 1899*

"I think there is a world market for maybe five computers." *Thomas Watson, chairman of IBM, 1943*

"Computers in the future may weigh no more than 1.5 tons." Popular Mechanics, *forecasting the relentless march of science, 1949*

"Louis Pasteur's theory of germs is ridiculous fiction." *Pierre Pachet, professor of physiology at Toulouse, 1872*

"I have travelled the length and breadth of this country and talked with the best people, and I can assure you that data processing is a fad that won't last out the year." *Editor in charge of business books for Prentice Hall, 1957*

"But what is it good for?" *Engineer in the Advanced Computing Systems Division of IBM, commenting on the microchip, 1968*

"Stocks have reached what looks like a permanently high plateau." *Irving Fisher, professor of economics at Yale University, 1929*

"Heavier-than-air flying machines are impossible." *Lord Kelvin, president of the Royal Society, 1895*

"There is no reason anyone would want a computer in their home." *Ken Olson, president, chairman, and founder of Digital Equipment Corp., 1977*

"We don't like their sound, and guitar music is on the way out." *Decca Recording Company, rejecting the Beatles, 1962*

"DOS addresses only 1 megabyte of RAM because we cannot imagine any applications needing more." *Microsoft on the development of DOS, 1980*

"I'm just glad it'll be Clark Gable who's falling on his face and not Gary Cooper." *Gary Cooper, on his decision not to take the leading role in* Gone with the Wind

"A cookie store is a bad idea. Besides, the market research reports say America likes crispy cookies, not soft and chewy cookies like you make." *Response to Debbi Fields's idea of starting Mrs. Fields' Cookies*

"Drill for oil? You mean drill into the ground to try and find oil? You're crazy." *Drillers whom Edwin L. Drake tried to enlist in his project to drill for oil, 1859*

"640k ought to be enough for anybody." *Bill Gates, founder of Microsoft, 1981*

"Who the hell wants to hear actors talk?" *H. M. Warner, a founder of Warner Brothers, 1927*

"Windows NT addresses 2 gigabytes of RAM which is more than any application will ever need." *Microsoft on the development of Windows NT*

Timeless Encouragement

"They are ill discoverers that think there is no land when they can see nothing but sea." *Francis Bacon*

"To spell out the obvious is often to call it into question." *Eric Hoffer*

"Discovery consists of seeing what everybody has seen and thinking what nobody has thought." *Albert Szent-Györgyi*

"Half the failures in the life arise from pulling in one's horse as he is leaping." *Julius and Augustus Hare*

"Es irrt der Mensch so lang er strebt" ("Man errs so long as he strives"). *Johann Wolfgang von Goethe*

"The man who makes no mistakes does not usually make anything." Edward J. Phelps

"We often discover what will do by finding out what will not do; and probably he who never made a mistake never made a discovery." *Samuel Smiles*

"If at first, the idea is not absurd, there is no hope for it." *Albert Einstein*

"Problems cannot be solved by thinking within the framework in which the problems were created." *Albert Einstein*

"Discovery consists of looking at the same thing as everyone else and thinking something different." *Albert Szent-Györgyi*

"Think before you speak is criticism's motto; speak before you think, creation's." *E. M. Forster*

"You see things: you say 'Why?' But I dream things that never are: and say 'Why not?'" *George Bernard Shaw*

"Don't worry about people stealing your ideas. If your ideas are any good, you'll have to ram them down people's throats." *Howard Aiken*

"Commonplace minds usually condemn what is beyond the reach of their understanding." *François de la Rochefoucauld*

"Imagination gallops; judgment merely walks." *Proverbial*

"As a rule, men worry more about when they can't see than about what they can." *Julius Caesar*

"It is with ideas as with umbrellas, if left lying about they are peculiarly liable to change of ownership." *Thomas Kettle*

THE CREATIVE PROCESS

Even when an idea is good it is still challenging to transform personal creativity into economic or societal gain. Hence the maxim that creativity is 1 percent inspiration and 99 percent perspiration. This is one of the areas where eLearning can have the biggest impact on an organization—by familiarizing people with the creative process, helping them navigate it, and influencing the environment in a way that makes it more receptive to creativity.

Understanding the Creative Economy movement and gaining a working understanding of what is meant by creativity were the first steps toward designing eLearning to take advantage of this new era.

The next step is to understand the creative process and see how eLearning can help at each stage. Surprisingly, most models of the creative process—whether they originate from academics, practitioners, ancient Greek philosophers, or modern journalists—bear striking resemblance to each other. We have elected to go with Csikszentmihalyi's model as it is elegant and simple.[8]

As you read the following creative process model, pay particular attention to the amount of preparation and effort that surrounds what people typically see as a spontaneous, Eureka event arising out of nowhere. It is true the moment when a new idea, insight, or solution hits is not only completely unpredictable but also likely to arrive when attention is diverted elsewhere. However, these sudden solutions rarely occur in minds that are unprepared, and the implementation of those Eureka ideas rarely happens in minds that aren't both prepared and disciplined.

Also bear in mind these steps are recursive, not linear. For the sake of explanation we present them as one following another, like reading the words in this sentence. In the real world these steps double back on each other, and during any one step a person could be going through all the other steps as well.

Concerning all acts of initiative and creation, there is one elementary truth— that the moment one definitely commits oneself, then Providence moves, too.
JOHANN WOLFGANG VON GOETHE

Step 1: Preparation

There is so much to be said about preparation, the first part of the creative process, that even if it took up the entire book it would only scratch the surface. In the next few paragraphs we will highlight what we consider to be the five or six most salient points for businesspeople considering the development of themselves and others. We strongly recommend reading the entire chapter titled "The Work of Creativity" in Csikszentmihalyi's *Creativity* to gain a deeper and more holistic understanding of the process.

A creative process is initiated when a person gets that first sense "there is a puzzle somewhere, or a task to be accomplished." At first this might be conscious or subconscious. Often this step is deeply personal in a way we are often not comfortable believing in in the work world, where checking emotions at the door is expected.

Typically the problems that arise from this route are those no one knew even existed. In other words, no one has even thought to ask the question yet, so no one even knows there is a problem. We will get back to this shortly.

The creative process people are more familiar with (and often more comfortable with) in a business setting is the one that addresses "presented" problems—ones that are already known to exist but that don't have any solutions.

Let's use an oft-cited business example to illustrate the difference. At 3M the presenting problem was how to improve tape, how to make new tape products that would sell. Since 1968, when a researcher had discarded a particular glue formulation as being not strong enough, several creative people had solved this presenting problem by introducing new lines of surgical, general purpose, construction, and other adhesive tapes.

But in 1972, a choir member (who just happened to also be a scientist working at 3M) was frustrated that his bookmarks were not staying put in his hymnals. He used the glue his friend had discarded. Although it took until 1980 to go through the rest of the creative process and bring Post-it notes to market, this is an example of a person who solved a problem no one even knew existed.[9]

In both cases, a critical part of the preparation for the discovery to take place is deep *immersion* in a particular arena. This can come in the form of years of formal or informal schooling, exposure to others who are in the arena, firsthand experience with the issues, or any other method whereby people can amass significant amounts of knowledge. While it is possible for creative solutions to be stumbled upon accidentally, with no prior knowledge of the subject area, it is extremely rare. The Toll House chocolate chip, modern art, the airplane, psychoanalysis, brainstorming, the theory of relativity, and almost all other solutions that have made a difference have come from people who had extensive knowledge and familiarity with a relevant arena or set of issues—even if they wound up breaking off and creating a new one!

Immersion in a set of issues typically encompasses the following (this is just a start):

- Getting to know others in the arena (especially recognized authorities)
- Learning the jargon and terminology
- Acquiring the practices, techniques, facts, figures, and so on that make up the arena
- Joining or participating in relevant associations
- Picking up the culture and unspoken expectations of the relevant arena

eLearning can clearly make a big impact in this area. First, it can do wonders toward helping people obtain the knowledge and experience they need to deal with a particular set of issues.

> *One does not become enlightened by imagining figures of light, but by making the darkness conscious.*
> **CARL JUNG**

> *Balzac observed all the things that Marx did not see.*
> **REGIS DEBRAY**

Second, it can help people figure out the best approach to presenting problems.

Third, and of particular relevance, it can help people come up with the problem in the first place, by creating an environment where assumptions are tested and expectations challenged.

Fourth, it can put people in the right mindset to tackle a creative problem.

Step 2: Incubation

Incubation is absolutely essential to creativity but little is known about the actual intellectual or emotional processes taking place during this time. From the viewpoint of an outsider looking in, it looks like the caulking between the tiles of preparation and insight—just a filler to keep the others on target. Incubation appears to be a time when nothing is happening, no progress is being made, and most important, no observable activities are being performed.

An understanding of incubation is one of the primary distinctions that set organizations that truly support and encourage creativity apart from those that don't—regardless of how much "innovation" lip service they spin.

Organizations that accept they don't understand what goes on during this mysterious period and also realize it might not result in a particularly creative solution—this time—but still give employees the leeway to be away from the problem, to mentally and physically change their surroundings, are ultimately the ones that win in the end. Participation in the Creative Economy is a marathon, not a sprint.

Csikszentmihalyi says that this phase occurs when "the process of creativity usually goes underground for a while." Experience has shown people who have just undergone an intense period of wrestling with a problem and then walk away from it tend to see the solution during this downtime.

One explanation is that their censors and inner that-will-never-work voices are distracted elsewhere, enabling the pursuit of solutions that would otherwise be quashed or dismissed as impossible, incorrect.

Another is that involvement in a different activity provides exposure to stimuli that to the logical mind appear completely unrelated but to the subconscious are absolutely relevant. This is tied into the belief, popular among several great creatives including journalist Arthur Koestler and artist Max Ernst, that bringing the dissimilar together is at the heart of creativity. In fact, *synectics* is an entire movement that has grown around this theory. It encourages people to use trigger questions that stimulate thought about divergent concepts.[10] For example, synectics suggests people take whatever subject they are working on and figure out what can be removed from it, figure out what human qualities the problem has, visualize it in a different environment, superimpose an incompatible idea on top of it, and so on. (See ". . . And Even More Reading!")

Whatever the reason, it is critical for people to have what we have termed reflection time and downtime away from the problem. We deem it so underappreciated an area that Chapter Fifteen is dedicated to helping you make best use of it.

> Between the idea
> And the reality
> Between the motion
> And the act
> Falls the Shadow
> **T. S. ELIOT**

Step 3: Insight

Insight is the step Hollywood lives for. This is Russell Crowe as mathematician John Nash suddenly realizing the solution to his formula. It's Archimedes running naked through the streets of Syracuse screaming "Eureka!" It's Sherlock Holmes declaring "Elementary, my dear Watson!"

We all love this moment. It is when our hard work pays off because a solution appears seemingly magically. People often refer to this as "the pieces coming together" or "an idea just hitting me, like a bolt from the blue."

eLearning has nothing to offer during this phase, other than to prepare people for it and help them make a solution a reality once it appears.

> An idea is a feat
> of association.
> **ROBERT FROST**

Step 4: Evaluation

One of us has a favorite expression, "Ideas are easy." The other one doesn't agree completely with that statement, but the point is well taken: the distance between getting an idea and implementing it is light years. Once the solution has "appeared" it is time to test its true worth. Csikszentmihalyi claims creative people are those who can tell the difference between an idea worth pursuing and one to let go.

Tests people will perform to check out the value of their ideas include

- Dialoguing with colleagues
- Market research
- Pilot testing
- Scenario testing (putting the idea, product, or whatever into different scenarios to see if it holds up)
- Internal checks (listening to gut feeling and intuition)

This is one of the areas where eLearning that addresses culture, self-worth, and the creation of an environment conducive to creativity is critical. People who have low self-esteem, lack of courage, or a negative self-image; who exist in an environment where new ideas are discouraged (or are derided or devalued); or who come from a culture or background in which standing out or suggesting new ways of doing things is frowned upon are much more likely to dismiss their breakthroughs as unworthy. Often this is more out of fear than it is a genuine, carefully reached conclusion that the idea is unviable.

Step 5: Elaboration

To the people who come up with a novel solution or idea the elaboration stage can be frustrating. From their perspective it may seem it took many months or even years to get to the point where the idea can be made into a reality, and now at last they are in the home stretch. In contrast, to newcomers, who often include stakeholders such as funders or project champions, the game is just beginning. They ask annoying questions that have already been put to bed and are sleeping soundly such as: Why do you think this will work? Why do we need it? Can't we just do X or Y instead?

Alas, this is just the first step on the long journey to making the idea a reality. Typical activities encountered in this phase are

- Getting buy-in from a wider circle of stakeholders or supporters
- Developing the required processes and accompanying documents to bring the idea to life
- Designing, building, testing, and modifying the implemented solutions
- Evaluating the end results

This is another step in which eLearning can aid creativity. A few specific examples are

- Providing project management skills
- Giving tips and advice on making presentations to stakeholders
- Connecting with others who have made similar pitches to stakeholders or who have successfully completed the planning and development processes

Table 2.1 details each of the phases of the creative process and how eLearning can facilitate excellence during that step.

The Knowledge Economy is dependent on creativity as a critical economic commodity. Although this has always been the case modern societies are moving into an era where this is more widely acknowledged and respected. The people and organizations that leverage novel ideas and solutions that have the potential to change people and systems outside an immediate circle of family and friends will realize better financial and societal gains.

TABLE 2.1 eLearning Solutions Mapped to Csikszentmihalyi's Creative Process Steps

Step	Description	Examples of Actions	How eLearning Can Help	eLearning Helping
Preparation "A sense there is a puzzle out there, a task to be accomplished" Attempting to come to terms with a personal conflict	• Real-world experience through exposure	• Living in India under British rule (Gandhi) • Having an unethical CEO or manager • Having respiratory problems because of smog • Losing good staff because of poorly executed merger • Suffering in school because there are no special programs for children with dyslexia or other special needs	• N/A (although people may use eLearning during their lives it can't give them personal experiences)	N/A
Preparation, Part Two Immersion in an area	• Learning about the area deliberately and formally	• Going to a university to learn physics • Attending conferences to learn eLearning design • Belonging to a listserv to stay current with the latest innovations in financial services and products	• Provide subject matter depth • Facilitate relationships and connections between people who might otherwise not be exposed to each other • Guide people through the process of discovering problems • Guide people through the process of taking ideas from problem identification to the production and evaluation stages • Provide emotional support and courage to people who have discovered a problem • Foster an environment where problem identification is not only supported but rewarded • Provide opportunities to practice critical thinking and deconstruction of other material • Present mind mapping and other visualization techniques • Discuss people who trusted their gut reactions and intuition and the changes they brought about • Use group idea generation techniques (for example, brainstorming) • Develop both divergent and convergent thinking	

(continued)

TABLE 2.1 (Continued)

Step	Description	Examples of Actions	How eLearning Can Help	eLearning Helping
Incubation "Mystery time," when rationality and the conscious mind cannot censure the solution	• Physical and psychological time spent away from the problem and settings where the problem is typically addressed (typically after extensive active engagement)	• Physically traveling to a place away from where the problem is worked on • Mentally turning attention elsewhere if even for a moment • Sleeping, eating, driving a car, taking a shower, or doing other daily activities • Immersing in an activity that requires deep physical attention (but is not related to the task at hand), such as a sport, craft, or other hobby • Doing an activity that requires enough conscious attention to block censors or other negative "will never work" messages	• Encourage activities that support uncensored thinking but don't relate to the subject at hand (for example, art projects, radio or TV shows, creative writing)	
Insight (called illumination by Wallis)	• The moment when the solution seems to "magically" appear	• Could be anything; Archimedes screaming "Eureka," and so on	• Foster synectic eLearning based on synectic principles (for example, using trigger questions)	
Evaluation Does the magical solution reached in the step before really work? Is it worth pursuing?	• Reality and the mental censor are welcomed back, and potential solutions are "tested" to see if they might really work	• Dialoguing with others, particularly respected people or leaders in the area • Doing pilot projects	• Teach people how to use tools (often computer sims) that can model potential solutions without costly repercussions	
Elaboration Making the solution a reality	• Once it is determined the solution does appear to be something that will be profitable or positively affect the chosen arena, it must be brought to life	• Designing and building the product or service • Testing the solution, product, or service • Personally using the solution, product, or service	• Provide people with planning skills • Teach people how to use the tools of their trade • Do a "reality TV" type of eLearning where other people can watch as the new idea is turned into reality and get inspired, and so on	
eLearning transcending steps				www.buffalostate.edu /centers/creativity /Education/Distance. html

eLearning can play a key part in helping people and the environments in which they function achieve greater results by tapping into creativity. At the preparation, incubation, evaluation, and elaboration steps in the process, eLearning designed properly for the Creative Economy can have a significant positive influence on business results.

NOTES

1. Richard Florida, *The Rise of the Creative Class* (New York: Basic Books, 2002).

2. Chris Smith, "Foreword," *Creative Industries Mapping Document* (U.K. Department for Culture, Media, and Sport, 2000), p. 2.

3. Peter Coy, Introduction, *Business Week*, Aug. 2000, No. 3696, p. 76.

4. Csikszentmihalyi is C. S. and D. J. Davidson Professor of Psychology at the Peter F. Drucker Graduate School of Management at Claremont Graduate University and director of the Quality of Life Research Center. He is also emeritus professor of human development at the University of Chicago, where he was a professor and chair before retiring. Most recently he has been retained by organizations such as Nissan, the World Economic Forum, and the John Paul Getty museum, as well as by a project dedicated to understanding how professionals do good-quality and socially responsible work. His book *Creativity* looks at over thirty years of research on how creative people live and work.

5. Mihaly Csikszentmihalyi, *Creativity: Flow and the Psychology of Discovery and Invention* (New York: HarperCollins, 1997). All quotations from Csikszentmihalyi's work that appear in this chapter are from this book.

6. These two ideas come from Csikszentmihalyi, *Creativity*, Part 1, "The Creative Process."

7. Many leaders of the Creative Economy movement use Csikszentmihalyi's definition of creativity in their publications and events.

8. Most of the ideas elucidated in this creative process section also come from Csikszentmihalyi, *Creativity*.

9. Not only do examples of this type of creativity abound, they are typically the ones that get the most respect and recognition.

10. Which brings up yet another point that we wish we had the time and space to address but don't: convergent thinking versus divergent thinking. This is an important component of creativity.

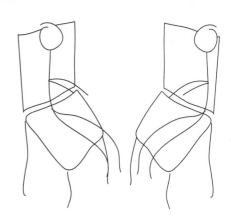

EDDY BAYARDELLE

Director of Merrill Lynch Global Philanthropy
(creator of the IPO eLearning program)

ON THE CREATIVE PROCESS . . .

[What's] wonderful about this place is that the resources of ideas are just incredible. People know we are responsible for the giving part of a firm so everybody has an idea. One approach would be to say, "Oh no! There's all these people with all these ideas and that means so much work." Or you could see it as an asset to have all these ideas.

We look at every proposal we receive, every single one, and there is a purpose behind it. Aside from the fact that a lot of people with regular time, effort and energy and resources write these things at least you can look at it. The other reason to look at it [is it] might spur you on to other ideas. We all have good ideas and no one person has a monopoly of ideas. We hear ideas from everywhere, literally, everywhere. An email, a phone call, you run into somebody in an elevator, ideas are everywhere.

With technology these days, it is not burdensome [for people] to send you a quick email when they have an idea. It's so wonderful. Everyday, there is not a day that goes by that I don't have someone calling me with a new idea. What is nice about it, while we may not be able to do something with that idea here, we refer that person to someone else.

ON PARTNERSHIPS . . .

We are kind of hands on. We want to be in partnership. It's not our style to say, "I'll write you a check and good luck to you and no more work for us." It doesn't make it fun.

If you really want to get to a point where you are always excited about what's going on, you enter partnerships. Together with your partners you will come up with ideas that you would never have thought of alone. Since they also have partners that they work with, the ideas just increase. It is just incredible.

There are only so many places you can go for talent and other resources. If you do not have the expertise nor the capacity at this moment to do something and someone next door to you does and they are doing a heck of a job and have the capacity and the track record and are also willing to share—why wouldn't you partner with them?

If I do A better, then you can give your population A. If you do B better, then my population can get B from you. That is what we have done and it's fascinating. This has taken us to a level that we couldn't even imagine.

For example, we are involved in a program called Food from the Hood, in Los Angeles. These are high school kids that work in a garden and then make salad dressing. Then they sell the dressing. I observed them at a business meeting where a fifteen-year-old is sitting at the table with other teens saying, "All right, let's hear from the Marketing Department, let's hear from the . . ."

When I was fifteen I was not talking about that stuff. They are so articulate, so smart, and so creative. They make a profit, they reinvest it in their company so it can continue to grow, and they take another portion for themselves to save for college. How can you beat that?

ON PEOPLE . . .

Everything starts with respect. People take such care and effort to put proposals and other ideas together. Purely out of respect, at the least you should view it and give your feedback. Beyond that, if you are a learning person, regardless of your direct job responsibility, if you just like learning, you would want to have new sources of ideas. This new stuff that comes up is just fascinating.

You may have to say it doesn't fit with our mission here. But you can also tell the person about someone else who might need it.

To do what we do here [needs] no particular background but the very basic characteristic is attitude. I come here every day feeling very lucky. When I don't feel so lucky, I look at a picture on the wall of these street kids with no place to go, no food to eat, no family, no shelter, and I look at the smiles on their faces.

It makes you realize you may have a problem, but that you also need to be thankful for everything you have.

The other thing about attitude is that it is the only thing that you can control. You cannot control what is going to happen during the day. I don't care how much you are planning; there is absolutely nothing you can do about it. But the way you approach people, the way you look at them, how you respond to them, that makes a big difference. If you walk around with a sour face, no one wants to talk to you.

We need to be able to lift each other up, because once you have that kind of positive attitude everything else falls in place. You can have all the degrees and all the skills, if you don't have the right attitude you are not going to make it. Your success will be limited. If people see what you are doing is mechanical: see the draft, read it, send a note back, and so on, you won't be respected. There is not a day or minute that goes by that I don't find something to learn. It is such a complex organization.

ON GESTATION OF THE eLEARNING PROGRAM . . .

We said why not create a program that gives kids and teens the information they will need about finances and decisions for college. They don't get it from school, some will not get it from home, even some adults don't know this kind of information.

I always believed the earlier you form good habits the better. The longer you wait, the harder it is to change those habits. So I said, "Let's start with the early ones, like *Sesame Street*, where kids are three, four." Then, for elementary and junior high kids, we developed the IPO program. We identified fifteen strategies to give kids the kind of knowledge and skills they need to compete and succeed in this global market. These fifteen strategies each take about forty minutes, which is not a lot.

The idea is to get the kids engaged. There is a role for the parents or the guardians or caregivers, and there is a role for the school and the volunteers out there. Together I think we can create a Circle of Champions and make a difference for kids.

FROM ANDRAGOGY TO HEUTAGOGY

Consider True Self-Directed Learning, If You Dare

▷ ▷ **Fast Forward** *People who are not a part of the training or education profession might want to go on to another chapter. This is a purely theoretical discussion. We introduce an emerging learning paradigm that can inform eLearning design during the era of the Creative Economy. It is not necessary to know any of this information to create great eLearning.*

IN THE 1940s AND 1950s, education was still under the spell of behaviorism. Teachers brought their own version of stimulus-response-reward or punishment into the classroom. Listen to the lecture, do homework, study hard, and you'll get good grades and star stickers. "You'll be a success!" Misbehave, fall asleep, don't study, and you'll get the belt, the ruler, or a dunce cap. "You'll never make anything of yourself!"

While adult education didn't have the same threat of physical punishment or drill and kill routines, it too operated under the same teacher-knows-best paradigm. During that authoritarian era, it was simply natural to hand control over to the experts who knew best, be they doctors, politicians, or teachers. Would you ask patients to select their own operations or prescriptions? Factory workers to manage their own production schedules? Certainly not back then. And so it was thought teachers were the best judge of a student's what, when, where, and how. This attitude has come to be labeled *pedagogy* and was the dominant teaching paradigm until Malcolm Knowles flexed his creative muscles and "solved" a problem others didn't even realize existed.

BOOKSHELF BEST BETS

Forthcoming book on heutagogy, Stewart Hase

How We Think,
John Dewey

Many books by
Edward de Bono

Gods of Management,
Charles Handy

THE WINDS OF CHANGE BLOW IN

In 1946, Knowles, the head of adult education at the Boston YMCA,[1] responded to the growing number of requests from adults wanting to learn more about the stars by hiring a Harvard astronomy graduate student to lecture. Participants were bored and soon alienated. Unconstrained by the social, financial, and legal shackles children and employees face, they dropped out almost immediately.

With demand for information about the stars still high, Knowles tried something more experimental. The local enthusiast hired to take over took participants up to the roof at night. He asked them to discuss whatever came to mind or piqued their curiosity. The notes he took were the foundation for the classroom conversation. On subsequent occasions participants were invited to his private observatory.

As Knowles watched enrollment increasing, he attributed success to control being given to the participants and the teacher's role being more that of a peer than an authority.

This experience was Knowles's first step on a journey that included formulating an alternate learning theory (which has since become the de facto standard). His new theory, labeled *andragogy* (*andra* deriving from a Greek word for "man"[2]) to stand in stark contrast to *pedagogy* (*ped* deriving from a Greek word for "child"), was founded on the belief that adults learn most when they are self-directing, when they, in other words:

> take the initiative, with or without the help of others, in diagnosing their learning needs, formulating learning goals, identifying human and material resources for learning, choosing and implementing appropriate learning strategies, and evaluating learning outcomes.[3]

Knowles provided support for self-directed learning by citing five critical characteristics of adult learners. They are, in his own words:

1. Self-concept: As a person matures his self-concept moves from one of being a dependent personality toward one of being a self-directed human being.

2. Experience: As a person matures he accumulates a growing reservoir of experience that becomes an increasing resource for learning.

3. Readiness to learn: As a person matures his readiness to learn becomes oriented increasingly to the developmental tasks of his social roles.

4. Orientation to learning: As a person matures his time perspective changes from one of postponed application of knowledge to imme-

diacy of application, and accordingly his orientation toward learning shifts from one of subject-centeredness to one of problem centeredness.

5. Motivation to learn: As a person matures the motivation to learn is internal.[4]

ANDRAGOGY IN THE eLEARNING AGE

eLearning owes its existence to andragogy. It was born out of the dream that computers would provide people with a new and exciting way to take control of their own learning. Informal, or less structured, eLearning has done wonders for learners' ability to be self-directed. This is particularly true for people seeking information or communities of practice.

On the formal eLearning side of the continuum, especially among the asynchronous, off-the-shelf collections, such as Skillsoft and eCornell, self-directed is the exception and not the norm.

Many programs operate under the phantom teacher paradox. The physical teacher and the mechanisms formerly under the teacher's control (such as the sequencing of the curriculum and permission to speak with other students) have been eliminated. But the voice of the teacher, which is now a diffuse and abstract presence, has become even more authoritative by virtue of its being depersonalized.

When there was a teacher standing in front of a classroom, the participants had the option of thinking, "This is just one person and one person's opinion. When I took such and such a class from so and so, she clearly didn't take this approach," or, "When I spoke to so and so, she had a very different take on this . . ." Physically having a teacher in the room preserved the participant's critical assessment skills and rights: she could determine whether she agreed or disagreed with this one person's opinion. More important, she could probe further for clarification or dialogue, with the actual person communicating that something is expected to be done a certain way.

When an asynchronous, off-the-shelf type of eLearning is used that has a teacher-knows-best tone, it not only is *not* self-directing, it is actually disempowering. Here are three of the many reasons why this is the case:

1. The participant assumes the organization *as a whole* agrees with and condones the messages of right and wrong stated in the program because the organization is encouraging the program's use.

2. Without a person to attribute the correct and incorrect messages to, there is no vehicle for discussion, disagreement, probing, or otherwise coming to conclusions different from those communicated by the program.

> *A teacher should have maximal authority and minimal power.*
> **THOMAS SZAZ**

> *Education is a state-controlled manufactory of echoes.*
> **NORMAN DOUGLAS**

> *If I wished a boy to know something about the arts and sciences . . . I would not pursue the common course, which is merely to send him into the neighborhood of some professor, where anything is professed and practiced but the art of life.*
> **HENRY DAVID THOREAU**

3. When a participant does have the courage or energy to critically assess the actual messages in the program, via a message board or chat room, there is typically a moderator who subtly diverts discussion back to less controversial or mutiny-laden areas.

PEDAGOGY IN PRACTICE

Education is an admirable thing. But it is as well to remember from time to time that nothing that is worth knowing can be taught.

OSCAR WILDE

The best way to describe this phenomenon is through example. eCornell's course in time management is typical of asynchronous library classes where a pedagogical tone is present. There is no avatar or graphical representation of a teacher or facilitator, no teacher specifically called out. However, the design and content implies a voice of authority who knows what's best for the participant.

Look at the following phrases, taken verbatim, including emphasis, from the eCornell program (see the sample screenshot in Figure 3.1):

"Few things are more important for supervisors than time management."

"This is NOT the preferred response. This is incorrect."

"This answer is NOT correct because the manager needs to take a pro-active role in this situation. . . ."

"Your time management habits are poor, and need immediate attention."

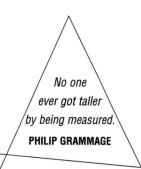

No one ever got taller by being measured.

PHILIP GRAMMAGE

An employee receiving these messages (especially accompanied by an authoritative narrator's spoken voice) will quickly be transported back to grade school. We've even seen people squirm as if they are uncomfortably sitting in a desk in grade school while the omnipotent teacher tells them what is best and right.

This disempowerment is diametrically opposed to the goals of people who support eLearning for their organizations. They were sold on the idea that self-directed eLearning would better prepare and support people in the Knowledge Economy. In some cases, especially information and community building–based eLearning, they got great value for their money. In other instances they would have been better off sticking with a classroom instructor. This is part of the reason for the backlash against eLearning we are still experiencing.

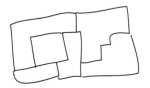

eLearning that takes away critical thinking, the ability to form one's own conclusions about the intelligence of a particular course of action, the need to organize, structure, gather, analyze, and select information—in summary to master a complex, dynamic world of increasing information

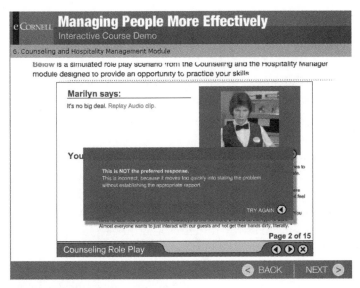

FIGURE 3.1 eCornell Screenshot

Copyright © Tower Innovative Learning Solutions, Inc.

and autonomy—actually hobbles the organization. It is better to provide nothing.

A new direction in eLearning development has to take place. Specifically, programs need to be designed that (1) go beyond the current application of self-directed learning and (2) are better aligned with the challenges, realities, and opportunities of the knowledge economy. Above all else, the learning process itself needs to follow that old tenet, treat thy neighbor as thyself. If we really want to develop people who will have what they need to make the most of this creative economy, we need to begin by treating them as if we are thoroughly committed to their ability to thrive in this new environment.

You expect to be treated as a competent, independent thinker who can adapt to change, manage complexity, and take control of your own world. When you participate in learning experiences that respect you and your abilities, this increases your self-confidence and ability to master the task at hand and all other tasks. When you are confronted by a learning experience that insults your intelligence or expects you to be an obedient pupil with limited control over the process, you feel disempowered. Sure, you might still learn the content, but you will hardly be inspired to take charge of the dynamic world out there. The short-term goal may have been met but the overarching one is completely undermined.

> *The secret of Education lies in respecting the pupil. It is not for you to choose what he shall know, what he shall do. It is chosen and foreordained, and he only holds the key to his own secret. By your tampering and thwarting and too much governing he may be hindered from his end.*
>
> **RALPH WALDO EMERSON**

> *Power can be taken but not given. The process of taking is empowerment in itself.*
> **GLORIA STEINEM**

> *He most honors my style who learns under it to destroy the teacher.*
> **WALT WHITMAN**

> *Education is learning what you didn't even know you didn't know.*
> **DANIEL BOORSTIN**

eLEARNING EVOLUTION

A new learning theory has been proposed that maximizes not only retention of content but adaptation and success in the twenty-first-century economy. Some will dismiss it as too idealistic and populist. Others will fail to see the difference between it and andragogy. Those who are able to get past the initial skepticism will be rewarded by gleaning some valuable inspiration and guidance.

Stewart Hase, a well-regarded professor at Southern Cross University in Australia, used his background in complexity theory, organizational learning, and adaptation to suggest a new spin on andragogy. He returned to the roots of self-directed learning to modernize it for the twenty-first century. His theory, named *heutagogy* to reflect a further evolution in the -agogy chain, will be briefly summarized here.[5]

Just as the Creative Economy is more refinement than replacement of the Knowledge Economy, heutagogy is more an expansion and reinterpretation of andragogy than a replacement of it. Hase's theory is incredibly rich and complex. We are going to summarize only a few key points, for the purpose of illustrating how following the principles of heutagogy can lead to the development of more effective eLearning—specifically, eLearning that ultimately makes people better equipped to thrive during the Creative Economy.

On the surface, heutagogy appears quite similar to andragogy. Hase's definition of it, "the study of self-directed learning," could easily be mistaken for a restatement of andragogy. However, there are some important differences between the two. For example, heutagogy specifically emphasizes the following:

1. *Learning how to learn.* Hase considers learning how to learn an integral part of any modern education initiative. Where andragogy focuses on the best way to help adults acquire and retain content, heutagogy requires the inclusion of an autodidactic component. Participants must walk away better able to master the process of acquiring knowledge, not just with more knowledge.

2. *Double loop learning.* Hase considers learning how to examine one's own internal assumptions, values, and beliefs a key part of learning how to learn. Argyris and Schön coined the term *double loop learning* to describe this method of solving complex problems that are constantly changing and ill structured. Specifically, they described four steps that can be done privately initially but must be repeated publicly to qualify as double loop learning (that's the double part):[6]

- Discovery of espoused theory and theory-in-use
- Invention of new meanings
- Production of new actions
- Generalization of results

3. *Universal learning opportunities.* Heutagogy speaks to a holistic and all-encompassing form of learning. Whereas andragogy focused on formal, structured education, heutagogy sees all experiences whether informal or formal as chances to learn. Specifically, there is a heightened emphasis on the importance of organic and informal learning experiences, including everything from internships and apprenticeships to everyday activities or events (such as interacting with others or environmental scanning).

4. *A nonlinear process.* Andragogy seems to imply people learn by following a logical, linear, conscious process. Knowles's description of self-directed learning reveals a deconstruction of a process that implies the learner is fully conscious of each step and is doing it in a linear process:

> The process in which individuals take the initiative, with or without the help of others, in diagnosing their learning needs, formulating learning goals, identifying human and material resources for learning, choosing and implementing appropriate learning strategies, and evaluating learning outcomes.[7]

A whale ship was my Yale College and my Harvard.
HERMAN MELVILLE

Hase asserts most learning not only doesn't follow this logical process but many of its steps are done either subconsciously or not at all. A supreme example of this principle in action is the expert who looks back on a mentor to whom she attributes much of her success. She will speak of the lessons she learned that were clearly by-products at the time but in retrospect became career makers.

5. *True learner self-direction.* The final point is a reiteration of what we said earlier. There is a large gulf between the theoretical adherence to andragogy and the actual practice. Hase tackles this head-on in heutagogy. He asserts that regardless of ideological bent, most learning programs today are teacher centered. Many eLearning developers and teachers are still controlling what is being learned, why it is being learned, how students are to behave during the course of instruction, and the criteria chosen to demonstrate whether the content has been learned.

The chief object of education is not to learn things but to unlearn things.
C. K. CHESTERTON

In practice the only real control that has been handed to eLearning participants is where they accept the delivery of that stream of

> A professor is one who talks in someone else's sleep.
>
> **W. H. AUDEN**

> One thorn of experience is worth a whole wilderness of warning.
>
> **JAMES RUSSELL COWELL**

instruction. Home? At the office? At night? During the day? Letting Hase's words do the talking:

> Teacher centered learning has to be organized by others who make the appropriate associations and generalizations on behalf of the learner. Thus, random individual experiences are taken to be inadequate sources of knowledge, the educational process is seen to need disciplined students, and literacy is seen to precede knowledge acquisition. Success is based upon attending to narrow stimuli presented by a teacher, an ability to remember that which is not understood and repeated rehearsal.
>
> Self-determined learning assumes that people have the potential to learn continuously and in real time by interacting with their environment, they learn through their lifespan, can be led to ideas rather than force fed wisdom of others, and thereby enhance their creativity, and relearn how to learn. Heutagogy recognizes that people learn when they are ready and that this is most likely to occur quite randomly, chaotically and in the face of ambiguity and need. The challenge becomes to maximize its potential.[8]

CONNECTING HEUTAGOGY TO eLEARNING TO THE BOTTOM LINE

Hase may be painting a picture as utopian as Walden or Valhalla or Nirvana. With wholesale adoption of all his ideas, most organizations may not be able to achieve their mission. Chaos is introduced when each individual is given free rein to determine her own learning path, method, and measurement criteria. How many people would want to get open heart surgery from a doctor who may not have elected to learn the basic canon of anatomy or biology? How many organizations could make a profit if their sales team was allowed to stumble across new products instead of deliberately being introduced to them and their features (come to think of it that's actually how learning happened in some organizations in which we worked, but we digress . . .)?

The critical gem contained in heutagogy is the power of individuals over systems. It speaks to the effectiveness of organic and complex learning processes that allow growth to emerge naturally.

There is much to be said for this method. Anyone who been around a toddler for an extended period of time has a deep respect for the individual's ability to drive her own learning and development. We never bought our daughter those enrichment videos or tapes or took her to classes to learn colors, shapes, words. She was not even a member of a playgroup. And yet when whatever that internal switch experts have yet to even begin to understand flipped, she'd irrepressibly start naming objects, shapes, and letters; counting blocks; pointing out colors. The process was magical and spoke to a primeval visceral quest to master the world around her.

At the very least we hope learning professionals begin to question and dialogue about the disconnect between the talk of self-directed learning and the implementation reality.

At the very most we hope they experiment with the creation of more organic situations, in which people can stumble into and guide learning according to their own needs and wants.

The ability to incorporate heutagogical principles is a critical part of developing eLearning that will foster the development of applied creativity, the kind that will add to organizational bottom lines. As we discussed in the previous chapter, a critical part of creativity that goes somewhere is discovering solutions to problems people didn't know existed, figuring out solutions to problems everyone knows exist, evaluating the feasibility of different solutions, and modifying solutions to be more workable. The core competency required in each of these situations is the ability to critically examine one's own assumptions, methods, values, and approaches. And that is exactly what heutagogy encourages.

It's time for the learning world to wake up and smell the coffee. Even though andragogy is ideologically terrific and gets a great deal of lip service, the vast majority of eLearning still does not even approach being self-directed. Heutagogy is not a magician solving this problem with a magic wand. However, it does provide a framework and inspiration for people to begin exploring an eLearning world where participants take charge of much more than whether they press the forward or back button.

> *Creative minds have always been known to survive any kind of bad training.*
> **ANNA FREUD**

> *The purpose of education is not to fit the individual for a place in society, but to enable him to make his own place.*
> **BOYD BODE**

> *Instead of pouring knowledge into people's heads, we need to help them grind a new set of eyeglasses so that we can see the world in a new way.*
> **J. S. BROWN**

NOTES

1. Robert Carlson, "Malcolm Knowles: Apostle of Andragogy," *Vitae Scholasticae*, Spring 1989, 8(1).

2. See the *Oxford English Dictionary*.

3. Malcolm Knowles, *Self-Directed Learning: A Guide for Learners and Teachers* (Upper Saddle River, N.J.: Prentice Hall/Cambridge, 1975; revised), p. 18.

4. Malcolm Knowles and Associates, *Andragogy in Action* (San Francisco: Jossey-Bass, 1984), p. 12.

5. Stewart Hase and Chris Kenyon, "From Andragogy to Heutagogy," http://ultibase. rmit.edu.au/Articles/dec00/hase1.pdf, accessed July 2004.

6. Chris Argyris and Donald Schön, *Theory in Practice* (San Francisco: Jossey-Bass, 1974).

7. Knowles, *Self-Directed Learning,* p. 18.

8. Hase and Kenyon, "From Andragogy to Heutagogy."

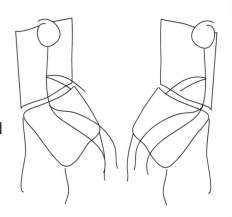

KIRK RAMSEY

Director of Learning Technologies of learndirect scotland

ON RESULTS . . .

We now have a stable operation with 410 learning centers branded with the learndirect scotland quality mark. Having that mark means they passed quite a difficult assessment and ensures us those centers actually have the open, welcome, and supportive environment that is needed to get people involved in learning. It is particularly important to our mission, which is to get people who have not been typically involved in learning back into learning. Our mission is less about doing more for those who do it anyhow and more about actually getting people started who either have never started in their whole lives, who may have never achieved anything educationally at school, or may have never achieved anything educationally since.

ON THE GESTATION OF THE IDEA . . .

The majority of learning-focused organizations have a very clear population group to work with. It could be by industry, age group, or whatever interest, but ours is very horizontal. It crosscuts right through all subject areas, all population groups, and every interest area, pleasure and professional.

That is what got me involved. It is a hard thing to do but then again I don't get a lot of pleasure in doing things that are that easy. I would much rather do something very difficult and get pleasure out of it even if I didn't completely succeed in accomplishing the goal.

Actually I think that is a motivator for many of the learndirect employees. We are very fortunate. Our activities and the groups we serve have attracted people who are much more likely to be interested in dealing with difficult things and finding solutions. We don't have too many people who just want to get the points.

ON PEOPLE . . .

Persistence is how we got where we are. The world is still filled with interest in short-term gain and certainly no interest in long-term pain, and that breeds an attitude that is not good for anyone. When something new comes along it tends to be greeted with the "not invented here" syndrome. People who otherwise may be very enthusiastic about that very activity oppose it because it hasn't focused on them and they haven't gotten a short-term profit from it.

When we started off there were many people who saw the dangers and the difficulties and the monumental undertaking we were attempting. They realized they could fail spectacularly and decided they did not want to be associated with us. But then over time, small success reaps bigger success, which convinced more people to be involved in us. We took the approach: let's not try to conquer the world, let's just identify small areas where we can genuinely make a difference and build those up. At the same time we decided to try just a few things that had a high probability for failure, because without trying we would never be able to deal with them. We then didn't fail, we succeeded!

I tend to say quite often, "Why do you think businesses were called companies in the first place? Because it is a company of people." It is not an institution, not an edifice, and it is not an account. It's a company of people that have come together because they have common interests. People deal with people, organizations don't deal with organizations. People make the difference. If you are going to be in a risk situation you only get to stay there if you've got an association with the right kind of people who recognize and understand and are prepared to tolerate that risk.

Five characteristics we look for in a potential employee. Nonconformist. Doesn't just accept opinions. Enthusiasm shows; it tends to come through very, very quickly and it doesn't matter in what form. Risk positive. I like people who enjoy risk. Interested in things.

I ask people about some of the things that they have done in their life. Usually I start off asking them to give me a two-minute thumbnail of themselves. Most people are quite good at doing that. They may not like to do it, but they are good at it.

Typically they will pick out the things that are of interest to them. We are all very self-centered, we all love to talk about ourselves, so given that opportunity in that two-minute thumbnail we'll talk about things that really interest us. If we don't, it is very, very obvious. You'll get the guys that come in and have thought this through very carefully. They come in thinking, "I know what his hot buttons are going to be and I am going to talk to those hot buttons." I put those candidates out the door immediately.

The technique is really to get people to do what they are good at and just talk about themselves. If they actually have been honest in that summary, you'll get what you need; if they have been dishonest in the summary and they have done their homework and they are trying to please you, it will be very obvious. There are people who love it when the candidate is just saying stuff to please them. They just want to hear that stuff and they'll hire those guys. I'm not one of those people. The people who have succeeded in the past have been honest. Otherwise they ain't going to succeed with me.

ON CREATIVITY AND THE DEVELOPMENT PROCESS . . .

My approach is very much experimental, let's try it. Who cares what the "*experts*" say. I don't think there are any experts and I wouldn't claim to be an expert either, just an interested experimenter. If we keep experimenting we will find some things that work and we'll find some things that don't, but even the things that don't work will lead us to find other ways that we can make things work in the same area. We just need to keep trying enough different options. Out of that will fall a number of successes. A small success will lead to a bigger success, and we can grow from there.

Once we were trying to introduce an eLearning program to centers where this was an alien concept. They hadn't done any eLearning. At the same time we were trying to drive them up that slope of managing the eLearning. We wanted to maximize the benefits and get leverage because we are not dealing with ten people. We are working with 10,000; 100,000; and a million.

In order to do that you need to leverage as many tools as you can. We saw managed eLearning as a good way to do that. Initially we tried to get the learning centers on board with that integrated program. It seemed doable. In practice it was very, very difficult. Part of the reason was because the majority of players in the eLearning market (even the ones who initially appeared to be on the ball and making good progress themselves) couldn't cope with the extent of our project and the rate we were trying to move.

It was a failure in the sense that we didn't get the number of organizations involved in the integrated eLearning solutions in the time scale we were looking for. But, on the other hand, it was a success because it illustrated to the whole community that there are other ways to do things. It showed everyone, yes, it is not easy, and yes, it does require commitment and time and energy. One of two colleagues ran for cover because it looked dangerous. But others remained involved and remained optimistic. We helped people who work with us make the leap across that chasm by learning from this situation.

ON PARTNERSHIPS . . .

Partnerships are crucial. You can't do everything. Even if you want to, you can't. Things move just too fast these days and there is such a huge variety of interest areas that we need to address. No matter what size organization you are, there is just no way you can ever do it on your own.

Partnership is a much overused word. When people talk about partnership, I think for the most part they rarely understand what it means. Partnerships are expensive. They are expensive in a number of ways: they are expensive in time, in energy, in resources, and they are expensive in critical success factors.

It is challenging because, as I said before, there are people who only want to be partners if the tasks are easy and they can share the success, not the pain and failure. Genuine partnership recognizes that each organization is going to have to share some of the key performance indicators.

For example, we work with organizations like Career Scotland, a new organization set up to centralize career services for people in Scotland. Since we need to work with many of the same people, it makes sense to have a partnership. Remembering that people work with people, organizations don't work with organizations, one of the senior people . . . and I work together to keep our organizations tight.

One of the first things we did was identify which publicly quoted key performance indicators we have in common and those which may not seem to be in common but actually are. We work on those together so everybody wins.

I don't think either of us sees this as career building. There are no politics or ego involved. It's back to a personal thing. People make things happen.

If people look at partnership from a political small perspective you again run into a big issue with partnerships. So few people share the attitude that working together you can do huge things quickly, that you can actually leverage the activities of both organizations. It's a law of squares: if you get two organizations in a partnership you'll get four times the benefit, if you get three organizations, you will get nine times the benefit, if you get eight you get sixty-four, and so on. One of the things people miss about partnerships is that in a genuine partnership your leverage goes way beyond anything that individuals or single organizations could ever achieve.

ON THE IMPORTANCE OF DRAMA/METAPHOR . . .

People lose interest in most eLearning today. And why is that? My conjecture is that digital natives are used to a highly interactive, multiple-channel world. Most eLearning extracts them from that and drops them into a very limited activity, single-channel world.

eLearning has generated this view that if it is not interactive then it is no good. What do they mean by interaction? Well, you tend to find most of the time they mean interacting by clicking a mouse. Well, that's not interaction and it is certainly not engaging. I am referring to real engagement; that is what we are interested in. In games and other narratives there is real engagement.

Since when was Harry Potter not engaging? You pick up a Harry Potter book, it is five or six hundred pages of closely printed text, and it's the kids who don't like to read who are reading it! Engagement is what we are after, but it has to be of the kind the individual is interested in. There is no point in someone who is fifty years old trying to use their view of the world to engage somebody who is five years old; that ain't gonna work. It is just as bad for somebody who is fifty years old to try to engage a twenty-five-year-old using the fifty-year-old's view. I am interested in games, not because they are games as such, because they are engaging. They engage many, many millions of people. In every country digital games are available and they engage tens of millions. The age group that is using games currently runs up to about forty years old typically, but there are older gamers too. Surveys have been done that 75 percent of gamers expect to play games for the rest of their lives. Eighty-five percent of the players of sims like SimCity are girls. It's an approach that really hasn't been exploited with adults for learning purposes. It has been toyed around with for kids, but it has never been mainstreamed. It especially has never been considered a mainstream option for adult learning. I seriously think that it ought to be. That's why we are working with games and I am doing it in a number of different ways.

Take the most successful games around the world. What has made them successful? Initial engagement? No. That doesn't sustain play. There have to be really good game play strategies and multiple experiences so it will attract and retain people with a huge variety of different engagement styles and types. What the games environments do is that they create very, very open systems. Yes, you have to achieve the goal, but there is almost no limit to the ways the goal can be achieved. The strategy and tactics the people are going to use are the ones that suit their skills and knowledge to best effect. As they become more and more involved in the game and become more experienced, they'll learn alternate ways to deal with these things. The levels will lead to more complexity. Beyond that, they will understand there are other resources that can be obtained from other people. The games developers have supported this form of learning through their community zones and networks. This allows gamers to communicate and share, to self-develop.

People might say, "I just had this great idea. If we just had this particular type of neuron shield we could get past that blaster with a whole team in one pass . . . how can we create one of them?" What the games developers have done is actually create development environments for their own games that the players can use so that they can go develop that neuron shield.

ON HEUTAGOGY . . .

One of the things that really annoys me is the constant use of the word *pedagogy*. No matter what age group you are talking about, pedagogy doesn't work. A fair number of people may talk about and refer to andragogy that Knowles made popular thirty years ago. But there are many people, traditionalists, who rejected it because it would mean students actually may have an opinion. We live in this digital world where everyone has an opinion and can express it. Andragogy may be where it starts, but if you are actually looking for learning theories that work, we are much closer to the heutagogical model. Heutagogy goes beyond andragogy. It is much more about self-directedness. It is really about the self-directed learner and the self-determined learner. You are building some resources around the learner and allowing them to self-determine, to actually take the lead. That aligns best to the digital native context we are in.

For example, a benefit of games is that digital gamers are really, really good partner workers because they have learned those skills through their gaming experiences. If they are in a team-based operation, the actual give and take that they need to succeed as a team is parallel to the behavior they used to succeed in gaming.

The press show gamers as if they are introverted oddballs, who sit in the dark corner with their nose up against the screen. They might do that. But they are actually developing really good-quality relationships, partnerships and techniques for working with others that are quite sophisticated.

In many of the online games you have to actually create an organization to achieve the goal of the game. That takes formation of a team of different people with different skills and characteristics. Which means you get individuals that as individual online gamers might be very successful in their own online world. But they then discover they can't go any further because one person is not enough. They need to find partners who will add to their capabilities.

They need to recruit partners; that's a skill. Having recruited them, now they need to engage them in their goal. That's team building, another skill. Then they need to work together to plan the strategy, fill the strategy with resource requirements, match those resource requirements to team member skills, and so on. They need to identify development requirements of their team members and help enhance those skills in order to meet joint objectives.

All of the aspects of building a team for business purposes are actually in there! They develop these business skills without being told what needs to be done or learned or how it needs to be done. The players are self-determining what they have and what they need. What game developers have done very cleverly is create an array of resources and tools around the core game to allow that self-determination. People in the education industry haven't caught onto doing this yet. Not recognized by the press or society but [these resources and tools] are there. There are real genuine, valuable business skills that are being developed in online gaming. That is being completely missed by the majority of corporations.

We want to create that organic model in eLearning. If we can, actually create an organic model for lifelong eLearning. We want to transform eLearning from a delivery channel to an engagement channel. It is only then that we will actually be delivering heutagogical models of learning.

PART 2
COMING ATTRACTIONS

Lights, Camera, eLearning!

 Fast Forward If you are convinced it's time to start developing eLearning that uses both cognition (intellect) and emotion as conduits to facilitate learning, skip all the justification stuff below and jump right into the main content by going to Chapter Five.

If you would like to hear a justification of why we think emotion needs to be tapped as a potentially important conduit for content presented in eLearning, begin with Chapter Four.

If you believe it is important to tap into emotions to enhance learning and are familiar with the basic components of narrative (plot, story, character, and setting), skip to Chapter Six.

Most complex skills, knowledge and attitudes, and interpersonal content, including management, development, higher-order thinking skills, and interpersonal and other social skills, fall under the purview of deep learning.

In the first section of this book we looked at the macro worldview. We put eLearning in the context of the trends and environmental forces that are influencing the direction learning needs to take in the near future.

In Part Two we zoom in our camera lens to focus on the micro level: the concrete application and practice needed to support the Creative Economy.

We begin by asserting that deep learning, learning that affects the learner's self-concept, is more likely to be effective when the process of acquiring the learning includes an emotional component. We show how this approach can result in not only increased retention, accelerated learning, and improvements in all the other ROI-type statistics but other, "invisible" outcomes that affect the bottom line as well: for example, it can stimulate individual and environmental creativity, generate enthusiasm and excitement for learning, and foster group cohesion.

Of the hundreds of ways eLearning can target the heart as well as the head, we opted for the dramatic.

Chapter Four illustrates our reasoning behind seeing emotion as a valuable conduit for learning.

Chapter Five establishes a common understanding of terminology and gives an overview of the building blocks that make up effective narrative (aka storytelling).

Chapter Six presents strategies for wielding narrative elements in eLearning.

The chapters in the middle section of Part Two examine character and figurative language in detail.

Chapter Seven introduces character development, touching on terminology, roles, and making the characters come to life.

Chapter Eight focuses on writing dialogue that is realistic and effective.

Chapter Nine follows along the same lines but looks more closely at the role of figures of speech such as metaphors.

The chapters in the last section of Part Two address the visual aspects of drama: how graphic design influences the effectiveness of eLearning.

Chapter Ten covers style and layout.

Chapter Eleven looks at type.

Chapter Twelve discusses perspective, color, and universal principles of design.

In Part Three, we will zoom the camera back out halfway between the macro world and the micro application to look at the immediate environment surrounding the eLearning initiative.

> For help finding resources such as graphic designers, novelists, playwrights, and screenwriters, see the "Casting Call" section in Chapter Thirteen.

TOPICS IN PART 2

**EMOTION MAKES
eLEARNING MORE
EFFECTIVE**

Page 53

**MAKING eLEARNING
DRAMATIC**

Page 63

NARRATIVE ARC

Page 65

**NARRATIVE
BREAKDOWN (PLOT
POINTS)**

Page 79

**CREATING CONFLICT
STEPS 1–5**

Page 89

**STEPS TO CREATING
A PROTAGONIST**

Page 107

**WHAT TYPE OF
NARRATION IS BEST?**

Page 113

**USING "IMMERSIVE"
METAPHORS**

**METAPHORS IN
DIALOGUE**

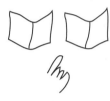

**VISUAL DRAMA:
SELECTING A VISUAL
STYLE AND LAYOUT**

**TYPE KERNING,
TRACKING, AND
LEADING**

"CAMERA" ANGLE

**COLOR AND
EMOTION**

**FIVE CRITICAL
DESIGN PRINCIPLES**

LIGHTS, CAMERA, eLEARNING!

Emotional eLearning

HOW DEEP IS DEEP?

FOR THE PURPOSES of this discussion, we are going to divide all learning into two categories: shallow and deep. Shallow learning concerns itself with those skills and knowledge that affect intellect almost exclusively. Activities that may or may not be physically or intellectually demanding but do not reside in a context that needs to be assimilated or considered on an emotional level by the learner are categorized as shallow learning.

Learning how to use a new computer program, assemble a product, memorize a password for a database, change a diaper, play a new guitar chord, find the best vendor for office supplies, review the latest advances in medicines for diabetes, and so on are largely shallow learning tasks. None of them appears at first glance to require much emotional energy or attention.

Deep learning, in contrast, not only affects intellect, it modifies an individual's self-concept. It affects self-esteem, identity, and other fundamental facets of the psyche. It is more likely to be greeted with an emotional response on the part of the learner and will almost certainly require a voluntary shift in self-perception if it is to have a long-lasting impact. Deep learning is more likely than shallow learning to have the following characteristics:

- It requires assimilation of multiple competencies, facts, and behavioral changes.
- It affects interpersonal behavior.
- It takes place over an extended time.

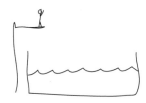

> The universe is made up of stories, not atoms.
> **MURIEL RUKEYSER**

BOOKSHELF BEST BETS

Emotional Design, Donald Norman

"What Good Are Positive Emotions?" Barbara Frederickson (in *Review of General Psychology,* 1998, *2,* 300–319)

Designing Pleasurable Products, Patrick Jordan

> *The best teacher lodges an intent not in the mind but in the heart.*
> **ANNE MURDOCH**

> *The strongest human instinct is to impart information, the second strongest is to resist it.*
> **KENNETH GRAHAME**

Managing people more effectively, strategic and scenario planning, understanding ethics, becoming a lifelong learner, raising venture capital, doing project management, and so on, are examples of deep learning.

BASKET WEAVING VERSUS BRAIN SURGERY

Shallow learning is easily learned. The content can be assimilated on an intellectual level, which means it can often be effectively learned without any translation or assistance. Deep learning, because it is unlikely to be accepted or even understood on an intellectual level, is facilitated by an assistant who helps the messages go from source to recipient.

Let's consider this metaphorically for a moment. Imagine the two types of learning to be appliances used in the typical North American home, which has outlets ready to run 110-volt AC electricity. Shallow learning appliances are the irons, DVD players, and KitchenAids of the world. They require 110-volt electricity, so it's just a matter of plugging them in and they're good to go.

Deep learning appliances, in contrast, are like computers and laptops. In order to work they require DC electricity. Because a typical home does not run on this type of electricity, a transformer is needed to translate the signal given out in the home (AC) to the signal that can be received by the appliance (DC).

If the signal to be learned is something shallow, something unlikely to wake our hibernating emotions, say determining where to put the company cafeteria, how to rebuild an engine, or which press release broadcast service provides the best ROI, the information can be given out on an intellectual level (charts, fact sheets, and so on) and assimilated seamlessly by the recipient.

Conversely, say the signal is deep learning. Perhaps a manager wants to encourage an employee to be more assertive in meetings; a project requires an individual, who has always had a fear of numbers, to learn how to create financial projections; a client tells a salesperson he lost the account because he didn't really listen to or respond to the client's needs. These signals can all be threatening to self-esteem, because this type of learning is often interpreted as stemming from criticism.

In a best-case situation the recipient will respond with ambivalence: perhaps a part of the message will be heard. But other parts will be rejected, at least initially. In most instances the person will respond with denial, anger, fear, uncertainty, disbelief, or confusion. If she has already perceived and accepted the need to learn whatever it is she needs to learn, then *it is no longer deep learning.*

As with the DC appliances we mentioned before, the signal needs a conduit, a facilitation device to provide a greater chance for the signal to have an impact. Purely providing intellectual information in cases of deep learning is just not as effective. People are not robots.

Think back to your own experiences. When others have provided suggested areas of improvement for you in a warm, friendly, and empathetic way, often accompanied by stories from their own lives, didn't you pay closer attention to their advice than when it was delivered in a cold, professional manner via statistics and out-of-context examples, usually by a person who expressed little to no emotion or concern?

Even when the subject matter is less about personal growth or interpersonal skills, for instance when the content is fundraising or advocacy, those approaches that include comedy or tragedy or play on any other emotion make the material easier to absorb. Emotions enable individuals to connect and identify with the content. They make it more memorable and increase the likelihood of long-term behavioral and psychological changes.

> *The intellect is always fooled by the heart.*
> **FRANÇOIS DE LA ROCHEFOUCAULD**

EMOTIONAL BRANDING

The former chief marketing officer at Coca-Cola, easily the world's most successful brand, points out the important role emotion plays in helping individuals form bonds with products or organizations:

> Emotional branding is about building relationships; it is about giving a brand and a product long-term value. . . . it is based on that unique trust that is established with an audience. It elevates purchases based upon need to the realm of desire. The commitment to a product or institution, the pride we feel upon receiving a wonderful gift of a brand we love or having a positive shopping experience in an inspiring environment where someone knows our name or brings an unexpected gift of coffee—these feelings are at the core of emotional branding.

"eLearning" could easily be substituted for "product or institution" in that statement. One of the main reasons to make emotion an integral and deliberate part of eLearning is to increase participants' trust that the program really does have their best interests at heart.

Calling All Drama Queens (and Kings)!

Whenever a significant or long-lasting change takes place within a person, it is almost inevitably accompanied by an emotional moment. It may be a small, seemingly insignificant emotional response, such as laughing at a poignant joke. Or it may be a profound one, a crisis such as loss of a loved one. Or a moment of profound joy, such as the birth of a child. But regardless of the profundity of the actual event, the emotions are central to the transformation that takes place.[1]

This leaves the person seeking to drive business results in somewhat of a quandary. The business world is largely inhospitable to emotions. Pushing for emotionally based learning experiences is unlikely to go over big. By the same token, even if some lone ranger gets funding and support for it, where would he turn?

Instructional design has a long legacy of focusing almost exclusively on cognition and motivation and neglecting or ignoring emotion.[2] As a result most of the deep learning–focused eLearning currently available also relies almost exclusively on cognition and ignores emotion.[3] Which positions a well-intentioned businessperson between a rock and a hard place.

It's understandable that eLearning vendors and developers aren't keen to jump into this ocean. Because corporations and government are their largest clients, their desire to play it safe is understandable. Most are simply importing their live instruction paradigm into the eLearning world: they are appealing to what they perceive to be clients' and participants' intellectual, logical, and rational selves.

This strategy of playing it safe by avoiding emotional appeals has merit when a human instructor or facilitator is an integral part of the learning process: most instructors, especially the good ones, will automatically infuse the curricula with an emotional charge. The emotional aspects do not need to be specifically called out or elaborated because with people as the delivery mechanism it will almost always be part of the experience.

Most software and computers providing eLearning today have no such predisposition, or even ability, which translates into a large opportunity not being widely recognized or addressed: playing to the heartstrings as strongly as to the headstrings.

> *Intelligence is almost useless to someone who has no other quality.*
> **ALEXIS CARREL**

> *We know too much and feel too little. At least we feel too little of those creative emotions from which a good life springs.*
> **BERTRAND RUSSELL**

Barbara Frederickson's broaden and build theory[4] has become the cornerstone for many academic theories about how emotion influences learning and behavior. Here is her later synopsis of that theory:

This model posits that, unlike negative emotions, which narrow people's thought-action repertoires (for example, fight or flight), positive emotions *broaden* people's thought-action repertoires, encouraging them to discover novel lines of thought or action. Joy, for instance, creates the urge to play; interest creates the urge to explore and so on. A key, incidental outcome of these broadened mindsets is an increase in personal resources: As individuals discover new ideas and actions, they build their physical, intellectual, social and psychological resources. Play, for instance, builds physical, socioemotional, and intellectual skills, and fuels brain development. Similarly, exploration increases knowledge and psychological complexity. . . .[5]

PUTTING THE "E" IN eLEARNING

A movement of exactly this sort is in its infancy, cultivated predominantly by Europeans and some of the bleeding-edge tech think tanks in the United States. Frank Thissen is a consultant and professor of multimedia communications and information design at the University of Applied Sciences, Stuttgart, Germany, and University of Karlsruhe, Germany. For the past several years he has been focusing on how emotion can make eLearning more effective. Recently his corporate sector experience prompted him to join forces with eleven international partners[6] to examine the theoretical basis for emotions as a key component in eLearning and to develop a concrete prototype.

His perspective is largely congruent with our own. In his words:

> Emotions are essential for the success of human learning processes. This well established idea has been confirmed by modern cognitive science, but is neglected in most of the models and implementations of computer-based and Web-based learning. Very often eLearning means the presentation of information and material on a very rational base. And communication between learners and trainers takes place in a much reduced form that ignores the fact that communication is always meta-communication (Bateson) as well.[7]

I think therefore I am is the statement of an intellectual who underestimates toothaches.
MILAN KUNDERA

Another key leader of this movement is Hermann Astleitner, an associate professor of education who specializes in research on educational technology and emotional education at the University of Salzberg in Austria. His research has shown making eLearning more emotionally engaging can reduce dropout rates and increase effectiveness. He explains the importance of incorporating emotion into eLearning:

Seeing's believing, but feeling's the truth.
THOMAS FULLER

> Despite the importance of *emotions* in daily life, for decades the focus in instructional design and technology was on the learner's cognitive and

In his book *Emotional Design,* Donald Norman cites Nathan Shedroff and Julie Khaslavsky's three basic steps to maintaining a deep emotional relationship between an item or experience and the person experiencing it: (1) enticement—make an emotional promise, (2) relationship—continually fulfill that promise, and (3) fulfillment—end the experience in a memorable way.[8]

You can learn more about a range of these approaches and the techniques they suggest in the ". . . And Even More Reading!" section of this book.

motivational processes (Reigeluth, 1997). Human *emotions* have not received adequate attention, not even in the latest comprehensive reviews of instructional psychology and design closely related to instructional technology (for example, Liebowitz, 1999; Tennyson, Schott, Seel, and Dijkstra, 1997). One reason for this situation might be that practitioners in the field of instructional technology do not call for knowledge and skills in emotional design of instruction. Many designers believe that the emotional education of students is the duty of parents or peers rather than computers, which are cold technologies without any *emotions* and will never be successful in this intimate area of human life.[9]

Rosalind Picard is one of the most famous leaders of this movement. The people mentioned previously are focused primarily on deconstructing and developing models that focus on how humans use emotion in learning and secondarily how eLearning needs to work within this framework. Picard, director of the affective computing group at the MIT Media Lab, comes from the computer's perspective. Specifically, her work in affective computing is focused on

> . . . creating personal computational systems endowed with the ability to sense, recognize and understand human emotions, together with the skills to respond in an intelligent, sensitive, and respectful manner toward the user and his/her emotions. We are also interested in the development of computers that aid in communicating human emotions, computers that assist and support people in development of their skills of social-emotional intelligence, and computers that "have" emotional mechanisms, as well as the intelligence and ethics to appropriately manage, express, and otherwise utilize these "emotions."[10]

Each group and each individual has a specific conception of how emotion can enhance eLearning. Almost all the deep learning content covered in eLearning could benefit from some of the points made by the people mentioned here and others in the area.

EMOTION IN MOTION
The following are all examples of successful products and organizations that have recognized emotion as a critical market driver.
Swatch. Donald Norman reports that Swatch was "not a watch company; it was an emotions company. Sure, they made the precision watches

and movements used in most watches around the world (regardless of brand displayed on the case), but what they had really done was to transform the purpose of a watch from timekeeping to emotion. Their expertise, their president boldly proclaimed, was human emotion, as he rolled up his sleeves to display the many watches on his arm."[11]

iPod. There is absolutely no technical or financial reason to make headphones white. In fact, given that the majority of the world's headphones are gray or black, making them white probably costs extra. However, as Steve Jobs would concur, the white headphones operate on a deeper level. Even the people inside Apple nixed it at first, as happens with many innovations. Jonathan Ive, the guy who designs many Apple products, recalls a conversation that included the statement, "Headphones can't be white; headphones are black or dark gray." Now, the trademark white headphones have come to be emotional branding. People with white headphones (even when you can't see the player) are somehow cooler, better. A recent article in Britain's *Evening Standard* noted how people with the white headphones are being singled out by muggers. Ironically, this can be the ultimate compliment: the white headphones are such a status symbol, demand for the iPod among thieves has easily surpassed demand for other types of music players.

Milk and juice cartons. We don't know exactly how milk and juice came to be housed in cartons. However, for many years that packaging was synonymous with those products. With today's technology there are several other casings that would serve juice as well as or better than the traditional cardboard one. However, the only change that has been made in recent years is the addition of a round plastic spout in the middle of the carton top. It makes it easier to pour the juice and keeps it fresher than opening the flaps on the side. Why not just change the entire package to a plastic jug or some other container? Emotion. People equate juice and especially milk with cartons. Many, too young to remember glass bottles and too old to lack a sense of what milk belongs in, have become accustomed to milk in cartons. Rather than risk breaking this attachment, and potentially the trust, of consumers, producers simply added that round spout. This is an excellent example of evolution taking precedence over revolution.

JetBlue and Song Airlines. Sure, JetBlue is a low-priced airline but its success has hinged on a profound understanding of the markets it is serving: New Yorkers and Californians. These groups buy not only with their

pocketbook but with their emotions: the experience is an important aspect of any undertaking whether it be purchasing a pocketbook or plane ticket. Unlike other low-priced airlines, JetBlue tapped into this emotional nerve by creating an experience that included what the people in these markets wanted, and eliminated what they didn't want. The satellite television and leather seats made flyers feel more at home; the elimination of airline sub-standard meal service was a welcome good-bye.

Song is Delta Airlines' answer to JetBlue. Delta recognized the importance of emotion and has attempted to trump JetBlue's card by introducing elements of design and style specifically targeted at female upscale travelers. Kate Spade uniforms, organic fruit, and treats from the chic Dylan's candy store in Manhattan are all tangible evidence of the recognition of emotions as important parts of any experience.

NOTES

1. There is extensive support for the connection between emotions and learning in most fields except instructional design. One of the most popular proponents among the business community is William Bridges, who focuses on transition as an opportunity for learning and growth. A recent book by Bridges is *Managing Transitions* (New York: Perseus Publishing, 2003).

2. C. M. Reigeluth, "Instructional Theory, Practitioner Needs, and New Directions: Some Reflections," *Educational Technology*, 1997, 97(1), 42–47; Jay Liebowitz, *Building Organizational Intelligence: A Knowledge Management Primer* (Boca Raton, Fla.: CRC Press, 1999); R. Tennyson, F. Schott, N. Seel, and S. Dijkstra (eds.), *Instructional Design: International Perspectives* (Mahwah, N.J.: Erlbaum, 1997).

3. This makes sense if you look at the most likely chain of logic: instructional design has a long legacy of focusing almost exclusively on cognition and motivation. Some instructional designers have even "intentionally neglected emotions because they fear interference with cognitive or motivational objectives" (C. M. Reigeluth and L. M. Nelson, "A New Paradigm of ISD?" In R. M. Branch and B. B. Minor (eds.), *Educational Media and Technology Yearbook* [Englewood, Colo.: Libraries Unlimited, 1997]. This is no doubt a survival tactic for an industry that is dependent on the business world for its survival. The workplace is inhospitable to emotions. An employee who cries readily, a CEO who shows fear during the annual shareholders meeting, a negotiator who expresses boundless enthusiasm before a deal is closed, an employee who yawns in a one on one with her supervisor, a doctor who tells his patient about his home life—all would be quickly labeled unprofessional and suffer the consequences. Daniel Goleman (the author of *Emotional Intelligence*) and the hundreds of

others involved in the movement have done much to raise the esteem accorded to emotions and the way they contribute positively to the bottom line. Unfortunately, emotions still get more lip service than genuine attention. Conventional wisdom still frowns on too much "drama" in the workplace.

4. Barbara Frederickson, "What Good Are Positive Emotions?" *Review of General Psychology*, 1998, *2*, 300–319.

5. Barbara Frederickson and Thomas Joiner, "Positive Emotions Trigger Upward Spirals Toward Emotional Well-Being," *Psychological Science*, Mar. 2002, *13*(2), 172–175.

6. Hermann Astleitner, University of Salzburg, Austria; Gerhard Fischer, University of Colorado, Boulder, U.S.A.; Edmund Kösel, University of Freiburg, Germany; Kai Krause, ByteBurg, Bad Breisig, Germany; Frieder Nake, University of Bremen, Germany; Rosalind Picard, MIT Media Laboratory, Cambridge, Massachusetts, U.S.A.; Gerhard Roth, University of Bremen, Germany; Klaus Scherer, University of Genf, Switzerland; Manfred Spitzer, University of Ulm, Germany; Agency Wagner + Coerdts, Karlsruhe, Germany; Henrik Walter, University of Ulm, Germany.

7. Frank Thissen, "Project: 'Understanding the Role of Emotion in eLearning,'" http://www.frank-thissen.de/english/concept.pdf, accessed May 2004.

8. Hermann Astleitner and Detlev Leutner, "Designing Instructional Technology from an Emotional Perspective," *Journal of Research on Computing in Education*, Summer 2000, *32*(4).

9. Donald Norman, *Emotional Design* (New York: Basic Books, 2004), p. 112.

10. Affective Computing Research Group, "About Affective Computing," MIT Media Lab, http://affect.media.mit.edu/AC_about.html, accessed May 2004.

11. Norman, *Emotional Design*.

5

AS SEEN ON TV

Using Narratives and Drama in eLearning

THIS CHAPTER and the next address just one approach to using emotion to make eLearning more effective. It's no less or more important than any other emotional conduit method suggested by the people in this area. It simply fits in well with our fundamental thesis of the need to prepare for success in the Creative Economy.

We see dramatic eLearning as a key method of infusing learning with emotion. Therefore we see dramatic eLearning as a critical path to achieving business results as a result of learning.

Our approach is to inject emotion into eLearning through drama.

When we refer to drama we are really referring to the dramatic: eLearning that is "arresting or forceful in appearance or effect." In other words we are suggesting people start developing programs that more closely approximate that addicting "grab you" factor commonly found in music, film, literature, theater, comedy, and other performance arts. That factor is the result of a well-constructed narrative. Also known as storytelling, it is the drug that keeps an audience glued to books, songs, movies, video games, and the like.

Narrative (aka *storytelling*) broadly encompasses all the elements that make up the telling of a tale or story. We focus on five of the most significant: plot, story, genre, setting, and character.[1] These components work in unison to set the cycle of immersion in motion and to keep it spinning. The cycle (Figure 5.1) can be described by these steps. (1) The audience members become engaged with the content because they see something that catches their attention. (2) After their attention is captured they begin to

Drama is life with the dull bits left out.
ALFRED HITCHCOCK

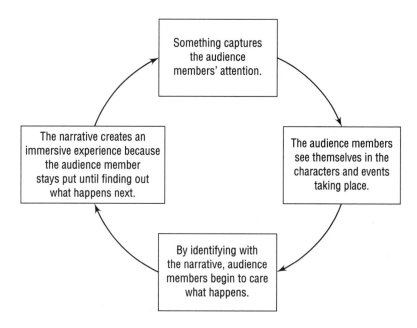

FIGURE 5.1 Cycle of Immersion

see parts of themselves in the characters or story. (3) Once they have identified with the narrative, they begin to care about the characters and the story. (4) This caring leads them to become more immersed in it as they wait to find out what happens next.

Understanding how to create dramatic eLearning requires an understanding of the components that make up a good narrative. Here we introduce those components—plot, story, genre, setting, character—through the lens of a narrative event familiar to most readers, the Broadway musical. The rest of the chapter will be devoted to a detailed presentation of methods of leveraging these narrative components in an interactive learning program.

Journalism allows its readers to witness history; fiction gives its readers an opportunity to live it.

JOHN HERSEY

▷▷ **Fast Forward** *Readers who are confident of their grasp of the elements of narrative should skip to Chapter 10.*

NARRATIVE INGREDIENTS

The original Broadway cast performance of *Les Miserables* is a particularly good example to use to illustrate compelling narrative. The fundamental *Les Miz* story, in each format—book, movie, musical—has achieved widespread popularity and success. However, many of the narrative elements were completely different in each retelling.

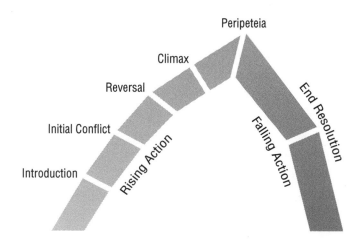

FIGURE 5.2 Classic Dramatic Structure: Freytag's Triangle

And so it is with eLearning. The eLearning content as it already exists may be the same old same old. When communicated through an exciting narrative, the experience can be a transformative one that is significantly more immersive and impactful.

Narrative Arc

Aristotle was one of the first people to codify the narrative arc, which is the process from start to finish that a story goes through. At its most stripped-down level, a classic narrative arc includes

- A line of action: also referred to as a plot and subplots
- A form of conflict: a crisis or problem the characters encounter
- A climax: when the crisis comes to a head
- A resolution: the cessation of the crisis

A more recent figure to address the narrative arc was Gustav Freytag. His contribution was to reconceptualize narrative as three dimensional. In what has come to be known as Freytag's triangle (Figure 5.2),[2] the plot is shown as something that physically rises and falls like a thrown ball. The narrative rises and falls according to the tension occurring at that moment in time.

According to this model, the narrative consists of three parts:

1. Desis: rising action and complication
2. Peripeteia: climax and crisis
3. Denouement: falling action and unwinding

Heffernan:
What are the formal distinctions between "The Sopranos" and network shows?

Chase:
Network television is all talk. I think there should be visuals on a show, some sense of mystery to it, connections that don't add up. I think there should be dreams and music and dead air and stuff that goes nowhere. There should be, God forgive me, a little bit of poetry.

NEW YORK TIMES INTERVIEW WITH DAVID CHASE

A look at virtually any popular narrative—a sitcom, a novel, a song—will reveal this process. A sitcom, since it is so compact and so formulaic, is the best illustration of this narrative process in action.

DESIS (SETUP)

The desis, or setup, shows the familiar characters doing something ordinary. At home during dinner, at their desks in the office, and so on. Almost immediately something happens that clues the audience into a crisis waiting to happen. Maybe the husband picks up an ad for a new car and starts dialing the dealership? The employee makes a slight change to an important report without telling the boss? A teenager sneaks out the window at night?

PERIPETEIA (CLIMAX)

Before you know it, the problem comes to a head—often with a confrontation. The spouse sees the new car in the driveway and a fight ensues; the boss gets a phone call about the giant mistake in the presentation; the teenager is arrested by the police.

DENOUEMENT (RESOLUTION)

In good TV fashion all is made well again. The car goes back to the dealership; the boss gets a phone call from the CEO congratulating him on the brilliant report addendum that closed the sale; the teenager is given a later curfew. This is typically followed by the final scene, which brings us full circle: the husband and wife are joking at dinner; the boss and employee are talking about their next proposal; the teenager is chatting happily during the family breakfast; and so on.

The most common structure for a narrative is the three-act formula. Stated simply, the narrative has a beginning, middle, and end. Not accidentally, this formula maps well onto the narrative structures described by Aristotle and Freytag. The first act is considered the setup, with an introduction to the characters, setting, and crisis, or problem. The second act is a further elaboration on the problem—it may be a further complication or it may be the same problem rearing its head in different ways. The final act is the conclusion, where the crisis comes to a head, is resolved, and we see a glimpse of postproblem normalcy once again.[3]

Although there are many ways this structure can be changed or adapted, the building blocks of setup, crisis, and resolution will almost always be present in any narrative. We will elaborate on the three components in Chapter Six.

Plot and Story

The plot of a narrative is the step-by-step action as presented by the author. It consists of the three elements introduced earlier (desis, peripeteia, denouement) albeit broken down into many smaller events and actions. When Victor Hugo wrote the novel *Les Miserables*, he presented a sequence of hundreds of events recounting the trials and tribulations of Jean Valjean, a man in prerevolutionary France who lives a double life as a result of stealing food. That is the plot.

It can be broken into three acts to correspond to Freytag's triangle.

1. From the time the man is freed from prison until the night before the revolution
2. The revolution
3. After the revolution

In contrast, the story is the sequence of events the audience pieces together to make a congruent whole that follows a logical time progression.

For example, in the musical version of *Les Miserables*, Fontine is fired by the foreman once it is discovered she has an illegitimate child. She is forced to sell her jewelry, hair, and eventually body to support her child (Cosette). She sings a song that tells how she was seduced and abandoned, which accounts for her present situation. The plot, on the one hand, is the sequence of events as they appear on stage. The story, on the other hand, is what the audience would piece together. Fontine is a young maiden who is pursued by a man. They fall in love and produce a child. When summer comes to an end, he deserts her. She is left needing a way to support herself and her child. She works in a factory until the foreman, whose advances she had rejected, fires her. She is eventually forced to sell her body until she gets in a fight with a customer, is taken to the hospital, and eventually dies.

The difference between story and plot is chronology. The story is the logical timeline going from past to present that the audience pieces together. It goes from the start of a character's life to the end of the narrative. In contrast, the plot is the order in which everything appears from the beginning of the book, movie, song, or other work to the end.

The best way to understand this subtle difference is to look at a character's life span. For the writer, the character's "life" as seen through the plot begins with her first activity and ends with her last one. For the audience the character was alive before the narrative and will remain alive afterward. The book, movie, song, or other work is showing merely a snapshot of a much fuller, longer life.

George Franju: *Movies should have a beginning, a middle and an end.*

Godard: *Certainly, but not necessarily in that order.*

INTERVIEW WITH JEAN-LUC GODARD

We have highlighted this distinction because it is an important component of interactive narrative. People typically think of interactivity as having to do with pushing buttons and controlling functionality, but it is also an intellectual task!

The audience member, for eLearning purposes the participant, is accustomed to fitting together a story from the disparate pieces presented by the author. She expects to be challenged in this way. Part of the reason she becomes engaged in a movie, song, TV show, and the like is the subconscious puzzle she is configuring. Provide an eLearning plot that is different from the story line and you'll make the learning process more interesting and engaging.

Genre

A related component of plot is genre. Genre is best explained as the style used to tell the story. When friends ask, "What are you in the mood for?" while choosing a movie, they are really asking, "What genre do you want to see?" There are thousands of genres, with more being introduced every few years. The most popular include comedy, mystery, sitcom, science fiction, horror, romance, documentary, action adventure, reality show, and so on.

In "The Moving Image Genre-Form Guide," Brian Taves, Judi Hoffman, and Karen Lund of the Library of Congress have created an outstanding guide to hundreds of genres and subgenres (available at http://lcweb.loc.gov/rr/mopic/miggen.html). The compilers describe genres as

. . . recognizable primarily by content, and to a lesser degree by style. Genres contain conventions of narrational strategy and organizational structure, using similar themes, motifs, settings, situations, and characterizations. In this way, the makers of moving image works use recognizable patterns of storytelling that are readily understood by audiences. Typical formulas range from the varieties of Hollywood feature films to modes of nonfictional discourse.

Any plot can be communicated through any genre, but it is typically the genre that clues in audience members about the emotions they are to feel. The death of an animal in a drama or crime mystery leaves people sad and curious. That death in a comedy, such as the film *A Fish Called Wanda*, is funny.

The audience is clued in to the genre of a narrative by recognizing the conventions typical of that genre. For murder mysteries, people might expect a single, often disillusioned retired or disparaged detective. For action or adventure, some hallmarks are car chases or other fast-paced scenes using expensive or flashy moving vehicles. For fable, there has to be a moral. Each genre has conventions and characteristics that define it.

If forced to characterize most of the deep content eLearning that currently exists, we'd have to consider it fable. Typically there are characters that represent an abstract idea, often taking clearly right and wrong views, and a pronounced (often explicitly stated) moral about what happens to people who do something the way the organization thinks best and what happens to those who don't.

Part of what makes *Les Miserables* the musical so compelling is the way it juxtaposes multiple genres. Like a roller coaster, it not only exposes the audience to just the right amount of emotion for just the right amount of time but also creates an overall balanced emotional experience by juxtaposing genres that work together well. Just when the audience is almost in tears from Fontine's sad tale, they are rescued from despair through a comedic illustration of prostitutes plying their trade. Lest we get carried away with that lighthearted jesting, the next scene plunges us into a moral quandary: Should Jean Valjean blow his cover to prevent an innocent man's going to jail?

Setting

The setting is both where the action physically takes place (planet, country, building, room, and so on) and when it takes place (century, year, time of year, time of day). *Les Miserables* is set in Paris during the French Revolution. Part of its appeal is the variety of physical locations. The audience is alternately at the work site of a prison chain gang, in a wealthy man's house, on the docks with prostitutes, at the barricades, in the woods, in a slum, in a café, and in a wedding banquet hall.

Most eLearning is set in a typical workplace during the modern era. When we discuss setting again, we are going to encourage breaking out of this typical, and therefore expected, setting.

Characters

Italian poet and novelist Cesare Pavese wrote, "We do not remember days, we remember moments." His remark carries a strong message for people seeking to drive business results through eLearning: create poignant moments. No one is going to remember every single thing she was exposed to in the program—no matter how great or dramatic!

Think back to your favorite movies, books, or plays. You do not remember every single scene but you do remember a few key scenes that were particularly strong. One of the main reasons people remember scenes is that the characters did something potent or outstanding. Good character development is so critical we are dedicating an entire chapter to the topic and its derivates, point of view, dialogue, and tropes (figures of speech). For now we just want to underscore the importance of character by illustrating how well *Les Miserables* wields this narrative element.

Character development is one of the most critical ways of getting an audience to identify with (and therefore care about) an experience. There are millions of considerations in creating a compelling character. Three of the most important are multidimensionality, realistic goals (at least realistic within the confines of the story), and point of view.

Cameron Mackintosh's *Les Miserables'* characters are strokes of genius. It is rare for an audience to be able to empathize, and identify, with so many characters at once. But that is part of the musical's genius—each of the characters is multidimensional to the point where people can see a part of themselves in each one. Let's consider just two of the multifaceted main characters, the hero, Jean Valjean, and the villain, Javert.

Initially the audience roots for the criminal, a role people are predisposed to disliking, because he was simply stealing bread to avoid starving. The audience members can all see themselves doing the same. In contrast, they immediately dislike the police officer, a role they are predisposed to liking, because he comes across as an arrogant, cold-hearted authority figure with no empathy for the plight of the poor.

As the story progresses the audience's initial loyalties waver: Jean Valjean steals from a compassionate man who helped him, and he exploits the poor once he attains a position of power. This makes the audience slightly less understanding of his situation and less empathetic.

Conversely, Javert comes to be seen as a product of his own limitations and therefore an object of pity and empathy. The audience learns his rigid adherence to the law is a survival mechanism: having been born in a prison ("with scum like you, I am from the gutter too") he must strictly adhere to the letter of the law lest he slip and become the criminal he was born to be. Eventually he commits suicide, after his belief system is shattered: the sinner he spent his life chasing might just be a savior. By that point the audience members can identify with him: How many times have they been just a little too dogmatic and suffered the consequences as a result?

I made mistakes in drama. I thought drama was when actors cried. But drama is when the audience cries.

FRANK CAPRA

People's empathy and identification with Javert never attains the strength reserved for the hero, as expected, but by the end of the play they respect both men. They see both villain and hero in themselves.

Up Next

We have now provided a basic overview of narrative and the five key elements that fuse to create an immersive experience. We have shown examples of each one in action in the musical *Les Miserables*. Chapter Six is going to focus on specific guidelines and techniques for enhancing your eLearning programs with narrative elements. Then Chapters Seven, Eight, and Nine are dedicated to the topic of character.

NOTES

1. In a traditional work most audience members are aware only of the gestalt, the overall effect of the elements. The enraptured audience member does not isolate the power of a particular setting or costume design or tone of voice from the dialogue or the plot or moral. It is the writer or director or singer or other creator who carefully sculpts the experience for the audience member. Although there are some ways in which this contrasts with interactive narrative, which we will be introducing after we cover traditional narrative, there are many ways it is similar. In some ways this could be considered a contrast to interactive narrative, where the user is given a stronger hand in sculpting his or her own experiences.

2. Gustav Freytag, *The Technique of the Drama* (New York: Johnson Reprints, 1968, originally published in 1863).

3. There are many narratives that don't follow this exact formula. For example, Edgar Allen Poe moved the order of the components in several of his works, making for an even more interesting drama. As Mark Stephen Meadows explains in *Pause & Effect* (Indianapolis, Ind.: New Riders, 2003): "Poe simply lopped off the Desis and the most revealing portion of the Peripeteia, allowing the gradual solution of the problem to serve as the story itself. He was interested in what cause produced which effect. . . . Poe wanted to bring his readers closer to the story. To do this, Poe turned the reader into an investigator."

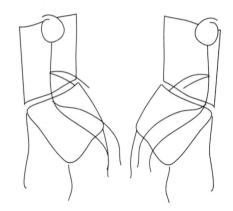

DANIEL BERNARDI

Professor of New Media Studies
University of Arizona

ON THE GESTATION OF THE IDEA . . .

As a professor with a specialty in new media, I began to think about ways
to combine this specialty with teaching. This was at a time when the university system saw distance learning as a cash cow. The first thing I realized
was the student's learning had to be the primary goal. The student had to
be at the center of the experience. The university will always make their
money if the student is at the center of the experience and actively involved
in learning. When the student doesn't see it as a waste of his or her time,
thinks it is challenging and feels he or she has gotten something out of it,
something that has helped them reach their goals (be it getting a degree,
or getting a job, or a skill that they would need in a certain job), they will
keep coming back. And the university will always make money.

The first course I built was mostly HTML. Students loved the interactive
part of it in live chat rooms, and so on, but I wasn't really tapping into the
way many students learn online, which is visual. Since the course was generating revenue, other people asked me to build something similar for them.

I wanted to tap into what it could be visually, not just what it was. So I
decided to come up with a template that satisfies two goals. The first [was]
facilitating conversion of the courses so people wouldn't have to start from
scratch. The second was keeping it flexible enough visually to fit the other
teacher's interests and course content.

I let the content drive the form, not the other way around. WebCT and
Blackboard have a template where you shove content into a form. I didn't
think the virtual classroom, that visual interactive element, that place
where all the students went to take the course should interfere with the
content of the course and in fact it should complement it.

I looked for money and everyone said no. Finally I wrote some grants and got a few. I think I got $25,000 cash and access to computer labs and classrooms and offices. That was to build four courses. We were actually able to build eight because the template made the process so streamlined and efficient. It also empowered faculty who were otherwise apprehensive about teaching in an online environment.

They saw two things. One, they could control form and content, which means it could be their course. Secondly, students were responding in positive ways.

ON RESULTS . . .

We did a study and found first that 82 percent would take another course. We recently did the study again and now it's over 90 percent. We had a less than 5 percent dropout rate, which for business learning, particularly at that time, was remarkable. The average for others was around 28 percent. The students all said these courses were more difficult than traditional courses, but at the same time 95 percent were saying they couldn't wait to take their next class!

I'm not talking about professional students, like a dentist might need a certification; I'm talking about undergraduate students, who want to pursue a BA. When these students spend their money they want their money's worth. And since we built our own system instead of going with a Blackboard or WebCT we can pass the savings on.

We made $125,000 for the university last year off that initial grant. The faculty were well paid for their work and so they were happy, and the students didn't pay anymore than they would for a traditional course.

ON THE IMPORTANCE OF DRAMA AND METAPHOR . . .

We didn't go with WebCT or Blackboard because they don't effectively facilitate what I think is amazing and revolutionary about business learning, especially at a research university such as mine. You're trying to reach students who are in an environment that's supposed to be cutting-edge research. You can't go with the cookie-cutter approach used by WebCT and Blackboard. . . .

I have a Ph.D., I'm from UCLA, in film, so I'm also a visual person. I get cinema and understand why television, film, and the novel work better for more people than reading. I sat back and said, "OK, the metaphor that drives the Web and by proxy distance learning is the page and therefore the book, Web pages." Most of the material the student was engaging with was text, and I realized that was the problem! It should be visual. The metaphor should be cinematic, which is why I went with Flash. Flash makes movies and it's visual . . . it's cinematic.

The student walks into a building, they don't have to think about the building, threshold of the door, the chair, where the professor is. But the aesthetics of the room, the ambience contributes to their mood, adds to how students learn.

If the light's too bright or if there's no light you bring the mood down. I wanted the same effect. I wanted students not to have to spend extraordinary time thinking about how to get around the virtual classroom, but at that same time I wanted that virtual classroom to sort of complement, motivate, and direct them to learn in specific ways. WebCT and Blackboard fail to do that.

First, cinema is a time-based medium. So you want things to come at you within a certain narrative time frame. Narrative is time. Second is the visual, and not just visual from a simple design perspective. The difference between a designer and a filmmaker is that the designer is going for one look where the filmmaker is going for looks that change over time.

Knowing Flash really emancipated me. The program essentially allows you to build Web pages as if they were movies with interactive components. This allows the student to access different elements of the timeline, different angles of the plot, all within layers. In other words, you get narrative and visual information that complements the nature of learning through the computer screen. It's a style that young people get; it's intuitive to them.

ON HEUTAGOGY . . .

The reason you go to my virtual classroom, my Web environment, is because you're going to interact. You're going to see information narratively, visually, and you're going to read. Every one of my lessons has an article that I convert to HTML. I make them read. At the same time I make them watch clips, do interactive modules, go on a Web board to have a threaded asynchronous discussion, go into a chat room and argue.

If you do all those things—and most of them are very inexpensive— you've gotten the visual learner, the tactile learner, the student who learns from listening by going to audio lectures, . . . and the dialectic learner (the student who like me doesn't get a lot out of reading, but gets a lot out of arguing). If I'm in there arguing and debating with a classmate or the professor and it's structured, I'm going to walk away with some serious retention.

A lot of systems like WebCT really do not facilitate argumentation. The conversations are one to one or they are done in a way that is meant to avoid argument and debate. That's another problem I had with distance learning in general. Many universities went to automated systems to save money, thinking that students would get really into it like correspondence courses. If you look at the numbers for them, they aren't all that high because the payoff isn't all that great. It actually ultimately undermines the three things that are absolutely unique about online learning.

One is visual, I already talked about that. The second is live interactivity. Three is global. For example, in all of my classes I've had students from around the world. When I did courses for the Global Film School there was a student in China having an argument with a student in France, with a student in Mexico, with three students in the United States, with one in Australia and two in London—all live. We had them working on projects together. The only limitation was language at that point. Space and distance were not an issue.

To summarize, I wanted to build a system that was visual and complemented ways in which students learn, facilitated interactivity, was open, inexpensive, and brought diverse people together to give them an opportunity to think and study together. Sort of a constructivist model of learning.

ON THE CREATIVE PROCESS . . .

It's fundamental. As important as content. I would say creativity is absolutely vital. Look at Hollywood. Why do they pay their people so much money? There's nothing worse than an ugly film. It doesn't work from an inspiration perspective.

I tell my students, Professor M. wants us to build an interactive module, a course on cinematography. Here are the basic principles of cinematography, a sketch of how I think this module should work. Students should be able to do this or that. Now go off, take two weeks, play, debate, do research, test certain little designs, then come back to me and our team with a mockup.

I let them know they have the freedom, if you think what I'm saying is wrong or if an aspect is not working, to take it out. Let the best idea win! If the person really trusts you and you really mean to give them that freedom, then you've captured what is essential to any creative process: inspiration.

For example, with the depth-of-field module, it was built by a young woman who was a student of mine at the time, Eliza Robinson, who's now running my UCLA design class because she is so brilliant.

She came back with this incredible mockup. Several ideas I'd never thought about although I'm the expert! That was great. Then we tested the hell out of the course. You just can't do without the testing. We brought other students in; we brought other faculty in. We constantly have this debate going on. There is always feedback, but the initial germination of the idea was a little of me and a lot of her inspiration. You've got to create a process that facilitates out of the box, inspirational speaking.

ON PEOPLE . . .

First, I try to identify people to work on my project who are diligent. I want to know if the person is professional, can meet deadlines, and follow through.

The second thing I look for and encourage is creativity. The last thing I ever look for is skill, because a smart student, who works hard, who could think out of the box will develop skills eventually. In fact, skills should always chase ideas. Once I get the person I give them a document that says, "Here's what we've been asked to do." Say it's an interactive module on narrative structure. Here are the fundamental learning objectives that the student who has experienced this module must come away with, know this, know that, and so on.

Here's the basic structure of what I think it should look like. Then I tell them to take it, go away. When they come back I want a flow chart and a mockup. The flow chart is for the interactive elements, the mockup for design.

When they come back, I bring in a great team of people. We analyze it together and always give three compliments for every criticism. This is especially important with the creative people.

From there we go for a first draft and again we bring in other people, the experts and people who don't know crap about it—people who are going to come to it fresh (like a student). We decide what needs to be changed. Typically we go through that process twice and then it's a done deal. This can move fast because the people who work for me trust me. I mean, I guess the question from a manners perspective is how do you facilitate trust, so that the person working for you feels that they can go ahead and go out on a limb.

ACTION!

Storytelling

6

IN CHAPTER FOUR we asserted that eLearning that taps into participants' hearts (emotions) as well as their heads (cognition or intellect) will have the greatest impact on business results. Of the many ways to tap into emotion we suggested (in Chapter Five) taking a dramatic approach: using narrative (also known as storytelling) to present content in a way that is "arresting or forceful in appearance or effect." We deconstructed five important components of narrative (plot, story, genre, setting, character) and illustrated how they are used in a traditional dramatic performance, such as the musical *Les Miserables*.

Now we dive into the praxis: how to wield the first four narrative elements to make eLearning that positively affects the emotions and the business results of an organization.[1]

The first step in creating narrative eLearning is to create a *high concept* that summarizes the story to be told and the genre in which it will be told.

HIGH CONCEPT

Writing objectives is one of the first steps to take when developing eLearning. To design good dramatic eLearning, a high concept needs to be developed, either before or in parallel. The high concept is a pitch or elevator speech that quickly gives listeners enough high-level information to pique their curiosity and potentially earn their investment or support.

At the beginning of the Chapter Five we explained that narrative plots all contain the same elements: the introduction, the crisis, the solution, then a return to normalcy. In Hollywood the high concept is the one-sentence

BOOKSHELF BEST BETS

The Writer's Journey: Mythic Structure for Writers, Christopher Vogler

The Hero with a Thousand Faces, Joseph Campbell

Technique of the Drama, Gustav Freytag

Pause & Effect, Mark Stephen Meadows

For more help sourcing books, try the experienced folks at the Drama Bookshop (212-944-0595) or The Writer's Store (866-229-7483).

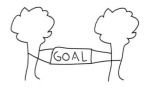

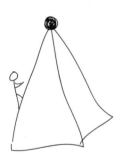

> One of the best ways of communicating knowledge is through stories, because good stories are richly textured with details, allowing the narrative to convey a stable ground on which to build experience and allowing multiple interpretations.
>
> **NATHAN SHEDROFF**

summary that summarizes the story and excites the listener (often enough to get "greenlighted"—the signal and budget to move forward).

The high concept should be the one-sentence summary that takes the listener on a tour of the main attractions of your narrative. Those main attractions answer these questions:

- Who is the protagonist?
- What is his or her goal?
- Why does he or she want to achieve that goal?
- What is standing in the way of achieving the goal?
- How does he or she deal with the problem?

Linda Aronson, in her book *Screenwriting Updated*, provides one of the best templates available to the narrative designer:

Protagonist faced with disturbance which creates problem and surprised by first act turning point responds and is foiled by a series of action set-backs, often triggered by the antagonist but also by fate, etc. reaches a low point of physical danger or despair when second act turning point but fights back by a series of actions in act three leading up to the climax and finally deals with problem by climax.[2]

If we transform this sentence into a list, the ingredients of a good narrative break down into the following:[3]

Act One

1. Normality: the status quo.
2. Disturbance: the first change that breaks the status quo.
3. Protagonist: the character or combination of characters that will drive the action forward.
4. Plan: what the protagonists intend to do as a result of the disturbance (typically the first response is to attempt to get right back to the status quo).
5. Surprise: an unanticipated physical or emotional event that will lead to the obstacle.
6. Obstacle: the situation that arises as a result of the surprise and that requires resolution.

Act Two

7. Complications: all the barriers that will prevent the protagonist from achieving his or her goal(s).

Act Three (complications continue)

8. Climax: the problem comes to a head, typically in a physical or life-or-death situation.

9. Resolution: the problem is solved and life has a new status quo level.

When pitching the idea to others you might cut this template down to its essence, but for your own internal use, this fill-in-the-blank sentence is a terrific guide to ensure the main elements of a good narrative are captured.

Here, for example, is the high concept for a popular movie that was pitched to others.

The Fugitive

Chicago physician Dr. Richard Kimble finds himself wrongly convicted of killing his wife. When the prison bus crashes, he escapes and vows to find the actual killer—a mysterious one-armed man—even though he must also avoid recapture by a relentless U.S. Marshal.[4]

The following high concept is an example of a type more likely to be used internally, as it captures more of the plot points:

Arthur

Drunken, lovable millionaire playboy Arthur must choose between obeying his father's injunction to marry a woman Arthur doesn't love and thereby retain his inheritance or following his heart with a poor but electrifying woman from Queens. After much vacillation he chooses love, only to discover that he gets the wealth as well.[5]

If you want to see an example of a high concept applied to an eLearning program, there is one in the next to last paragraph of this chapter.

It is challenging to write this high concept statement if you are not familiar with the elements of narrative it calls out (such as conflict, character development, and so on). First, we are going to discuss each of the elements and demonstrate how they have been used (or not been used) to make eLearning more dramatic. We will then come full circle at the end of the chapter and write a high concept for the major example discussed here.

STORY

Before you can write a high concept you must decide what story you want to tell and in what genre. Here we run into good news and not so good news. The

TABLE 6.1 Eight Fundamental Stories

1. Achilles	The fatal flaw that leads to the destruction of the previously flawless individual. This is also the cornerstone of the crime drama—the flaw here belonging not to the hero but the villain. Example: *Law & Order.*
2. Candide	The innocent abroad; naive optimism triumphant; the hero who cannot be kept down. Examples: *Batman, Mission Impossible, Chariots of Fire, Bend It Like Beckham.*
3. Cinderella	The dream come true; unrecognized virtue recognized at last; goodness triumphant after being initially despised; rewards achieved through transformed circumstances.
4. Circle	The chase; the spider and the fly; the innocent and the victim; mostly the temptress ensnaring the love-struck male.
5. Faust	Selling your soul to the devil may bring riches but eventually there is a price to be paid; the long-term debt; the uncovered secret that catches up with us sooner or later and damns us; the inescapability of fate.
6. Orpheus	The gift taken away; the loss of something personal. Either about the tragedy of the loss itself or the search that follows the loss.
7. Romeo and Juliet	Boy meets girl, boy loses girl, boy finds/does not find girl—it doesn't matter which.
8. Tristan	Triangles (eternal or otherwise); man loves woman and unfortunately one or both are already spoken for.

Source: Adapted from Raymond Frensham, *Screenwriting,* Teach Yourself series (London: Hodder Arnold, 1996).

good news is there are really only about eight stories that can be told. The bad news is there are an infinite number of ways each story can be told, and it requires real talent to write the actual incarnation of any particular story.

Think of a story, any story. It can come from a book, movie, tale a friend told you, magazine article, campfire ghost story, whatever. We guarantee whatever story you remembered is a derivative or retelling of one of the eight fundamental stories listed in Table 6.1 that cut across all cultures and historical eras.

These stories are templates that are not to be taken literally. For example, the Romeo and Juliet scenario does not have to feature a boy and girl. It could feature a boss who finds a great talent and wants to recruit her into the company but she is happily employed elsewhere. It could focus on an idea that continues to evade an R&D employee. Perhaps it comes to him in a dream, then the next morning he can't read the notes he scrawled, so he tries to get it back. It could present a salesperson who knows a particular prospect would be much better off if she switched to the salesperson's company's product and does whatever possible to win this prospect.

Any of the story lines will work for any topic, given a talented scriptwriter. That is part of the beauty of these stripped-down stories; they can be used as skeletons upon which any manner of body can be put.

One of the wonderful aspects of a glamorous profession is the surplus of extremely talented people who are barely able to make a living. There are thousands of screenplays and stage plays written for every one that is bought (and few of the ones bought actually get made!). This means the number of very talented writers who would be grateful to help develop an excellent story for eLearning programs in exchange for a minimal fee is plentiful.

People who are not seeking to develop their fiction-writing skills should read the rest of this chapter to get a foundation in the process and elements and to generate some high-level ideas on what might be an interesting narrative or fiction treatment. Then they should find a talented screenwriter or scriptwriter who can transform the vision into a ground-level reality. Using some of the recruiting techniques mentioned in Chapter Thirteen, one could hire a good writer for between $3,000 and $5,000 (depending on the scope of the work, of course). This is a win-win situation. The writer gets support until she wins an Oscar, and your eLearning achieves significantly better results.

GENRE

The next step is to decide which emotion to tap to best communicate the learning. This is the purpose of genre, to tell a story in a way that evokes a particular emotion. After you have decided on the fundamental story you want to tell, you combine that with the way you want to tell it, based on the emotion you want to evoke. Comedy evokes silliness or humor; action, excitement; crime, fear; romance, love or affection; suspense, anticipation; and so on.

Often the genre you select will have more to do with the eLearning participants' predisposition and the culture of the organization. At the risk of stereotyping, a predominately young, male audience *may* (for the record, we said *may*) respond to action adventure, an older female audience may respond to romance. The company culture, however, may also dictate avoidance of violence or romance. A simple way to select a genre is to do an informal or formal survey to learn participants' top five movies, books, and television shows. A few patterns of preference will emerge. Take into account the company's culture, the eLearning stakeholders' preferences, the appropriate fit between content and genre, and any other relevant influences (including selecting a scriptwriter whose talents rest in your preferred genre).

TABLE 6.2 *Genre Choices*

Popular Genres (genres most likely to be useful to eLearning developers; excluding such unlikely choices as pornography, slasher, horror)

Adaptation	Journalism	Public affairs
Adventure	Jungle	Reality based
Biography	Legal	Road
Buddy	Magazine	Romance
Caper	Medical	Science fiction
Comedy	Melodrama	Situation comedy
Crime	Music video	Soap opera
Disaster	Musical	Speculation
Documentary	Mystery	Sports
Espionage	News	Survival
Experimental	Opera	Talk
Family	Operetta	Trigger
Fantasy	Parody	Variety
Game	Police	Western
Gangster	Prehistoric	
Historical	Public access	

Genres Currently Used by eLearning

Educational	Interview	Social problem
Ethnographic	Lecture	Sponsored
Industrial	Propaganda	Training
Instructional	Social guidance	

Each genre (see Table 6.2) has certain characteristics that the audience uses to guide its responses. For example, comedy must have gags, parody, wisecracks, or jokes; action must have some form of chase; horror must have screams, usually a strong female protagonist, and in our opinion, gratuitous gore. Attaining the right balance of conventions is tricky and one of the key areas where a talented professional writer can assist. Use too few conventions, and the participants can be left hanging, uncertain what emotions they should be feeling. Use too many conventions and the piece becomes clichéd or, worse, an unintentional parody of itself.

The Library of Congress offers a well-organized directory of genres and subgenres—each definition containing clear descriptions and a list of representative films. Looking over this list provides guidance on the elements to include for each genre.[6] Because there is no universal standard for genre, it is wise to look at other film-related resources as well to see other categories or approaches: for example, the Library of Congress does not treat cult film as a genre but the British Film Institute does. The ". . . And Even More Reading!" section in this book is a good place to start. The more adventurous, or film buffs who just want to legitimately spend hours watching movies on company time, can rent several videos belonging to the genre of interest and view them with an eye to detecting patterns.

EXAMPLE

Earlier in this chapter we said that the Romeo and Juliet story could be told with a salesperson seeking to convert a prospect away from a competitor. Now let's say the particular eLearning content is to focus on competitive intelligence.

First, let's say you want to cater to an audience that would respond best to excitement and energy. The genre you might use would be action adventure. The prospect does not know it, but the salesperson has been put in a predicament: if she doesn't convince the customer to switch vendors within a week and the other company's product is released to market, a giant computer virus epidemic will be unleashed in the general population. This kicks off a series of physical activities including capturing secrets and the like under duress.

Alternately, let's say your audience is more prone to analysis. The genre you might select is documentary. Create a story in which a reporter is exposing how a prospect was converted from one vendor to another through competitive intelligence techniques.

As a final instance, let's say the audience members are keen to have their curiosity and figuring-it-out emotions stimulated. A good genre might be mystery. The participant looks through the eyes of a detective to piece together why a salesperson received a death threat. The answer of course will be an unraveling of all the steps the salesperson took to win over a rival's prospect—which led the frustrated rival to issue a threat.

Suggestions

- Think ice cream. One genre should be dominant, but any good narrative contains ribbons of other genres. Espionage will have humor; speculation will have news. The dominant genre is like the base flavor (vanilla) and the others are flavor accents (chocolate chips, caramel, and so on).

- Remember, some genres use content generally not viewed as appropriate in the business world (murder, rape, incest, certain diseases, and so forth). Have some ideas at the outset for what you will use instead of these charged topics.

- It is easy to get carried away and use too many genre conventions, which fast makes the eLearning narrative clichéd. Unless your genre is parody, avoid overreliance on a particular package of conventions.

SETTING

If readers can make only one change to their eLearning after reading our book, changing the physical location or era, or both, of the action would be a good choice. This change requires virtually no additional resources and doesn't tax the creative or writing muscles the way the other suggestions might. This little guy provides quite the bang for the buck.

Almost all eLearning is set in an office, factory, or other corporate environment in the current year. News flash: most people would prefer to be somewhere other than their workplace. At the very least, moving the setting out of the office to a more desirable location (from the participant's point of view) will encourage a fresh approach to the learning process. More likely, it will also induce relaxation, decrease defensiveness, open minds, and generate more interest (leading to positive word of mouth).

If done in conjunction with some of the other dramatic techniques, moving the setting can encourage participants to see connections they didn't before and approach problems from a different angle, foster their creativity, put them in an entirely different mindset, and even excite them about using the program or even learning in general.

The secret to choosing an appropriate and effective setting is to look to your participants and the organizational culture, as you did for genre and story. Unlike story or genre, the content will dictate some constraints on the setting.

Stepping in the Right Direction

A good first step is to look at what knowledge, skill, or behavior you are trying to help participants acquire or develop. Look for the places where the knowledge, skill, or behavior could *not* be used as well as where it could be used. On the one hand, if the skill is building high-quality cabinetry, making the setting a political campaign headquarters in a poor neighborhood is quite a stretch. If the knowledge to be acquired is computer programming, a raft on the Amazon during the Middle Ages is a stretch. Sure, it's not impossible—a creative writer could no doubt make it credible (think *Back to the Future*). But it's also a lot of extra work with little chance of a big payoff.

On the other hand, building cabinetry is a skill that is needed anywhere cabinets are needed: if participants are sports fans, set it in a home where the challenge is to build cabinets to hold a brand-new, bleeding-edge, giant screen plasma TV and all the additional components before the Super Bowl starts. If the computer programming participants enjoy traveling, the setting might be a sonic jet in 2050 traveling around the world from assignment to assignment.

The setting issue is particularly relevant for personal growth, interpersonal learning, or management skills development. Virtually anywhere there are people the same skills are needed. Just today we learned of a man who was grateful for his expertise as a logistics professional after fertility treatments blessed him and his wife with sextuplets. Communication, conflict management, negotiation, project management, mentoring, strategic planning, goal setting, recruiting—all of these skills and many of the others needed in a business environment are also used in many of the millions of interpersonal situations people find themselves in when they are not at work.

Transplant your participants from the workplace to a leisure location or another place that captures their imagination and attention: put them in charge of NASA's latest project, elect them to the board of a golf club, make them the producer of *Iron Chef* or owner of a new couture fashion house. Send them back in time to manage Darwin's Galapagos expedition, or forward in time to set up an extraterrestrial dog fashion show—whatever!

As long as your setting can include a group of people who are working toward a similar goal and who are involved voluntarily (in other words, they are not physically or mentally compelled to remain a part of the group), it's a viable option.

After creating a list of settings (ranging from the outrageous to the mundane) you can test the concepts with your participants—again with a quick informal survey. Or you can wait to see which works best with the plot points you will create, as discussed later.

Break down the walls and let your participants travel to situations they want to be in!

EXAMPLE

Revisiting the Romeo and Juliet scenario and the salesperson who is trying to woo the competitor's client, one aspect of competitive intelligence that transcends time is the networking or person-to-person research involved. But an equally important aspect is the Internet and the ability to gain information electronically. This means it is easiest to set the program in the modern age or the future. This is the main constraint placed on the setting. (See Table 6.3 for more setting suggestions.)

BAM! POW! ZOOM! AND OTHER EVERYDAY OCCURRENCES IN THE WORLD OF MOVIES

By this point in the process you will have selected the high-level story, genre, and setting of your program. It is now appropriate to attend to the

TABLE 6.3   Ideas for Genre Settings

Genre	Setting 1 Idea	Setting 2 Idea
Action or adventure	A futuristic world where the "companies" are governments and the threat is to the population.	Current day. A quaint village that will be destroyed by chemical leakage if the salesperson cannot convince the mayor to buy solar panels from her instead of granting a contract to a nuclear reactor.
Documentary	A small European city experiences a major economic and cultural boon when a famous football (soccer for U.S. readers) player is recruited away from a rival team (from a major city). This documentary spotlights how one person used competitive intelligence to woo the player.	Los Angeles, modern day. A reporter reveals how an online music purchasing company (à la iTunes or BuyMusic) convinced a major star to sell a new collection of songs exclusively through the company's service instead of making an album with the star's current record company.
Mystery	A person traveling in Asia senses he is being followed and fears he might be in danger. An investigation reveals he has won a very important client away from a major competitor and has become the subject of a Web site on cutting-edge competitive intelligence technique—the person following is a reporter trying to get an exclusive, the inside scoop.	A document is emailed to the chief of police in an African city. It seems to be evidence of international corporate espionage by a sales person at a multinational conglomerate. An investigation reveals it was a fraudulent attempt to frame a rival salesperson who managed to legally and ethically woo a major customer.

actions that will move the story forward. This process is the dramatic world's equivalent of creating an outline for a presentation or report. It is the roadmap the writer will follow when creating the narrative.

When this process is completed the writer is ready to write the script, using this outline as her roadmap. The writer or designers would typically already have a vision of the characters and their characteristics. Because a separate chapter is dedicated to this topic we will go on the assumption that the characters have already been created and will not elaborate on the process here.

When this roadmap is completed a high concept statement is completed. The following are arranged in order of presentation in a typical narrative.

Normality, Status Quo, Introduction, or Setup

The introduction is the opening of the eLearning program. It will provide participants with expectations and give them their first impression of the rest of the program. The setup should immediately tell the participants

- The physical location where the action is going to take place
- The era in which it is happening
- Who the main characters are
- What the genre is

Take this opportunity to capture attention and connect emotionally with your audience. You will also want to focus on establishing what "normalcy" is.

Because drama is dependent on conflict and the eLearning you are designing will contain some form of conflict, your participants will need to know what sea level is before they can understand how high a mountain is or how deep an ocean is. This normalcy gives the participants a quick glance at the status quo so they can become familiar with the current state of affairs.

Some important pointers:

- Establish normalcy quickly, then move on. You will lose an audience's attention if too much time is spent showing the lay of the land.

- Determine what information is necessary. In most cases this will include at the least a glance at the main characters' personalities, the learning objectives, the setting, the goal, and motivations.

- If the eLearning is going to be disseminated visually, it is essential that a compelling graphic accompany any action. This captures the participants' attention and allows them to identify the situation they are joining.

- Use music. The temptation is always to go after the lowest common denominator, avoiding technical or social requirements such as sound cards or facilities where the sound will not bother others. Music is one of the most evocative, and inexpensive, ways to create mood and convey emotion (especially excitement). Research has shown music is closely tied to emotion. Fast music arouses, slow music calms. Increase efficacy by making sound the default mode but building in a silencing mechanism to allow users to turn off the sound if necessary. There are extensive libraries of shareware, stock, and royalty-free music that costs nothing or next to nothing.

Disturbance

Drama is diametrically opposed to real life. In their own lives people try to minimize conflict. In drama they want to see conflict—lots of it.

Few people would trade their own life for that of a soap opera character if they really had to deal with the aftermath of finding out their father's brother's son is really their sister who was married to their ex-husband who actually turned out to be the robber baron who single-handedly master-minded the downfall of their corporate and philanthropic empire.

Then again, few audiences would sit glued to their television or pay $10 plus the price of popcorn to tag along as we change our daughter's diaper,

---

Learning objectives can be communicated without specifically saying, "By the end of this module . . ." We encourage creative presentation of learning objectives. The classic example of this is the varied ways the *Mission Impossible* statement, "Your assignment, should you choose to accept it, . . ." was introduced.

Look in the books in the ". . . And Even More Reading!" section to find shareware or stock music that costs next to nothing.

TABLE 6.4 Escalating Crises

Disturbance

- An unusual thing happens that breaks the status quo and either foreshadows what is to come or is the cause of subsequent crises.
- It is the participants' first introduction to the action and acts as a setup.
- It must be described using an action verb (such as write, decide, hire, receive).
- It must disrupt the current state of affairs in either a negative or positive way.

Surprise

- A consequence or result of the disturbance—it would not be able to happen if the disturbance hadn't taken place.
- It takes the story and protagonist in an unexpected direction.
- It is the reason why the entire second act happens.
- According to Linda Seger (*Making a Good Script Great*), it:
  Kicks the action in an unexpected direction
  Pushes the protagonist deeper into the problem
  Raises the central question again but with added, surprising complications

Obstacle

- The situation that arises as a result of the surprise.

Complications

- The tangible concrete ways the protagonist is prevented from accomplishing his or her goal due to internal limitations, external circumstances, or other people.
- Ensure obstructions are genuinely different, not just different versions of the same obstruction.
- Complications should be barriers and reversals, again according to Linda Seger.
- Each complication must be more difficult to overcome.
- Some of the complications should be setbacks—two steps back in order to take one forward.
- This is where the point of no return comes in. The complications must put the protagonist in a position where he or she needs to take one road, which will effectively cut off the other forever.

Climax

- The protagonist reaches his or her lowest point—emotionally or physically.
- This will be the last big struggle, resulting in literal or figurative life or death.
- It must answer the problem presented by the surprise.
- It must be the biggest challenge of all the crises presented.

walk the dog, write this book, clean the house, talk to our parents on the phone, coordinate flight schedules, meet with clients—zzzzzzzzzzzzzz—are you asleep yet?

As Hitchcock said, "Drama is life with the dull bits left out." In order for an audience to stay engaged with the content there has to be conflict. It moves the story forward and gives people someone to root for. The protagonist must have a believable goal, and there must be credible barriers standing between her and the goal. These are necessary to increase the participants' engagement. The "conflict" is actually a combination of several conflicts that all relate to each other.

Table 6.4 shows how conflict stretches over five action points: disturbance, surprise, obstacle, complications, and climax. The differences between these conflict points lie in their intensity and their location within the plot.

One of the best ways to understand the connections between the crisis points is by comparing them to the progress of a marathon. It requires a minimal amount of energy (relatively speaking) for a runner to get through the first leg of the run. As the race progresses it takes an increasing amount of energy to complete each succeeding leg, until finally the runner must muster all her energy and reserves to make it through that last leg.

As Freytag's triangle (Figure 5.2) illustrates, the participants need to be sucked into the drama through a small initial conflict, but over time the crisis needs to get more complicated to hold their interest. The stakes need to get higher until eventually the conflict becomes a literal or metaphorical life or death struggle.

Looking again at the musical *Les Miserables*, the goal is for the protagonist (Valjean) to raise Cosette, as he promised the dying Fontine he would do. Unfortunately he is a fugitive running from the law. A few of the physical, logistical, and psychological barriers that stand in his way are

- A lawman who is trying to arrest him
- The people who are keeping Cosette, refusing to give her up
- His discovery that an innocent man is on trial for his crimes

> Just a reminder: at this point the characters will already have been created and fleshed out, as it is impossible to design conflict without having an image of the characters in mind.

Conflict is one of the key areas where traditional drama and dramatic eLearning diverge. In a traditional noninteractive narrative the author must devise both the conflicts and the resolutions to the conflicts. When we see a movie or read a book the author has created the barriers that stand in our hero's path and the ways he or she overcomes the difficulties.

In an interactive narrative, particularly one focused on development and learning, the writer needs to not only create the conflict but also create the space for the participant to sculpt the solutions. The way this is typically done is by presenting a scenario of a problem and then asking the participant to choose a solution from a multiple-choice list. We think there are ways to use crisis and the opportunity to overcome it more effectively (and convincingly) than this formula does.

It is more challenging to accomplish this in asynchronous simulation type learning than in eLearning with active facilitator involvement. However, employing artificial intelligence tools is still outside most people's grasp. Which means the writer needs to be particularly creative in sculpting crises so they can be resolved within the format and constraints of the eLearning.

Make 'em laugh; make 'em cry; make 'em wait.
CHARLES READE

The fundamental premise of conflict is that it changes a character in some fundamental way—once he has gone through the journey he can no longer revert back to his old ways. This is useful in learning not only because it provides a role model but also because if the participants are using the program properly—and therefore playing a strong hand in the solution of the conflicts on a repeated basis—it should change them as well. Clearly the participants will not change overnight or even in the course of the program—they are not fictional characters. But if the conflict and resolution process is realistic it is almost certain to guarantee a deeper impact than is achieved by the majority of today's shallow multiple-choice attempts.

Steps for Creating Conflicts

STEP 1: DETERMINE WHAT YOU HAVE

Begin by drawing a representation of some sort (it could be a MindMap, a flow chart, a list—whatever suits your style) of the elements you already have:

- The story
- The genre
- The characters
- The learning objectives, or content goals
- The introduction, or setup

STEP 2: ESTABLISH THE GOAL

Look at all the elements you have and make a list of the goals people would typically have in those situations. You should have goals both related to the learning content and unrelated. Now ask why would the character want that goal? Be sure the motivation is realistic from the character's perspective.

STEP 3: LOOK FOR HIGH-LEVEL CONFLICTS

The high-level conflicts are often obvious: money, time, space, intelligence, and the like. Make the goal distant. Write down a list of the high-level conflicts that might stand between the character and her goal.

STEP 4: CREATE MICRO-LEVEL CONFLICTS

Participants engage with conflicts at the micro-level, not macro-level. They identify with individuals and their itty-bitty renditions of larger problems everyone faces. Audiences don't identify with Jean Valjean because he is involved in solving world hunger. They identify with him because he is trying to steal a few nibbles of bread to stay alive. They identify with him because he wrestles not with generalized morality and ethics but with the difficult decision of giving up his freedom and the riches he has amassed in order to prevent an innocent man from being convicted in his place as a result of mistaken identity.

The high-level conflicts you listed in step 3 need to be broken down into discrete tangible conflicts anyone could realistically encounter were he or she to be in that setting. In the case of dramatic narratives, however, the word *realistic* can be more broadly defined than it can in the typical learning situation. If participants are engaged in the program their willing suspension of disbelief will kick in, giving writers a wider berth. People want to be taken beyond everyday reality—but not into a stratosphere so far beyond realistic that it ruins the *illusion of reality*.

This is yet again an area where a talented scriptwriter will be able to flesh out specific crises that will fit into the narrative, grab the participants' attention, and serve the learning objectives. As you think about the potential conflicts, bear in mind that almost all conflict can be grouped into one of these categories:[7]

- Person versus person
- Person versus self (internal conflict)
- Person versus society
- Person versus natural forces
- Person versus spiritual entity or cosmic forces

STEP 5: EXPAND ON THE CONFLICTS TO CREATE THE STORY LINE

After you have come up with your initial list of conflicts, you will have to modify them and adjust them to fit in the slots for the five conflict action points of disturbance, surprise, obstacle, complications, and climax (as outlined earlier in Table 6.4).

EXAMPLE

Continuing to use the Romeo and Juliet scenario involving a salesperson, we are going to walk you through the process of creating crises for a protagonist. For the sake of the example, let's say the learning content is competitive intelligence, including acquisition of the following knowledge, skills, and attitude (our definition of KSAs):

- Pinpoint competitors' soft spots, blind spots, and strategic vulnerabilities.
- Evaluate your own company's strategy and its blind spots, as well as pinpoint its vulnerabilities.

Raymond Frensham's way of categorizing conflict is easier to use at a glance:[8]

Protagonist versus

- Something physical
- Other characters
- Something cultural (different nations, organizations, belief systems, and so on)
- Something supernatural
- Time (a deadline)

- Dissect the numbers, and use them to construct and assess what is really happening in a competitor's business.
- Understand competitors' behaviors, and predict significant competitive moves.
- Advise on business decisions in the light of competitive intelligence analysis.

Let's also say that using the mystery genre, you created the plot outline described earlier: a document is emailed to the chief of police in an African city. It seems to be evidence of international corporate espionage by a salesperson at a multinational conglomerate. An investigation reveals it is an attempt to frame a rival salesperson who managed to legally and ethically woo a major customer.

And let's say you have sculpted your characters to include a protagonist, who is the detective working on the case; an antagonist, who is to be the salesperson who sent the fraudulent letter; and a third character, who is to be the salesperson who won the client.

Motivation or Goal   The goal for the detective is to solve the case. Let's give her the motivation that she once had a coworker who falsely accused her of something that cost her the job she had then. She is motivated to find the truth not only because she wants to clear the case, but because she is dealing with the unresolved internal conflict of having been unjustly robbed of her professional reputation and self-esteem.

Normalcy   You might establish normalcy, the setup, by showing the protagonist chatting with a coworker on the way to her desk. Participants see a desk that reflects her personality (more on that in character development), the phone rings, and they hear her having a conversation that fleshes out her normal day.

Disturbance   The disturbance is a mysterious package arriving and her realizing there is something strange about the document and other contents. This disrupts the status quo because it has the potential to send her down the path of a new case.

At this juncture the first interactive learning would be introduced, perhaps an activity to figure out who sent the letter, what the letter contained, and so forth. This would be designed as a way to provide the first level of competitive intelligence skills.

Surprise   After the detective (the participant) does some research, the program throws a twist: the document leads to questioning of the salesperson who supposedly wrote it. As this is taking place one of the authorities the

Just a reminder, Chapters Seven, Eight, and Nine cover character and define terminology such as *protagonist* and *antagonist*.

detective had consulted in the previous module (where the participants were learning competitive intelligence skills) cuts in and says the document is a forgery and was never written by the salesperson suspect.

As a result of that surprise, the detective and salesperson 1 need to find out why a forged document trying to get salesperson 1 arrested was created and sent and by whom.

Complications   Now you need to come up with several potential complications that could get in the way of a person trying to find out who wrote a forged document to frame a salesperson. Here is a small sampling of the activities the participants might do to learn some competitive intelligence skills and see how those activities can translate into crises or solutions to crises.

- Searching databases and other places to find a list of competitors
- Scanning through newspapers to find articles about the rival company and rival salespeople
- Finding locations where networking is likely to take place
- Networking with others to uncover relevant information
- Locating mentors or retirees who would want to share information and advice
- Finding sources of major legal, political, and societal trends and regulations
- Developing and maintaining a database of collected intelligence, sources, and so on
- Crunching numbers and analyzing data
- Presenting data and getting feedback

The next step is to ask yourself what could prevent a person from doing some of the activities listed above. For example:

- After a person makes contact with a mentor and gets some initial guidance, the mentor dies or is bribed to stop speaking with the person, or the like.
- An ethical dilemma occurs. The person is offered information and advice derived from competitive intelligence that violates ethical standards or legal ones.
- Small crises arise. An individual or group with important information that the person is going to interview cannot be interviewed (due to logistical or other reasons); the library that had the needed books is closed for renovations or the books have disappeared; a computer crashes after the data have been entered; a government official refuses to release records because the person does not have proper ID.

- A manager or boss hears an initial report and thinks it needs much more work. The person is sent back to get more support, and so forth.

- Time constraints surface. A manager or boss tells the person she no longer has X amount of time, now she has only twenty-four hours or whatever before she will be reassigned, due to an influx of new demands.

- Matters come to a climax. Salesperson 1 does not have authorization to use a certain database and is caught trying to use it. She is arrested, and the detective is unable to help her—perhaps disbelieving her innocence. As a result she is fired, which cuts off her ability to use any of the databases and her financing to do the other forms of competitive intelligence. She must now turn to guerrilla tactics in order to clear her name and make a case.

This is just the start of what could possibly stand between the detective (the participant) and success. Depending on the exact content you wanted to teach and what resources and knowledge you wanted the participants to pick up, these crises would be individualized and rearranged so they become increasingly more difficult to overcome and demand more of the participant.

PROTAGONIST

The next chapter will address the characters, including the protagonist.

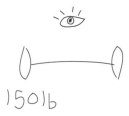

150|b

Mark Meadows, in his book *Pause & Effect,* describes four steps of effective interactive narrative. Let's review these in light of eLearning:

1. Observation: when the learner is hanging back just trying to assess what can be done ("what is possible").

2. Exploration: when the learner starts to interact with the eLearning program to see the limits of what she can do with it.

3. Modification: when the learner changes the system in a way that makes him feel more involved in the process and more invested in his own learning.

4. Reciprocal change: when there is true interactivity, not just what people commonly consider interactivity. Programs where a user can click on something to turn a page or get a verbal response have no more educational impact than a TV remote control. However, systems where the user can make a change and the system then changes based on her action present true potential for learning.

BrainPOP is an excellent example of a system with all four elements. BrainPOP users can observe what is possible by clicking and pointing as they would do with any program. Exploration happens as they play with the various elements to see what can and can't be done. In BrainPOP's case they are able to select an area of interest, pick a subtopic within that area, play short movies, do experiments, get a basic understanding of the subtopic, hop to related topics, and so on.

Becoming a member is the entrée to the modification level. A fact that makes BrainPOP stand head and foot above other educational Web sites is the strong person-to-person interaction facilitated by the site. This is not just peer-to-peer interaction where members talk to others. There is actually a large human staff responsible for answering emails that come from kids. Some of the emails are just seeking advice on how to find information or on how to use BrainPOP. But many of the emails modify the system. The most important modification might just be that they actually influence the content of the site—by asking questions members change what movies, topics, and experiments are put up on the site. And we're not talking about the usual "your feedback is important to us" BS. BrainPOP's people genuinely change the content every day, based on the thousands of emails they receive.

The final level, reciprocal change, comes about by driving the email behavior. The learner is changed by the system because she cannot follow the typical path used on the Internet—searching for information—and must instead develop a research and critical thinking skill—formulating the question.

Unlike the massive world called the Internet, BrainPOP provides only brief, introductory-level coverage of a particular topic. It is designed to provide just enough to get kids excited about learning more. If they want to learn more they must (and do!) send an email. Although this may not seem terribly significant, it is. As the kids are forced to inquire about the information they are seeking, they will not only learn the topic material. More important, they will learn how to formulate questions articulately so a reader is able to respond quickly and accurately. They will learn the first step of a critical thinking process they will rely on for the rest of their days. (Figure 6.1 presents a sample screenshot.)

PLAN

The plan describes how the characters will overcome the crises standing in their way. In traditional narrative forms the author dictates both the obstacles

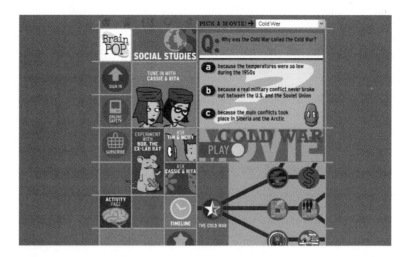

FIGURE 6.1 BrainPOP Screenshot
Brainpop.com, LLC

and the resulting actions (the plan). This in and of itself is challenging. Add the interactivity variables—where the division between participants and author blurs—and the challenge becomes exponentially more difficult.

In interactive eLearning, the best a designer can hope to do is sculpt an environment and experience that accommodates, preferably welcomes, each participant's unique solutions.

Creating this flexible interactive narrative eLearning is difficult, time consuming, and experimental. No Web-based training cookbook has a magic formula or recipe to solve this dilemma. Most eLearning programs try to get around this challenge by allowing only highly structured responses or requiring intensive facilitator involvement The first quashes creativity and screams "contrived!" The latter is expensive, time consuming, and potentially constrained by the facilitator's value system or knowledge level.

For the near future these will remain the mainstream form of interactivity in eLearning—at least until there is some unanticipated major advance in artificial intelligence or discovery of some heretofore unknown simulation technology that makes computer responses indistinguishable from human ones. We don't have a silver bullet to solve this problem, but we do have a few ideas designed to stimulate alternate implementations.

Those who don't have the time or desire to make eLearning more effective by following these interactive response techniques should stick with some of the less resource-intensive options described previously in this chapter (changing the setting and the like) and the next (for example, making more convincing characters).

There are many well-documented, large-scale ways to increase interactivity in digital narratives. The complexity and detail of most of them precludes covering them here, but because they are so important, visit the ". . . And Even More Reading!" section to learn more about them.

STIRRING UP THE POT: MAKING eLEARNING MORE INTERACTIVE

Following are some more contained fringe ideas about how to make dramatic eLearning more interactive (and therefore more effective). By more effective we mean

- Allowing for more realistic responses
- Valuing individual expression and creativity
- Requiring deeper processing
- Requiring real-world activities performed outside the eLearning module

Idea 1: Freeform Experimentation

The best learning allows participants to experiment with different cause-and-effect situations. As they experience the outcomes of their actions, their judgment skills, in addition to all other desired learning, are strengthened. One effective way to do this is to provide freeform play spaces, where the participant makes her own judgments about what is good or not good.

EXAMPLE

Root Learning's outstanding simulation on executive decision making offers numerous occasions when the participant is given several variables and asked to manipulate each of them based on complex information. The results are not a multiple-choice right or wrong but an impact on share price. Participants are then asked to discuss their actions and the results by responding to open-ended questions such as, "When you got the results, which elements surprised you?" and, "What would you do now given the existing results and information?" The narrative then changes based on the participants' complex and unique solutions to the crises. (See the sample screenshot in Figure 6.2.)

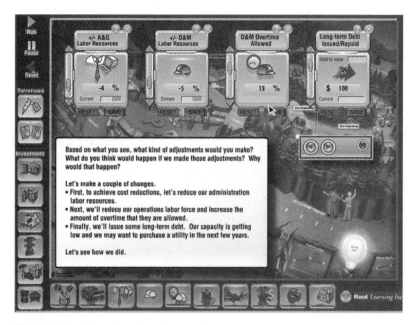

FIGURE 6.2   Root Learning Screenshot

Copyright © Root Learning, Inc.

Idea 2: Hurdle

The participant is given a task and has a wide variety of ways to accomplish the task. There might be literally hundreds of possible combinations of actions she could take to accomplish the task. She is not given specific feedback on the actions taken. Instead, she encounters a barrier that either disappears as the result of her actions or does not. Most video games follow this premise. The players rarely know exactly why they made it past a certain door or over a certain terrain until they analyze their actions, applying hindsight and looking at what was done through trial and error.

EXAMPLE

The few examples of eLearning that contain this form of interactive narrative are either integrated into video games or focused on children's development. In the first instance is learndirect scotland's literacy module, which fits seamlessly into the popular video game Deus X. An example of the second comes from Broderbund's Logical Journey of the Zoombinis. In the beginning of the program the children make ten characters by selecting a hairstyle, a nose, and other body parts for each and a transportation method. The ten characters travel to a distant land where they encounter several discrimination tasks: some of the characters will make it over the hurdle and others won't. It is up to the children to learn over time what body parts or combination of parts led to success at each crisis.

Idea 3: Hurdle with Debrief

A related method is to accompany the hurdle approach with feedback from others. In this case feedback is not provided immediately. The participant is expected to go through several crises and attempt to analyze why he did or didn't overcome each. At the end there is a debriefing session with a facilitator or other participants where actions and choices are analyzed.

Idea 4: Increasing Difficulty

One of the tasks computers are well suited to is following rules. One rule that could make eLearning far more effective would involve adjusting levels of difficulty based upon prior responses. For many years standardized assessments such as the GRE have been adjusting the questions presented to test takers based on their prior correct or incorrect responses. This structure could just as easily be applied in simulations, blackboard-type environments, or other forms of eLearning where there is a pool of crises to be overcome, each of which has a varying degree of difficulty. Instead, most eLearning programs present the activities according to a different order. With the technology available today there is little reason why programs shouldn't adjust to learners' progress, not just by redirecting them to different content but by adjusting challenge difficulty.

EXAMPLE

The Educational Testing Service describes how the GRE's questions change in response to the performance of the test taker.

> Your scores on the verbal and quantitative sections of the computer-based General Test depend on your performance on the questions given and on the number of questions answered in the time allotted. Because both of these sections are computer adaptive, the questions presented are selected to reflect your performance on preceding questions and the requirements of the test design. Test design factors that influence which questions are presented to you include (1) the statistical characteristics (including difficulty level) of the questions already answered, (2) the required variety of question types, and (3) the appropriate coverage of content.[9]

Idea 5: Checkpoints

Once participants attain a certain level of proficiency many learning institutions have checkpoint programs for them. The participants spend most of their time independently gathering information, testing theories, overcoming obstacles, and basically experiencing life. Every once in a while they check in with a mentor or adviser to ensure they are gathering the proper information. This approach has been applied well in some blackboard-style eLearning programs minus the narrative. One way to increase interactivity is to add the dramatic layer and then build in the checkpoints in character.

EXAMPLE

Almost all graduate programs at universities follow this model. A simple example comes from the University of California at Berkeley. Students in UC Berkeley programs do research all over the globe and check in or have discussions with professors via email and instant messaging. This is a great example of eLearning being so thoroughly incorporated into the day-to-day operations of an educational program that it appears almost pedestrian.

Idea 6: Real People

Another way to increase the interactivity of narratives and decrease the perception of contrivance is to use real people and real people's words. For example, one approach is to capture on a video or tape recorder actual conversations between people, after you've given them prior notice, of course. When possible use these actual conversations as the dialogue in the program. When this is not feasible because editing is required, either make small digital modifications to these dialogues and then use the recordings or transcribe the words and use an edited written form of the actual discussion. The next step is to capture all the responses the participants make. Eventually, when you have recorded enough of these conversations and participants' responses, you will have a huge selection of much more realistic choices for the participants.

EXAMPLE

The Royal Bank of Scotland took this approach to management development. They recorded real people in real situations and used those modules as the basis of their management training programs.

Idea 7: An Inkblot Test

A slightly off-the-wall idea is to do an inkblot test reminiscent of the Rorschach®. Consider the written text to go in only one direction: from participant to characters. After participants have been given a task or guidance, have them type in freeform words to start the dialogue. Beforehand, create a series of visuals that will convey responses from the characters. Each visual should clearly communicate a certain emotion or mix of emotions. Images allow for interpretation in a way that text does not. Establish a way for participants to speak with each other about their reactions to the visuals. Not only will this foster development of self-analysis and reflection, it can help reveal and resolve issues too sensitive to be addressed directly.

WRITE THE HIGH CONCEPT

To return to the point we made in the beginning of this chapter, the high concept is the sentence that summarizes the story and excites the listener. Based on the information we just covered, the high concept for the Romeo and Juliet mystery used as an example in this chapter would be stated this way (using Aronson's template[10]):

> African detective faced with apparent corporate fraud which creates a reminder of her past career fall from grace and surprised by the document's having been forged responds and is foiled by a selection of the crises and solutions described earlier and along with salesperson 1 reaches a low point of physical danger or despair when the salesperson is arrested for hacking into confidential databases she is not permitted access to but both fight back by learning about competitive intelligence tactics and finally deal with case by proving another salesperson sent the document to frame salesperson 1.

Up Next

In the next three chapters we introduce character development. Chapter Seven, up next, provides an introduction to characters and the way point of view sculpts the participants' experience.

NOTES

1. The last element, character, is the subject of the next chapter.
2. Linda Aronson, *Screenwriting Updated* (Los Angeles: Silman-James Press, 2001), p. 83.
3. Aronson, *Screenwriting Updated*, p. 101.
4. Charles Miller, *Screenwriting for Film and Television* (Needham Heights, Mass.: Allyn & Bacon, 1998).
5. Miller, *Screenwriting for Film and Television*.

6. Brian Taves, Judi Hoffman, and Karen Lund, "The Moving Image Genre-Form Guide," Library of Congress, http://lcweb.loc.gov/rr/mopic/miggen.html, accessed May 2004.

7. Miller, *Screenwriting for Film and Television*.

8. Raymond Frensham, *Screenwriting*, Teach Yourself series (London: Hodder Arnold, 1996).

9. "Frequently Asked Questions About the General Test: Scoring and Reporting," http://www.gre.org/faqnew.html, accessed May 2004.

10. Aronson, *Screenwriting Updated*, p. 83.

PART 2 CONTINUED
COMING ATTRACTIONS

What a Character!

Participants who see reflections of themselves in an eLearning program's characters will be deeply influenced by the content. Creating convincing characters builds an emotional and intellectual bridge between the participants and the learning material.

It increases the participants' willingness to analyze their development needs, decreases resistance to the content, reignites passion for learning, and decreases the learning curve. At the very least, it decreases the dropout rate and inhibitions about online learning and generates positive word of mouth about the organization sponsoring or developing the eLearning.

Chapters Seven and Eight will provide those managing writers and those considering creating their own characters with an understanding of the key elements of characterization and some guidelines to more effective character development and dialogue. Chapter Nine moves into the functions of figurative language, which delineates character but has uses beyond that as well.

For help in finding resources experienced in character development, such as novelists, playwrights, and screenwriters, see Chapter Thirteen.

WHAT A CHARACTER!

The ABCs of Character Development

MICHAEL CAINE'S WORDS apply equally well to eLearning as to film. Participants who see reflections of themselves in an eLearning program's characters will be more deeply affected by the content than those who are merely observing others in action. This is because convincing characters touch participants' capacity for empathy, enable them to question their own beliefs and actions in a nonthreatening context, build confidence through vicarious success, and model a different (typically improved) approach. In short, they decrease defensiveness and increase interest.

Ideally, an eLearning program with compelling characters will increase the participants' willingness to analyze their development needs, decrease resistance to the content, reignite the passion for learning, and flatten the learning curve. At a minimum, convincing characters decrease the dropout rate, sustain interest in learning, decrease inhibitions, and generate positive word of mouth about the organization sponsoring or developing the eLearning.

People connect with content on a personal, down-to-earth, individual level, not a macro one. Abstract business concepts such as ethics, success, business results, the bottom line, creativity, and management skills mean little in the day-to-day world. They are too big to be digested or grasped. Abstract concepts need to be brought down to a level where they directly affect the lives of participants in order to be taken personally, to be seen as relevant and critical.

Which would affect you more: a module on business ethics that describes in intellectual terms some of the consequences of not following ethical

> *People go to the cinema to see themselves on the screen. As an actor, people must identify with you. You cannot hold up a picture and say "this is me." You hold up a mirror and say "this is you."*
>
> **MICHAEL CAINE**

A professional can accomplish this task on a shoestring, making this one of the wisest, no-brainer eLearning development investments to be made. We strongly recommend having a professional writer as a resource.

procedures or one that shows a person you quickly identify as being like your grandmother or mother having her heat cut off because her pension had been raided by a corporate executive who used the money to furnish his mansion and fly mistresses around the globe? A module on time management that lists great techniques or one that shows a character you quickly identify as being like your child sitting at home alone watching television or surfing porn sites because his parents are still at the office?

Characters are the way learning content is made personal: the way you get participants to stand up and take notice, to care about their future. Participants are more likely to respond to and absorb the content when the characters are mirrors reflecting their hopes and fears and personally experiencing the benefits and consequences of an abstract issue.

This chapter assists those seeking to create more convincing characters, either by going solo or hiring a talented writer. Creating convincing characters is unquestionably an art that cannot be taught anymore than having an artist's eye or a chef's palate can be taught. Instead we seek to provide some guidelines and an overview of the building blocks that combine to make strong characters. The writer is the kayaker maneuvering down the river. This chapter is the riverbank, providing direction and structure but leaving the imagination and specifics to the writer.

DECONSTRUCTING CHARACTER

To an audience, a strong character is one organic entity, a person with all the history and idiosyncrasies and preferences that any other human being has. In reality of course a strong character is a brilliant illusion, as hard to pull off as any Houdini stunt. Even when the character is a real person (as in a documentary or reality show) or a portrayal of a real person, the character the audience sees is the end result of a construction project. The representation people see on screen or in a novel or a song (or any other narrative) is just select parts of a person put together and presented deliberately with the goal of communicating a whole image of who the person is.

In fictional works, like most eLearning, each character is pure fiction. There is no biography to work from. Not only does the writer need to select parts of a person and present them, she needs to conjure up the parts. The raw materials of fictional characters are just pieces of imagination.

If a character is a construction project, one way to start figuring how to create good characters is to deconstruct the elements that combine to make up the entity participants see as a whole person.

Here are some parameters for characters:

- *Multifaceted and multidimensional*. Real people exist on many levels. They have behaviors, preferences, beliefs, and characteristics, many of which conflict and all of which evolve over time. If a character comes across as having too few sides or as too black or white (always doing the right thing or always doing the wrong thing) or always stays exactly the same, credibility goes out the window. Participants identify with characters because they see parts of themselves in them, and no one can see himself or herself in a person who is unidimensional.

- *Appropriate actions*. A character's actions need to be consistent with his or her personality, skills, and beliefs, unless the author is deliberately making a point. The CEO of a multinational is just not likely to start throwing cookies during a board meeting. The expert competitive intelligence professional is not likely to ask for help in using a database even a beginner knows how to use. These would put a dent in character credibility, unless the inconsistency is intentional. When it is intentional, it must be directly relevant to the story and have an explanation. Typically it would be used to show that a character is growing or experimenting with different behaviors or that a disturbance is shaking up the status quo. For example, it might turn out that the CEO was trying to recapture the magic of the time when the company was a start-up and he used to lead food fights to get people's creative juices going.

- *A point of view consistent with the narrator's personality*. The perspective participants view the eLearning from is that of the narrator. We will discuss this in detail later, but we note here that the voice of the narrator must mesh with the participants' expectations of the narrator's personality. If, for example, the main character is a woman in her thirties and she is the narrator, the participants' belief in her will be shaken if she has a childlike voice or if she says things more consistent with a child's than an adult's behavior ("No, you can't have it! It's mine!").

- *Realistic dialogue*. The conversation between characters must seem like something that could easily be spoken by them.

- *Believable relationships*. The way characters interact with each other and other animate beings (for example, a dog) must be realistic. This is intimately connected to the dialogue and actions mentioned earlier. A manager who has just finished analyzing an employee's

productivity ratings and has found them lacking is unlikely to become (without explanation or cause) that employee's best friend or take him on as a protégé.

Now that we have looked at the elements audiences might see that would lead them to identify with a character and to find the character credible, we are going to approach characterization from the construction end. Here is a list of the building blocks a writer uses to sculpt characters. We will discuss each in turn.

1. Creating the protagonist and antagonist
2. Establishing point of view
3. Writing dialogue (tropes, especially metaphors)

CHARACTER ROLES

Unless the eLearning program is a major, high-budget, long-term-use production, there will be room for only three characters and perhaps some very minor bit players. The first character, the protagonist is always an essential. The second, an antagonist, is essential but is not always a person. The third, a secondary character, is a luxury unless this character plays a minor role.

The protagonist is the main character, the person the participants will follow most closely, the person around whom the story revolves, and ideally the person participants identify with most. In many eLearning programs the protagonist role will be split between two characters because one will be there almost exclusively to move the story forward whereas the other—by necessity—has to be a quasi-avatar of the participant. In our Romeo and Juliet mystery example the protagonist is the detective who will need to "learn" competitive intelligence skills in order to unravel the mystery. However, the successful salesperson who is being framed is also a protagonist, there to move the story forward and to share information on how she did the competitive intelligence, on her rationale for the steps she took, on her fear, and so forth. This avatar is part teacher, part story mover.

The antagonist is the antihero, more commonly called the villain. In traditional narrative forms—movies, books, and so forth, the antagonist is a person—in *Star Wars*, Darth Vader; in *Silence of the Lambs*, serial killer Buffalo Bill. In our example we created the shadowy figure of a rival salesperson who is trying to frame our protagonist to serve as the antagonist.

People developing eLearning can go two ways with the antagonist. Because organizations do not like their training to be seen as putting anyone down or being "negative," the antagonist role is often given to circum-

> I start with characters. I walk around in their shoes for a long time. I stay in my pyjamas all day talking to people who aren't there.
>
> **BARBARA TRAPIDO**

stances that get in the way and other obstacles. For example, time might be one component of the antagonist, lack of budget another, inclement weather yet another, and so on.

Another approach is to have multiple individuals make up the antagonist role. In effect, one character has been split into multiple incarnations. For example, in our Romeo and Juliet mystery example, the protagonist salesperson might be completing a database search when a librarian appears demanding she shut down the search immediately because she has exceeded her twenty-minute limit (here the antagonist is time and rules). In that same example, the officer who has this salesperson arrested for allegedly stealing proprietary information is another facet of the same antagonist.

Secondary Characters

The secondary characters are there to make the story more colorful or to help the protagonist accomplish her tasks. For example, our mystery might include the following secondary characters:

- A mentor to provide support and guidance
- A reference librarian
- A fellow trade show attendee

The amount of credibility a character needs to have is directly proportional to the weight he carries in the program. If learners are going to identify with our detective, who is also learning about competitive intelligence, he must be very believable. However, our hypothetical librarian, who appears only once and says only one line, can be fairly unidimensional. Those characters are like the extras in a movie or television program: they need be only convincing enough to *not* get too much notice.

Creating the Protagonist

The first step is to develop the protagonist: the person who carries the most dramatic weight and appears most often (has the most face time).

Here are some steps to guide that process.

STEP 1

Make a visual representation of the program's learning objectives, setting, genre, and any story ideas team members might have.

STEP 2

Use your imagination to make a list of the kinds of people who might want or need to learn the content that fulfills the learning objectives.

EXAMPLE

When we decided to do a mystery, we realized a detective might need to learn competitive intelligence skills in order to get to the truth. Other people who might need to learn the content are

- New employees
- Visiting dignitaries on a trade mission to learn how another group does something
- Government agents trying to assess another country's situation
- Research analysts setting up a scheme to inflate stock prices

Your list, like ours, should start with the realistic and become progressively more imaginative.

STEP 3

Once you select a few favorite types, create a tangible sketch of each of them, as they could be described in one sentence. Include

- Age
- Gender
- Height and weight
- Color of eyes, hair, and skin
- Nationality
- Physical build or body type

All of these elements will begin to transform an imagined type (for example, a detective) into a specific physical presence.

STEP 4

Start to imagine what would motivate each of your now fleshed-out favorites to achieve the goal you have created for him or her. Make a list of at least ten motivations, some realistic, some slightly more of a stretch.

EXAMPLE

Why would our short, twenty-six-year-old female detective in Africa want to take on, let alone solve, this case? And why would she want to learn competitive intelligence (CI)? She has a few motivations:

- As it turns out, if she had known how to do CI before, she might not have lost her job to the person who unfairly had her fired (she might have been able to prove what was happening).
- She wants to vicariously get her pride back by helping the salesperson.

- She wants people to respect her and praise her skills. Successfully solving this high-profile case would help achieve those goals.

After going through this process with each of your possible protagonists, one or two should be emerging as a best choice. Before completing the following steps commit to one protagonist.

STEP 5

Create the protagonist's history. Get to know your character and fill in as many blanks about his or her life as you can. Although this detailed information will never be provided to participants, having this profile in mind is essential when you are trying to select aspects of the character to use to create the illusion of a multidimensional person.

STEP 6

Brainstorm a list of outward characteristics that will quickly give participants a good sense of who the character is. These will include mannerisms, expressions, habits, clothing style, movements, and other observables that provide a good window onto a larger whole.

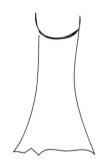

Each character should now be developed enough for you to move on to the next building block, point of view.

POINT OF VIEW OR NARRATOR

There are two components of point of view. One is physical perspective, which is present only when there is something for the eye to see (for example, a movie, an image on a computer monitor, and so on). We'll define this for our purposes as the manipulation of the viewer's thoughts by showing something from a particular angle. (We will be addressing physical perspective in Chapters Ten, Eleven, and Twelve.)

The other component of perspective is cognitive/emotional. This type of perspective is what laypeople typically mean when they speak of point of view: "the mental position from which the story is observed." Point of view in narrative means whose eyes the reader or viewer sees something through. For example, in the movie A *Beautiful Mind* the audience sees the story through John Nash's eyes until almost halfway through the movie. The point of view then switches to that of an objective third person.

In eLearning, point of view must be deliberately and carefully considered and constructed because most participants will assume that whatever the narrator says is what the company (or whoever participants think sanctioned the eLearning) condones. The narrator is the mouthpiece for the company whether the designer intends him or her to be or not.

Look Through My Eyes: Selecting a Narrator

The main purpose of the narrator on a simple level is to tell the story (someone has got to do it!). On a deeper level it is to define the relationship the participants have with the content. There are four basic forms the narrator can take. Neither is better nor worse than any other, but each encourages participants to approach the learning from a slightly different perspective.

There is no hard and fast rule for which point of view to use in an eLearning program. It will depend largely on the goal and preference of the development team. The main goal is to find the proper fit with the material.

Look at the sidebar describing ways the narrator can relate to the content. Consider your goals and how they can be best served by each of those elements. Then look at the types of narrators described here and pick the one that will work best.

English professor John Lye, of Brock University, does an excellent job of breaking down the ways a narrator can relate to the story:[2]

1. *Distance:* the narrator can be emotionally or in other ways distant from the story she is narrating, or very close, very involved. This can take a number of forms, including, for instance, . . . dialect, vocabulary or style . . ., distance in time, distance in culture.

2. *Interest:* the narrator may share the "stakes" of the story with the characters or may not; may show a great interest in the outcome of the story and the choices the characters make or may be clinical, reserved, apparently uninterested, or disinterested (that word means "impartial," not "uninterested").

3. *Sympathy:* not dissimilar from distance as emotional distance, this refers to how much the narrator empathizes with the characters, or judges them, or approaches them as a clinical observer. It differs from emotional distance in that the narrator may be emotionally close, but judgmental or antipathetic.

4. *Voice:* this refers to what the narrator is like, as it is conveyed by the language of the narration, the tone, the choice of comments and descriptions, and so forth: These may indicate

- what her personality is
- what her attitude is to the characters, to the subject of the story, to the readers
- what her ideological position, faith commitment, intellectual and emotional positions are

5. *Orientation:* this is a category which is useful, but may repeat aspects of the categories above: is the narrator approaching the story from a certain position of commitment and concern, for instance of ideological or sexual or theological or social or political commitment or concern. The term "orientation" can at times be replaced by the term "standpoint."

6. *Sense of Audience:* narrators may differ in their sense of who they are narrating to, and why. In this case the narrator of an embedded narrative (an account, a diary, a letter, etc.) will likely have a very different sense of audience than the primary internal narrator.

Third-Person Omniscient Narration

With a third-person omniscient narrator, the story is told from the point of view of a person outside the story with unlimited access to anyone and everyone, to all the characters' thoughts, motivations, actions, and any other information about the story. The two main advantages to this point of view are the ability to tell anything about anyone or anything at any time without breaking credibility and the ability to effortlessly shift from one character's thoughts or actions to another's. The only disadvantage is the potential for decreased participant connection to the material (like the distancing that might occur if a teacher instead of a fellow student were speaking to a group of students).

EXAMPLE

In a module from an Enspire Learning sales training demo, the genre is comic book (Figure 7.1). In keeping with that classic style, the narrator must be third-person omniscient. Indications of this narrative style (aside from the distinct look and feel of the graphics, an issue covered in Chapters Ten to Twelve) include the absence of "you," "I," and other first-person and second-person pronouns and the sense that the speaker is able to comment on the larger picture. He or she is removed from the immediate action. For

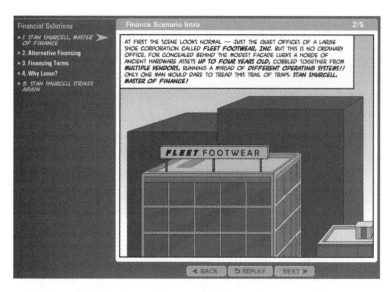

FIGURE 7.1 Enspire Learning, Inc. Screenshot
Source: www.enspire.com

example, in Figure 7.1, the narrator says, "At first the scene looks normal. . . ." The text for first-person narration would be, "At first I thought the scene looked normal, . . ." and for second-person narration, "At first you think the scene looks normal. . . ."

First-Person Narration

With a first-person narrator, the story is seen through the eyes of one of the main characters, who refers to himself or herself in the first person: "I." This book is written from a first-person point of view. (If just one of us were writing, you'd see lots of "I" statements. As two of us are writing, you see "we" statements, which are also first-person narration.)

One of the main advantages of this point of view for eLearning is the potential for intimacy and emotional connection. Of all the points of view, this is the one that most directly puts the participant in the character's shoes. The main disadvantage is that the narrator is not perceived as objective, and therefore the content may be seen as just one person's opinion.

EXAMPLE

Typically, when first-person narration is used the character is talking aloud, so there is no screenshot to show. An excellent example of this narrative style can be found on a PBS Web site for P.O.V.[3] On "The Talking Back Tapestry" section of this site, the women who participated in Eve Ensler's prison writing workshop read their works aloud.

Second-Person Narration

With second-person narration, the story is told as if the participant (audience) is the one doing the action. For this reason it is almost never used in narrative fiction as it sounds very awkward. It is by far the most commonly used point of view in instructional programs (live and electronic). The advantage is a connection the participants will find familiar and natural, as if they are being spoken to directly. The two main disadvantages are the risk of sounding paternal or condescending (it is tricky to pull off when the narrator is not present in person) and the risk of breaking the dramatic illusion.

EXAMPLE

Junction-18 created a small business eLearning program using the metaphor of a television show (Figures 7.2 and 7.3). Addressing the participants as "you" and using the second-person verb form are both dead giveaways that the narrator is speaking directly to the audience in second-person narration. Also notice in this case that the second-person narration is consistent throughout the program (in the introduction and in subsequent sections). Often in eLearning the narration will switch from second person in the introduction to another form in the actual program.

FIGURE 7.2 The Small Business Project Screenshot 1

Source: Created by Junction-18 for Learn Direct & Build

FIGURE 7.3   The Small Business Project Screenshot 2
Source: Created by Junction-18 for Learn Direct & Build

Third-Person Limited Narration

With the third-person limited point of view, the narrator is a character in the narrative who knows everything about himself but can see only a limited amount of the other characters' motivations, behaviors, and so forth. Most typically he can see only the same observable aspects of the other characters as the participant can. The main advantage of this point of view is that it balances objectivity with involvement. The participants see the story unfold from eyes that are slightly more distant than those of the first-person narrator. This has the potential to slightly decrease involvement or identification but it also increases credibility—the point of view is assumed to be more objective by virtue of the narrator's being less intimately involved in the story.

EXAMPLE

Third-person limited narration appears identical to third-person omniscient except for a subtle difference: the participants come to know *all* the internal workings of only one character.

Up Next

Chapter Eight, up next, continues our exploration of character development. It focuses on making characters believable by writing realistic and intelligent dialogue.

NOTES

1. Any of these rules can be violated to make credible and outstanding characters. However, they must be violated intentionally and an explanation must be provided to the audience. An excellent example is the relationship between Helen Hunt and Jack Nicholson in *As Good as It Gets*. The relationship between them is completely unrealistic until we understand Nicholson's personality disorder. If one of these elements is going to be violated, there must be a good, intentional reason to do so, and the participants must know it.

2. John Lye, "Narrative Point of View: Some Considerations," July 9, 2002, http://www.brocku.ca/english/courses/2F55/pt_of_view.html.

3. "What I Want My Words to Do to You," http://www.pbs.org/pov/pov2003/whatiwant/index.html, accessed May 2004.

ARE YOU TALKIN' TO ME?

Creating Convincing Dialogue

HUMAN BEINGS FORM images of others primarily by what they say and what they do. In Chapters Five and Six we covered actions. In Chapter Seven we covered point of view (which gives individuals the potential to learn about others by getting inside their heads, which people cannot do in real life, of course). This chapter covers the final avenue writers have to illustrate character: dialogue.

One of the main reasons why many of today's eLearning programs are ineffective is poor dialogue. The participants buy into the setting and are willing to accept the validity of the learning materials. Then the role play comes up or a character speaks, and the dialogue is so unrealistic, stiff, wordy, or just plain limited they question the integrity of the entire program if not the whole medium.

EXAMPLES

Trilogia's role-play module on sales skills shows a salesperson calling to sell role playing as a form of training (Figures 8.1 and 8.2). The manager's response might look fine at first glance (and would be fine if he were writing an email or a report). Speak his words aloud and they suddenly become very unwieldy and unlikely to be spontaneously generated in a phone conversation. The salesperson's response also sounds awkward rolling off the tongue. Both characters come off as one dimensional, as if they were just following written scripts. Two tip-offs are "furthermore" and "You are correct." These are conventional phrases in literary writing but are almost never used in informal conversations (such as phone solicitations).

BOOKSHELF BEST BETS

Writing Dialogue,
Tom Chiarella

*The Playwright's
Guidebook,* Stewart
Spenser

*The Art of Dramatic
Writing,* Lajos Egri

*Writing Dialogue for
Scripts,* Rib Davis

For more help sourcing
books, try the Drama
Bookshop (212-944-0595)
or The Writer's Store
(866-229-7483).

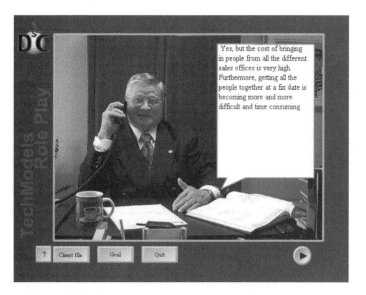

FIGURE 8.1 Trilogia Screenshot 1
Copyright © Trilogia Solutions Inc.

FIGURE 8.2 Trilogia Screenshot 2
Copyright © Trilogia Solutions Inc.

Contrast this with Enspire's eLearning program on quantitative analysis. A hotel manager has requested help from a consultant. He needs assistance forecasting occupancy in order to manage staffing requirements. In the screenshots (Figures 8.3, 8.4, and 8.5) he comes across as human; we are inclined to see him not only as real but as a person worthy of empathy because he apologizes for being short and shares that he is upset. He uses conversational slang, including euphemisms that are used in everyday conversation ("a little incident down in the restaurant"). He adds extra words, pleasantries people slip into conversation but usually edit out of formal written material (when he says, "Is there anything you can do to help me here?" that "here" is grammatically unnecessary but adds to the characterization and ambiance).

DIALOGUE FORMATS

In eLearning, dialogue can take any of the following formats:

1. Spoken word: used in programs that have audio. The dialogue can be heard aurally.
2. Written word: used in programs that have a display or monitor. The dialogue can be read as text on a screen.
3. Both spoken and written word: used in programs with both an audio component and a visual display. The dialogue can be read and heard.

The writer must know how the dialogue will be experienced by participants as this will strongly shape how it is written and subsequently how the characters and content are perceived by the audience. Writing dialogue that will be heard is harder than writing dialogue that will be read, because anything that sounds wrong will be easily detected. Written dialogue is more challenging because our sensibility about what "seems" right when we read interferes with judgment about what sounds right spoken aloud.

DIALOGUE DECISIONS

Beyond considering the format the dialogue will take there are five other decisions that need to be made. Although each has its own merits, the most important factor is that whatever direction is chosen should be used consistently throughout the program.

1. What tone to use (formality, grammar, vocabulary)?
2. What accent to use (especially if spoken)?

For those eLearning formats where audio is logical (for example, simulations) we strongly urge its use. We understand the concerns about lowest common denominator computers and environmental distractions to others that audio raises. However, the benefits of keeping dialogue in its natural format (spoken) and of having music to create the right emotion and ambiance typically far outweigh these concerns. There is no reason why the programmers can't (in most instances) include a component that automatically checks whether a system has the right capabilities and then blocks the audio if it does not.

FIGURE 8.3 Enspire Learning, Inc. Screenshot 1

Source: www.enspire.com

3. What type of dialogue to use (monologue, conversation)?

4. What purpose to assign to each spoken element? (Revelation: dialogue is a quick and cheap way to reveal events from the past, deepen characters, add to ambiance, give information.)

5. What tropes (literary devices such as metaphor) to use? (Tropes are discussed in the next chapter.)

Tone

Tone is how the writer communicates the emotional state or attitude of the speaker. It shows whether the speaker is happy, sad, frustrated, intrigued, and so forth, as well as indicating how the speaker categorizes the relationship between the speaker and the person being spoken to.

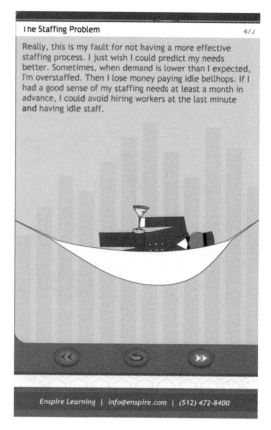

FIGURE 8.4 Enspire Learning, Inc. Screenshot 2
Source: www.enspire.com

Tone is made up of

- Degree of formality
- Level of use of grammar
- Choice of vocabulary
- Choice of style

Tone exists on a continuum from very intimate to emotionally distant. eLearning that seeks to establish an intimate connection with participants uses an informal style with loose grammatical rules and few or no obscure words. It uses slang and colloquialisms to establish a common ground, to indicate the writer literally speaks the participants' language.

eLearning that wishes to distance itself from participants does the opposite. The style is formal and even stiff, with rigid adherence to grammatical

> *If Galileo had said in verse that the world moved, the inquisition may have left him alone.*
>
> **THOMAS HARDY**

The Staffing Problem   6/7

Is there anything you can do to help me here? What
predictions about occupancy can I make based on advance
bookings? And how much can I trust them?

Enspire Learning | info@enspire.com | (512) 472-8400

FIGURE 8.5 Enspire Learning, Inc. Screenshot 3
Source: www.enspire.com

rules and enough large words to make it clear the program is not necessarily in the same league as the participants.

We have almost never run across an occasion when eLearning could
have been improved by using a more formal, distancing tone. The opposite
is more often the case: many programs are too stiff or formal and would benefit from more intimacy.

SPOKEN DIALOGUE

Where there is the option for spoken dialogue, there is also great potential
to convey not only degree of intimacy but emotional state. The rate, volume (as in decibels), inflection (aka *phonation,* for those seeking more info),
and variation in pitch (difference between the lowest the voice gets and the
highest it gets) give clues to the human ear that written dialogue cannot
about the emotional state of the speaker.

- The average person speaks at 175 words per minute. When dialogue is spoken faster, it implies stress, importance, the need to rush, and so on. When it is spoken more slowly, the emotion conveyed could be relaxation, being lost in thought, and so forth.

- When the speaker's pitch is similar throughout, the listener hears a monotone. This might be interpreted as boredom or condescension and is almost guaranteed to lose the listener's attention over time.

- Typically, words said more loudly are considered more important and those said more softly perceived as less so. This is a shaky rule as it is context dependent. All other factors being equal, keep the voice loud enough to be respected and attended to.

- Inflection arises from the physical shape of the mouth and vocal chords when a word is spoken. It is possibly the main reason why spoken words convey so much more emotion than written ones. Interestingly, there are several cultures in which one word may have three entirely different meanings depending on the inflection given to it by the speaker. When recording audio, encourage speakers to slightly exaggerate their inflections. Because people rely both on the heard word and the facial expression, when the latter is absent a slightly exaggerated inflection picks up the slack and communicates the emotion more easily.

- Genuine enthusiasm is by far the easiest way to keep participants' attention and win them over to the content. Whenever possible, for voiceovers use a person who might have benefited from the knowledge in the program or who has another reason to be passionate about the subject.

An important aspect of the tone of spoken dialogue is that it cues the listeners into what is important. When the speaker stresses a word, when she speaks one word more loudly than another, and so on, the participants listen more closely and are more likely to recall that word. This is a distinct advantage of speech and one that can prove very important for eLearning's impact.

WRITTEN DIALOGUE

When the dialogue is read and not heard by the participant it is difficult to assess emotion. Anyone who has ever had an email misinterpreted is intimately familiar with this phenomenon. The person who gets an email that was sent to communicate humor only to be misinterpreted as rudeness has been stung by this bee.

I have to watch my characters crossing the room, lighting a cigarette. I have to see everything they do, even if I don't write it down. So my eyes get tired.
GRAHAM GREENE

Because writing always means hiding something in such a way that it then is discovered.
ITALO CALVINO

The human voice conveys so much emotion in so few words that a font on a screen simply can't duplicate that richness. Some of the ways people have attempted to overcome this limitation in eLearning involve emoticons, font selection, and graphical display of words (making them **bold,** *italic,* <u>underlined,</u> or ALL CAPS, for example). To create a richer written communication experience, another important technique is to use slightly exaggerated dialogue (just as we suggested using exaggerated inflection when the facial movements were absent). As long as it isn't over the top, the exaggerated wording will remove some of the potential ambiguity and subsequent misinterpretations.

Style

Finally, style is an important component of tone as it will indicate to the participant what the genre of the program is. Much like music, vocal style (one appropriate to comedy, drama, or mystery, and so on) viscerally communicates what the participant should feel and expect. It is hard to communicate this on a printed page. Think back to the last time you listened to the news, classical music, or popular music on the radio. In each instance the voice of the announcer was dramatically different. The news reporters have that "I'm just going to read what's in front of me" sound. The classical DJs are always speaking in hushed tones, calmly (and typically without any editorial viewpoint) stating composers and titles. The pop station has some wild person excitedly rambling on about this or that in a relatively fast voice with lots of pitch variation and unbridled enthusiasm. In none of these situations would the listener need to be told specifically, "You are listening to a news [or classical music or pop music] program now."

EXAMPLE

Enspire Learning's sales training using the comic book genre was introduced in Chapter Seven (Figure 7.1). The next screen in this eLearning program(Figure 8.6) continues the comic book genre with dialogue representative of that style. The exaggeration, outlandish metaphor, and slight hint at suspense are all representative of a tone that works in comic books.

Accent

The issue of accent is fairly straightforward. When dialogue is going to be spoken aloud an accent should be chosen that either represents the accent found among the majority of participants or that is most pleasing to the largest number of participants. For English-speaking participants, the tendency is to use either an upper-class British or American (frequently male) voice for all the characters, especially the third-person omniscient narrator.

Cinema is the most beautiful fraud in the world.
JEAN-LUC GODARD

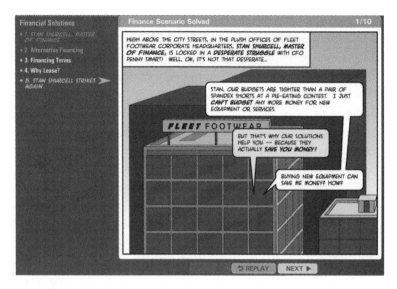

FIGURE 8.6 Enspire Learning, Inc. Screenshot 4

Source: www.enspire.com

There may be good reason for this in some instances, but a quick way to add engagement is to try people who speak with other accents (as long as they are understandable and not stereotypical).

When the dialogue is only visually communicated, it is still valuable to introduce accents. In order to keep your participants' interest (and not make it overly hard for them to read the dialogue) carefully select which key sentences are going to be written as if the speaker had an accent and put the rest in the standard accent. It is too frustrating for readers to wade through extensive amounts of transliterated accented words.

Type of Dialogue

Within the confines of the eLearning program there are only two people a character can talk to, himself or another character, who typically talks back (the audience of course hears what is said in both situations). There are obvious differences in writing for these two situations. In the first, a monologue, there are no interruptions from other people. Because no other character is available to break up the speech, either external interruptions need to be invented or the monologue needs to be well written to continue to capture the audience's interest and attention.

In the second, a dialogue, the relationship between the two (or more) speakers needs to be clear in the writer's head, and it needs to be consistently communicated through the conversation.

The typical choice in eLearning seems to be dialogue. One person speaks and another person responds (typically a person who needs help speaks and the person providing it responds).

There are two significant reasons to use monologue. First, it fosters intimacy or connection between the audience and the speaker. Second, it is a useful device for modeling reflective thinking and critical problem solving.

A monologue draws the participants closer because it allows them to see a side of the character she may not readily or easily reveal to another person. Because the character thinks she is speaking only to herself she is apt to be more honest, less guarded, and more direct. This is a fantastic device for establishing connection and trust between a character and the participants.

A monologue can be a more subtle (and sometimes more respectful) way to help participants learn because it lacks the baggage of the teacher-student or authority figure–recipient dynamic. When a person is talking himself through something, we do not feel threatened the way we do when a teacher tries to talk us through something. Compare the monologue and dialogue texts in Table 8.1. The factual content to be learned is the same, but in the monologue the participant sees another learner modeling the thought process of deducing information and also sharing parts of his or her personality and emotions.

A good question is never answered. It is not a bolt to be tightened into place but a seed to be planted and to bear more seed toward the hope of greening the landscape of ideas.

JOHN CIARDI

Purpose

Think how much harder it is to paint a picture of an apple than take a photograph of one. This is because in the photo the apple is a real object and the only question is what style in which to reproduce a real object. In painting an apple all stylistic questions come second to the primary one: how to generate the nonexistent so as to make it appear as if it exists. One could ask, "How do I create the illusion of an apple so effectively those looking at the picture barely remember it is just an illusion?"

This is the difference between real dialogue and dramatic dialogue. In everyday conversations, on the one hand, there is no need to construct anything. Like taking a photo of an apple, all that is needed exists. On the other hand, writing dialogue requires creating an illusion of real people having a real conversation. Like painting that apple, this is a much more complicated effort than simply recording real conversation and transcribing it.

Dialogue that works most effectively creates the illusion of a real conversation. All the sounds and pauses that are extraneous and counter to the purpose are removed. Like a chef making a good sauce, the writer reduces all the ingredients to their essence so only the essential, more flavorful tastes remain.

TABLE 8.1   Monologue Versus Dialogue

Monologue of Detective in Our Romeo and Juliet Mystery Scenario	*Teacher-as-Narrator Dialoging with the Participant*
It took me long enough to find the damn database now I don't have a clue how to use it. They could at least give—oh, those are instructions, looks like a coffee coaster to me. Hmm. OK, let's start fresh . . . go to the search palette, select Corpomatic Inc., click find financials. Something's not right here. These numbers are far lower than what they declared publicly last quarter. What did that guy say I do when this happens? Wait . . . wait. Oh yeah, I remember. . . . I compare these numbers to the SEC filings. Hmmm, the difference is $105 million; what might account for that? Taxes? No. Dividends? No. Oh yeah, depreciation! So they are actually valid numbers.	When you want to check last quarter's results for any corporation you go to the X database. Select search. A palette will appear. Select Corpomatic Inc., click financials. See if they match with the SEC filings. If not the main reason could be taxes, dividends, or depreciation.

Watch a favorite television program or movie and notice how an entire conversation might consist of ten sentences (or less) for each character, and still you feel as if you are in the room overhearing the others speaking.

Part of the science of writing eLearning dialogue is making sure each phrase serves a purpose. This purpose could be one or more of the following:

> *Example is always more efficacious than precept.*
> **SAMUEL JOHNSON**

- *Offering revelation:* revealing something from the past. This is a wonderful technique for eLearning developers to use as a way to avoid having to flesh out all events and activities from the beginning.

- *Deepening character:* adding dimensions to the characters by having them say things about themselves that give the participants a better sense of who they are.

- *Adding ambiance:* adding to the overall feeling of a particular scene. This is an excellent and fairly simple way to emotionally connect with the participants.

- *Giving information:* allowing participants to learn by hearing what the characters already know. The crime drama *Law & Order* does this throughout each program: the detectives might visit the coroner who shows them something on the dead person's body. The detective, who would lose credibility if she didn't know its significance, will say its meaning aloud to clue the audience in.

After the writer has finished creating the dialogue, it is worthwhile to recruit a second pair of eyes (and ears)—preferably someone unfamiliar with the project—to label each phrase with a purpose. If any are hard to label or could achieve their purpose better, consider rewriting them.

Up Next

In the next chapter, the final one covering character development, we delve into the heart of learning and drama: tropes. Specifically, we look at how figures of speech such as metaphors can be wielded to make characters more effective and learning more intuitive.

IT WAS A
DARK AND
STORMY NIGHT . . .

Metaphors and Figures of Speech Capture Attention

EVER BEEN SO embarrassed you could just die? Ever recounted a story in which you describe hearing something make the sound BAM! BAM! Asked a participant why it would be important to learn something? Said something sarcastic like, "So nice of you to be early for our meeting," when the attendee was fifteen minutes late?

In all these instances you used *tropes*. Tropes are integral to everyday conversation. People use tropes, as they do most second-nature behaviors, without recognizing it—or for that matter knowing what tropes are!

Trope is just a fancy rhetorical term for a figure of speech—for words people use to make conversation and language more colorful. Most tropes make dialogue more interesting and engaging, illustrate a concept, or heighten an effect. A few types of tropes were illustrated in the first paragraph of this chapter:

- *Hyperbole:* also known as exaggeration ("I could just die!")
- *Onomatopoeia:* use of words that mean what they sound like ("BAM!" "CRASH!")
- *Rhetorical question:* a question that does not require an answer ("Why should we care about interactive narrative?")
- *Irony:* saying something that is the opposite of the literal meaning (saying someone is early when she is late)

There is a tendency to avoid this colorful language in eLearning. Perhaps it is driven by the same fear that has precluded heavy use of emotion in eLearning: the fear of not being taken seriously or of being ostracized by

A different language is a different vision of life.
FEDERICO FELLINI

BOOKSHELF BEST BETS

Any books by Constantin Stanislavsky

Metaphors We Live By, George Lakoff and Mark Johnson

Metaphoric World, Samuel R. Levin

The Way We Think, Gilles Fauconnier and Mark Turner

133

those who don't feel emotion has a valid place in the workplace. We can see where some readers might remain uncomfortable about using tropes. We advise trying it at least once and seeing the response.

For readers uncomfortable with using tropes, we suggest an experiment. Participate in an eLearning program you would rate highly. Immediately afterward, watch a favorite television show or movie. The contrast will be stark. The eLearning will most likely be bending over backward to use only business-friendly language. The TV program or movie will be going slightly overboard with melodramatic dialogue. If your organization's cultural taboo against such tropes outweighs the benefits of disseminating content in a way that is sought after by the participants, don't use them. If, however, aligning the eLearning programs more closely with the participants' day-to-day, enjoyable leisure activities is more desirable than staying in the comfort zone, then go for it!

Intelligent use of tropes makes eLearning programs more interesting, dramatic, and memorable. It is particularly essential when writing dialogue. Because tropes are ubiquitous in everyday conversations, their absence will be particularly noticeable in dialogue—and that absence can be one of the factors that break the illusion of real conversation and decrease the dramatic effect.

METAPHORS

Since finding out what something is is largely a matter of discovering what it is like, the most impressive contribution to the growth of intelligibility has been made by the application of suggestive metaphors.
JONATHAN MILLER

Tropes add color and flavor. Some go beyond garnish to fill a more profound role. Two tropes in particular, *metaphor* and *simile*, actually shape the way most of us think about and approach the world. Because metaphors and similes have a direct impact on how people learn and how what people learn changes their behavior, deeper coverage of them is warranted.

Metaphor is the substitution of one concept for another in order to simplify an explanation or suggest similarity. For example, the phrase "the itours family" is a metaphor. The speaker is comparing the employees, system, and interactions at the corporation to a family. In this case the desired implication is a positive one: the warmth and loyalty of a biological family. A simile has a similar purpose but the comparison is typically made explicit by using words such as *like* or *is to*. If the speaker had said, itours is "like a big family," that would have been a simile. For the sake of simplicity, when we refer to *metaphor* henceforth, we are subsuming both metaphor and simile under that one term.

Metaphor might appear on the surface to be a poetic way of saying something—a rhetorical device to make something sound better, more romantic, more interesting, or more intuitively understandable. It is true metaphors do serve this purpose. For example, poetry could not exist without metaphor ("My love is like a red, red rose," "Shall I compare thee to a summer's day?" "Because I could not stop for Death / He kindly stopped for me"). Nor could many other narrative forms.

However, metaphors also have a more profound role. They frame all individuals' ways of thinking and shape their conceptual systems. They are a powerful force shaping the way people look at and interact with the world. Specifically, metaphors shape

All perception of truth is the detection of an analogy.
HENRY DAVID THOREAU

- The way individuals think
- The way individuals think about the world around them
- The actions individuals take that are based on the way they think about things

Our daughter's nickname is Sunshine. Like many nicknames this is actually a metaphor. She is not really a giant orb of gas living zillions of light years away (although if it is late enough at night and we are tired enough . . .). Nor do we think she is going to emanate significant heat or enough power to decrease our heating bills. In this sense we are using the metaphor as a poetic device.

However, our using this nickname reveals the profound way a metaphor shapes thoughts and actions. Somewhere along the line we both were taught the sun is similar to a big, jolly, warm, friendly, smiling person. We drew pictures of a big, bright yellow circle with a smile and rays extending down to cover our stick-figure families. Inevitably we would use a sun to indicate a happy scene. Of course the sun is not actually a person and we have absolutely no way of knowing whether the sun is happy or gobbling antidepressants. But what we do know is that in our culture it is taken for granted that sunshine embodies those positive traits.

Once this idea was internalized, we no longer even noticed it was a metaphor. We no longer consciously noticed we were making a comparison. It just became the way things are! We could just as easily have learned that rain is a positive force: water bringing life to everyone and everything. But how often do parents or lovers call each other raindrop? That is almost never heard because people's concept of rain is not one of enjoyment and pleasure but one of, at best, necessity.

It does not matter that Dickens' world is not life-like, it is alive.
LORD DAVID CECIL

There are a whole host of actions we take based on this sunshine metaphor. We smile and hug our daughter when she first wakes up because we anticipate she will bring us joy and happiness during the day. We tell other people how friendly and radiant she is. This may seem like the natural parental thing to do, and indeed we hope it is.

Compare our behavior to that of parents who see their kids as burdens or problems, the type of caregiver represented in Charles Dickens's *Oliver Twist*. The dominant metaphor they are operating under is that their kids are similar to a piece of equipment or other object that drains resources. Subsequently their actions are guided by the desire to minimize the use of food, love, time, or any other seemingly limited resources.

In both cases the metaphor parents use to conceptualize their children, childhood, and parenthood influences the way they view and treat their children, which of course shapes who those children are and what they do later in life.

How Metaphors Shape People's Worlds

George Lakoff and Mark Johnson, professors at the University of California at Berkeley and the University of Oregon, respectively, discuss the idea that metaphors are central to each person's understanding of the world. In their seminal book *Metaphors We Live By*, they illustrate how profoundly metaphors shape people's perceptions and understandings of the world around them, which in turn shapes their behavior. This is the main reason why people interested in driving business results through eLearning need to care about metaphor, because it profoundly and often invisibly affects the actions people take as a result of seeing something framed in a particular way.

> The metaphor is probably the most fertile power possessed by man.
> **ORTEGA Y GASSETT**

To drive the point home, look at how Lakoff and Johnson illustrate how the Western concept that "argument is war" influences people's thinking, which subsequently affects their words and the actions they take:

To give some idea of what it could mean for a concept to be metaphorical and for such a concept to structure an everyday activity, let us start with the concept ARGUMENT and the conceptual metaphor ARGUMENT IS WAR. This metaphor is reflected in our everyday language by a wide variety of expressions:

ARGUMENT IS WAR.

Your claims are *indefensible*.

He *attacked* every weak point in my argument.

His criticisms were right on *target*.

I *demolished* his argument.

I've never *won* an argument with him.

You disagree? Okay, *shoot!*

If you use that *strategy*, he'll *wipe you out*.

He *shot down* all of my arguments.

It is important to see that we don't just talk about arguments in terms of war. We can actually win or lose arguments. We see the person we are arguing with as an opponent. We attack his positions and we defend our own. We gain and lose ground. We plan and use strategies. If we find a position indefensible, we can abandon it and take a new line of attack. Many of the things we do in arguing are partially structured by the concept of war. Though there is no physical battle, there is a verbal battle, and the structure of an argument—attack, defense, counter-attack, etc.—reflects this. It is in this sense that the ARGUMENT IS WAR metaphor is one that we live by in this culture; it structures the actions we perform in arguing.

Try to imagine a culture where arguments are not viewed in terms of war, where no one wins or loses, where there is no sense of attacking or defending. . . . Imagine a culture where an argument is viewed as a dance, the participants are seen as performers, and the goal is to perform in a balanced and aesthetically pleasing way. In such a culture, people would view arguments differently, experience them differently, carry them out differently, and talk about them differently. But we would probably not view them as arguing at all: they would simply be doing something different.[1]

Metaphors and eLearning

Metaphors have a profound impact on eLearning because they can structure the way concepts are integrated into people's minds and the subsequent actions they take based on those mindsets. When you are seeking to add to or modify participants' concepts, as you will almost always be doing in deep learning, recognizing the metaphors others are currently working from and constructing new ones is required.

Suppose the content is negotiation. As Lakoff and Johnson discuss, negotiation may be seen as war, an adversarial process in which the goal is to get as much as possible from the other person while giving the least. If this metaphor is consistent with participants' concept of negotiation and the company wishes to keep this concept in its culture, it would be appropriate to build eLearning on this metaphor.

Now suppose the organization is dependent on having both parties bettered by the negotiation (as may be common in a political organization, a not-for-profit, and the like) or is seeking to change its culture to one that is more cooperative or has recently gotten into regulatory troubles stemming from its negotiation tactics—in all these instances it would be necessary to either change the metaphor from negotiation is war to some other image (such as negotiation is dance, as Lakoff and Johnson suggest) or to otherwise stay clearly away from associating negotiation with war.

In the first environment (the company that wants to act as though negotiation is war), eLearning that poses negotiation as a dance could be ridiculed or dismissed as out of touch. In the second environment (the organization that needs win-win negotiation tactics), eLearning that treats negotiation as war might be considered offensive and counterproductive. In both situations, eLearning made without awareness of the dominant metaphors framing the content and the environment would either have no impact or would stand in the way of results.

Layers of Metaphor

Looking at metaphor in eLearning involves seeing three layers:

1. Immersive structure
2. Dialogue
3. Visual metaphors

Visual metaphors will be covered in the next chapter. Although immersive structure is bigger than dialogue we cover it here because it significantly influences dialogue.

IMMERSIVE STRUCTURE

Immersive structure is the environment within which content is placed. Before addressing immersive structure in eLearning, let's look at a real-world example.

Most people are familiar with Disneyland. Walt Disney was a master of immersive structure metaphors. When he created Disneyland, the goal was to build a setting both physical and psychological, where people were mentally transported outside their everyday lives and into an entirely different world. The lands that were created, Tomorrowland, Frontierland, and so on, had every detail worked out to make the visitor feel she was a native (minus the discomforts of course). In Tomorrowland all the costumes, shows, rides, concession stands, stores, garbage cans, street signs, and so on have a futuristic theme. There are astronauts and space exploration, 3-D movies, and all the other accoutrements Disney imagined the future would bring.

Immersive structure in this instance is the combination of all the elements that come together and transport a person (at least mentally) into a physical rendition of a metaphorical world. Tomorrowland's metaphor is the space age.

Immersive structure as it relates to eLearning can be defined as the gestalt of an immersive experience that follows a particular theme. It is tempting to refer to it as the interface, but that is just one of the many elements that make up the immersive structure.

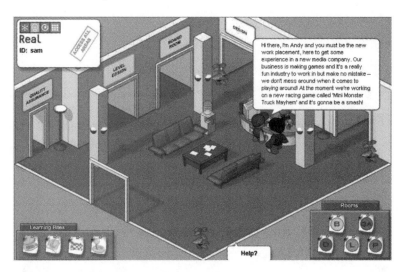

FIGURE 9.1   Real: Creative Learning Screenshot 1

EXAMPLES

A Disneyland-like metaphorical treatment is used to teach new media and architecture skills in two of Real: Creative Learning's learning bites. In the first, the environment is the office of a multimedia developer (Figure 9.1). The program begins with a sign-in process in which the participant gets a badge, as he would in many professional offices, and continues by allowing him to do the types of things a visitor could do in that setting: visiting different offices, meeting people who hold different job titles and roles, examining typical project documents (Figure 9.2), and so on.

A similar immersive structure is used for the architecture program: the metaphor is a football club bought by the participant, who then needs to build a stadium. In this case the model is a simulation (Figure 9.3).

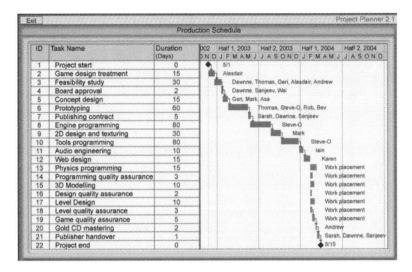

FIGURE 9.2   Real: Creative Learning Screenshot 2

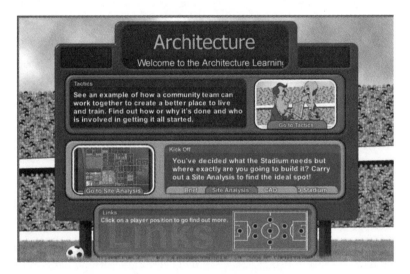

FIGURE 9.3   Real: Creative Learning Screenshot 3

In both the multimedia office and architecture training examples, as in Disneyland, the immersive structure metaphors are obvious and explicitly called out. They rarely require deep analysis or discussion.

SUBCONSCIOUS METAPHORS

There is another type of immersive structure that is more challenging because it plays on subconscious metaphors. Blackboard's eLearning programs and programs modeled on them are examples of this type. The pre-senting metaphor is a typical classroom blackboard where the teacher puts content and students solve problems or stand to do presentations, and so forth. But the metaphor actually has a much more profound connection. Blackboard's metaphor of a traditional school and traditional pedagogical relationship guides not only the interface but the organization's entire approach to learning—and ostensibly the approach people who elect to use its system take. In other words, the creators of Blackboard considered the ideas inherent in a traditional children's classroom to be the perfect metaphor for learning in a virtual world.

It seems no one considered whether this pedagogical metaphor would be appropriate for adults learning outside a classroom or outside a specific phys-ical environment. What also does not appear to have been considered is how the undesirable elements of the compared concept can overwhelm or put off potential participants.

Blackboard's classroom metaphor appears in the interface, the process, and the expectations about the way people will relate to each other. The interface shouts traditional classroom: buttons are labeled with terms such as "Announcements," "Books," "Assignments," and so on. The learning process is very traditional-school oriented: it begins with announcements, goes on to course content, and ends with an assessment and grades. Even the marketing materials betray how deeply embedded the traditional school metaphor is for Blackboard:

> *Blackboard Learning System* has been developed to provide instructors and students with a feature-rich learning environment, pedagogical flex-ibility, complete control of the course design. . . .

This sentence alone betrays how deeply rooted this traditional class-room metaphor is. Notice how the choice of the words "pedagogical flexi-bility" and "complete control of course design" reveal the bias toward the instructor as teacher in control and student as passive recipient. There is lit-tle said about the student at all, let alone about student empowerment or involvement in one's own learning.

This metaphor might work well in a traditional academic setting. It would certainly work against effective learning for participants who recall negative experiences with traditional schooling or for the disenfranchised, who don't necessarily thrive in that structured environment.

All these examples demonstrate how easily a metaphor (conscious or unconscious or a combination of both) can be used to create an immersive structure whose benefits include

I don't know the rules of grammar. If you're trying to persuade people to do something, or buy something, it seems to me you should use their language, the language they use every day, the language in which they think. We try to write in the vernacular.

DAVID OGILVY

- Acting as a shortcut to meaning and learning
- Modeling a world in which the new metaphorical structure exists
- Guiding much of the program's action and dialogue

At the same time, its drawbacks could include

- Triggering negative associations among participants
- Encouraging exclusion of information that is relevant but doesn't fit the metaphor

Selecting a good immersive structure and using it wisely is a great way to increase the efficacy of eLearning.

It provides a shortcut because instead of having to create and explain an entirely new situation or world to the participants, the eLearning borrows a world that is already familiar (and, one hopes, pleasurable). It models behavior because it illustrates people coping in a world where a new or different conceptual metaphor is dominant. It guides much of the action and dialogue to be used because each metaphor encompasses a list of expected characteristics.

> *Science is all metaphor.*
> **TIMOTHY LEARY**

For example, in the Real: Creative Learning football metaphor (recall Figure 9.3), the list of potential elements participants might expect includes a scoreboard, two commentators, an outline of tactics, a playing field, and so on—all of which the developers elected to include.

Immersive structure metaphors can enhance business results. The goal is to ensure the comparative concept evokes positive and not negative responses among the participants. Gain an understanding of the conceptual metaphors they hold and do some pilot testing of the concepts themselves to get the most from your eLearning!

METAPHORS IN DIALOGUE

Using metaphor on the ground level, when characters are speaking to each other or when the program is speaking to the participant, can reap many benefits. A few of them are

- Distancing participants from a problem or situation so they can be more objective
- Fostering recognition of connections between previously unconnected concepts
- Encouraging participants to use metaphors in problem solving and other areas
- Making content more memorable
- Providing a new understanding of experiences

- Significantly increasing efficiency in communication
- Making it possible for people to put into words feelings, thoughts, actions, and so forth, that are hard to state
- Making it easier to use unfamiliar ideas, equipment, and processes
- Encouraging strategic thinking by encouraging predictive behavior

There are four predominant ways to use metaphor in dialogue:

1. Explicitly pointing out how one concept is related to another
2. Implicitly having a character act as a metaphor and speak accordingly
3. As a matter of everyday conversation
4. As a poetic device (in other words, to make dialogue more interesting and memorable though unlikely to increase understanding or retention of actual content)

Explicit Comparison   One of the most useful ways to increase retention of eLearning content is to explicitly compare one concept to another, often for the purpose of simplifying the understanding of a concept.

This use of metaphor has always separated the best from the rest. In a traditional classroom it is not uncommon to see the facilitator or teacher constantly drawing explicit comparisons between the material to be learned and another concept. We have heard teachers say that mentoring people is like baking a cake, the Windows interface is like a desktop or a filing cabinet, a car engine is like the human body, and so on. We've even heard some our editor would no doubt delete, so we'll save her the effort and just leave them to your imagination.

The following two sentences come from PBS's eLearning program "The Voyage of the Odyssey" and from a NASA Web site, respectively, and both show explicit metaphor in use:

> "Mangroves are the coastal equivalent of tropical forests on land and are among the most productive ecosystems in the world."[2]

> "In the first exercise, the pennies will represent the photons, and the egg crate separators represent the receiving instrument on the satellite. Let students take turns tossing a few pennies at a time into the egg crate separator. Continue until all 100 pennies have been tossed. If some do not land in the crate, do not worry, not all photons hit the high-energy satellite."[3]

In the example we have been using thus far (the Romeo and Juliet mystery with competitive intelligence content), many explicit metaphorical comparisons could be made to positively affect learning. Here are two examples:[4]

- Doing competitive intelligence is like getting the "dirt" on a blind date or a person you recently began dating.
- Putting together a competitive intelligence library is like organizing a giant home media collection.

Characterization as Metaphor   The main character in an eLearning program may be a metaphor designed to constantly remind the participants of a particular environment or mindset. If the character speaks, he or she will often say things in keeping with that metaphor. This device serves at least four purposes:

1. It decreases inhibitions. By showing a user-friendly face, the character can help decrease user fears and the intimidation factor, especially when the content is likely to step on a nerve.

2. It increases the effectiveness of a help system. When a character takes the place of the usual monitor manual, it can decrease inhibitions about seeking help and can make the help easier to understand. Both of these make the system more effective.

3. It focuses attention. The character can appear to be a narrator or friend designed to focus the user's thinking in a certain direction, albeit subtly.

4. It creates ambiance. In some cases the metaphorical narrator can just add the *je ne sais quoi* that either personalizes the experience or encourages a deeper or longer interaction with the eLearning.

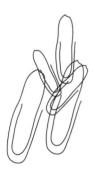

Arguably the world's most ubiquitous example of character as metaphor is Microsoft's paper clip help character. For anyone who has been living under a rock for the past ten years, the paper clip was an animation that appeared whenever certain Microsoft applications were launched or when the user indicated he needed assistance. (It left us completely cold. However, the new dog help character puts us in a significantly better frame of mind.)

Another example appears on the cover of Real: Creative Learning's "Sharpen Up!" workbook, which accompanies the online program of the same name. The lead character for this program aimed at helping people develop their learning muscles is a sharp pencil (Figure 9.4).

Everyday Conversation   We all use second-nature metaphors so effortlessly they are detectable in only two ways. One is when people are consciously looking to hear them because of a heightened awareness of their existence (as people who have read this chapter will have). The second instance, and the one that really matters in eLearning dialogue, is when they are absent.

FIGURE 9.4   Real: Creative Learning Screenshot 4

Look at the following sentences from eLearning programs (emphasis added):

"Self-esteem is how we see ourselves and how we feel about ourselves. It *shapes* the way we think and it can shape the way we behave" (Sharpen Up, Real: Creative Learning).

"To *move* through the story, use the 'next' or 'back' buttons" (Root Learning).

"I have *no clue* what I need to do" (Root Learning).

The italicized word(s) in each of these phrases demonstrates how deeply ingrained metaphors are in everyday conversation. Had we not pointed these out, most readers would never have even noticed them as metaphors. Of course people can't physically give a form to the way they think, unless they open their skulls and mush up their brains. But the use of *shape* as an ideological verb is so common it makes perfect sense. The same is true for the verb *move*. In the last instance, the phrase *no clue* has come to be a colloquialism that takes advantage of the word *clue*'s association with solving mysteries to indicate the reverse of a solution: confusion.

When creating dialogue in eLearning smart use of conversational metaphors—particularly colloquialisms and culturally relevant ones—is critical to maintain participant engagement with and immersion in the drama. Leave these metaphors out, and participants will feel the program is flat.

The saying "a picture speaks a thousand words" also illustrates why dialogue, where possible and appropriate, should leverage metaphor.

Poetic Metaphor   The final type of metaphor we are going to address that can enhance eLearning is the poetic use of words and phrases. These metaphors are predominantly literary devices that indirectly enhance the effectiveness of eLearning. Directly, they serve one of the following purposes:

- They make the program more enjoyable, just as poetic wording in a book or movie can make it more pleasurable to hear the dialogue.

I describe metaphor as an evolutionary knowledge process that combines brain, mind, and culture in the creative formation of language.

EARL R. MacCORMAC

- They put participants at ease and avoid monotony by verbally transporting them to a more pleasurable mindset.

We have yet to run across a good example of poetic metaphor in eLearning. Until someone submits one or we chance upon it, here are some examples from our favorite literary works and writers:

"My mistress' eyes are nothing like the sun" (William Shakespeare).

"Words and words and words, how they gallop—how they lash their long manes and tails. . . ." (Virginia Woolf).

"Because I could not stop for Death / He kindly stopped for me" (Emily Dickinson).

Perhaps one of the reasons poetic imagery has not been used more in eLearning is because it is not "efficient" and seems impractical. On a per word ROI basis, it is true it does not carry the weight of some other phrases. However, if the goal is genuinely to immerse participants in a dramatic experience that will have a profound impact on their behavior, which in turn will affect business results, pepper the program with some poetic metaphors. They might be just the thing to spice it up!

CHARACTERIZATION GUIDELINES

In the real world, actions speak louder than words. In the dramatic eLearning world, words and actions occupy equally important positions. If either one is not believable, credibility is shot. The illusion of reality, which is what drives an eLearning program's effectiveness, is broken and often can't be repaired. The following tips will help you sculpt better characters through actions, words, and every other element of character development!

1. *Show, don't tell.* When budget and time are very limited, the temptation is to tell the participants' something about the character. A more effective and believable way of connecting them to a character is to show them the actions of the character and allow them to come to their own conclusions. When this is done properly, they will come to the desired conclusion but will be more likely to put themselves in the place of the character. For example, the program could tell participants "Suzy in purchasing is an overworked manager." Or it could show Suzy at her desk, with the clock in the background saying 9:00 P.M. and pitch darkness outside the window. She is getting her coat on, her hair is messed up, and there are circles under her eyes. The phone rings. It's her boss thanking her for emailing the report a few

seconds ago and asking if she could just do one other small thing before she leaves. In most cases it is preferable to illustrate the character's actions and allow the participants to come to a conclusion about the character or her situation instead of flat out telling them.

2. *Create a detailed biography or history for each main character.* The only people who will ever have access to this entire picture will be the program developers. The point is not to give participants a full illustration of the person (that would bore them to tears!). Rather, this background will make it much easier for you to visualize and develop the actions and words each character will need to do and say to convince the audience of the reality of his or her motivations, background, personality, and so forth.

3. *Use real people.* Almost all good writers, whether they will admit it or not, base their characters on real people. This goes a long way toward giving the impression of depth and helps participants identify with the characters. Pick pieces of several individuals in your life and put them together to form a composite.

For example, in coming up with our Romeo and Juliet mystery we selected people to use as models for the two protagonists (the detective and salesperson 1) and the antagonist (the salesperson who sends the fraudulent documents). Here are some real-person traits we would use in the program:

- When we were in Mexico we visited a few properties available for purchase. The two individuals who took us around were stereotypical real estate agents. A notable incident occurred when they took us to the last property. The roof had caved in. They were as surprised as we were, and they blamed it on the very heavy rainy season. However, everyone else in the area had told us it had barely rained that year. We would want to remember their eagerness to sell at any cost and their blatantly incredible lies while writing dialogue for our antagonist.

- We know a woman who is extremely resourceful in finding out what her boyfriend is doing and when. She is constantly vexed by the mystery of what he is doing, and with whom, and behaves accordingly. We would want to borrow her stealth way of talking and the facial expressions she uses when she describes her actions.

- We know of a lawyer who was laid off for not billing enough hours; she spent too much time helping pro bono clients. In constructing our protagonists, we would adapt this woman's steadfast determination to both continue to help less fortunate people and regain a reputation in her field. We would look at both things she has said and steps she has taken.

In addition to internal characteristics, use selected, external ones as well: physical features, gestures, and so on.

4. *Always consider where the character is coming from immediately before entering the scene.* Did he just wake up? Go to the bathroom? Was he on the phone trying to fix his computer? Working on a long report? Just as what you do right before the next thing you do affects your mood and how you behave right afterward, so it is with your characters. It is only after thinking carefully about where they are coming from emotionally and physically that you are ready to create their dialogue and the actions they will take in the scene you are showing to the participants.

5. *Keep your characters real.* Don't make them too stiff or correct—even the best person has idiosyncrasies and foibles. A character doesn't need to have a fatal flaw, but she does need traits that the participants can relate to. A lead detective might also be a person who can't stop eating ice cream despite being told his cholesterol is off the charts and who spends too much time playing solitaire on the computer or reading car magazines. Avoid clichés at all costs: the detective who is a recovering alcoholic, and so forth.

6. *Listen to the people around you.* In the real world, nine times out of ten people's remarks display an interrupted syntax. People almost never speak in complete sentences. Making dialogue believable and real means making sure there are frequent interruptions and abrupt cutoffs.

7. *Don't include too much dialogue or text.* Unless the program is one that spans hours or involves thousands of scenes, keep the dialogue to a minimum or you will lose the participants (unless of course they are the ones writing the dialogue as they go).

8. *Don't show all at once.* Reveal ideas and events over time. If participants know everything at the beginning, they will quickly lose interest. But do put hints into the conversation at the beginning so participants are intrigued enough to continue.

9. *Look over the actions and words of the characters.* Make sure each action and item of dialogue does at least one of the following:

- Advances the action of the plot
- Requires the participant to do something to advance the story
- Illustrates something about a character

10. *Make sure the characters grow in some way from the start of the program to the end.* They must have new skills, knowledge, or attitudes, and they also must have changed in some fundamentally deeper emotional or psychological way.

11. *Plan to reveal different aspects of major characters over time.* Even if you reveal only three things about a character, doing it over the course of the program will make that character more interesting and add dimensionality.

12. *Try to use new metaphors or metaphors that come from the participants,* instead of recycling tired old ones (such as the computer as a mind). For example, if participants love cars or gardening, pick some facet of those interests to use as a metaphor.

13. *Remember that eLearning dialogue is not everyday dialogue.* Every word should be purposeful and important—you want to give the illusion of real conversation.[5]

Up Next

This brings to a close our coverage of character development. The final section of Part Two focuses on visual design: those elements of appearance that foster and support dramatic learning. We leave you with this final thought: in good narratives, the characters stay with the participants well after the book has been closed, the curtain has come down, or the computer has been shut off. Which is why, frankly, my dear, you should give a damn.

NOTES

1. George Lakoff and Mark Johnson, *Metaphors We Live By* (Chicago: University of Chicago Press, 2003), pp. 4–5.

2. Public Broadcasting Service, "The Voyage of the Odyssey," pbs.org/odyssey, accessed July 2004.

3. NASA, "Imagine the Universe," http://imagine.gsfc.nasa.gov/docs/teachers/lessons/picture/picture_main.html, accessed May 2004.

4. We are showing these as examples that might work for us. We remind readers to make sure the metaphors will work for their participants.

5. Raymond Frensham, *Screenwriting*, Teach Yourself series (London: Hodder Arnold, 1996).

PART 2 CONTINUED
COMING ATTRACTIONS

Looks Matter!

Producing visually appealing eLearning is more than an exercise in aesthetics. It is a critical way to foster positive attitudes about the content, promote creative thinking and problem solving, and increase acceptance and use of both eLearning and the learning content, according to the aesthetic-usability principle.

The next three chapters provide an introduction to some of the basic principles of graphic design to help readers who are not trained as designers make their written communications more effective, decrease participants' apprehension or fear of the content, increase participants' engagement, and work more smoothly and efficiently with graphic design professionals.

The first, Chapter Ten, addresses style and layout. The second, Chapter Eleven, type. The last, Chapter Twelve, visual perspective, color, and six of the most important universal principles of design.

For help in finding resources experienced in providing visual drama, such as graphic designers, see Chapters Thirteen and Fourteen.

 Fast Forward   If you're a graphic design pro or just don't really want to know anything about it, skip to Chapter Thirteen.

If you have time to read only one thing, read Chapter Eleven and the section of Chapter Twelve titled "Universal Design Principles." Okay, those two things but both are critical. The former is an overview of type elements, and the latter presents six essential principles of design.

VISUALLY ARRESTING

Good Graphical Style and
Layout Encourage Learning

WHICH ONE GRABS YOU? Figure 10.1 or Figure 10.2?

FIGURE 10.1 National Curriculum in Action Screenshot 1
With permission from QCA Enterprises Limited

> *Art is the lie which*
> *makes us realize*
> *the truth.*
> **PABLO PICASSO**

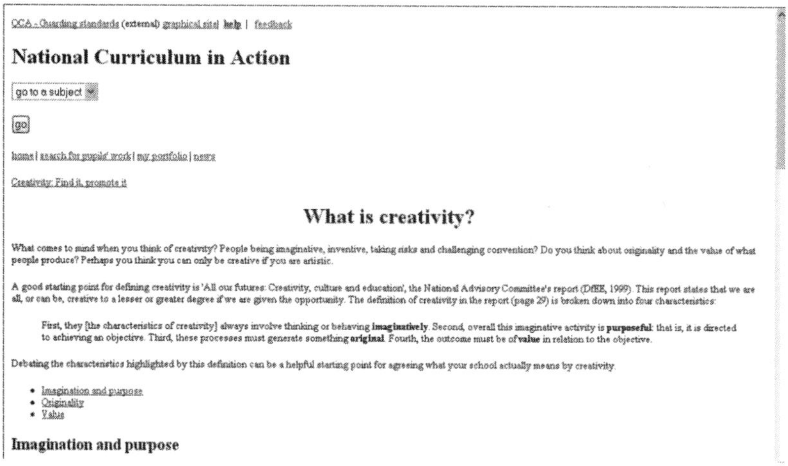

FIGURE 10.2 National Curriculum in Action Screenshot 2
With permission from QCA Enterprises Limited

BOOKSHELF BEST BETS

Design Workshop, Robin Williams and John Tollett

Information Anxiety, Richard Saul Wurman

Emotional Design, Donald Norman

Making a Good Layout, Lori Siebert and Lisa Ballard

The Graphic Design Cookbook, Leonard Koren and R. Wippo Meckler

Grid, Allen Hurlburt

The Visual Display of Quantitative Information, Edward Tufte

Reading Images, Gunther Kress and Theo van Leeuwen

On the one hand the screenshots in Figures 10.1 and 10.2 illustrate the importance of visual drama. The second one has the same content as the first but is intended for nongraphical browsing.

On the other hand there are some overzealous animation junkies who clutter their PowerPoint presentations with dogs flying planes, the question mark guy scratching his head, and other gratuitous graphics. Our clip-art-happy presenter thinks this will combat boredom and attention loss.

The irony is that poor graphic design (an overwhelming number of images and tenuous connections between graphics and text) actually distracts the audience. People's attention wanders at least partially *because of* the graphics.

The incorrect assumption that any technology capable of handling multimedia is *inherently superior* to any technology capable of handling only one form of media is becoming increasingly prevalent in eLearning. Whether they are employing PowerPoint, a simulation, or any other form of eLearning, people are starting to feel pressure to use graphics just because the technology can handle them. An incorrect assumption has emerged from this environment and is reflected in too many eLearning programs: any graphics are better than no graphics at all.

Consider for a moment two popular candy products: Nutella (in Europe) and Reese's Peanut Butter Cups (in the United States). Both are absolutely delicious mixes of nuts and chocolate. However, their invention did not make chocolate on its own or nuts on their own less delicious. In contrast, chocolate-covered Mary Janes (for the uninitiated this is chocolate covering a hard peanut butter and molasses mix) died a quick death. The fact that chocolate and nuts can be combined to make a great product does not mean that every time chocolate and nuts are combined the outcome will be good. Likewise, putting graphics in an eLearning program can actually make it less effective than word-only eLearning unless the visual element is designed properly.

Don't quite agree with us? Look at the modern evidence: ebooks. Despite a billion-dollar budget and multiple years of development the ebook reader and the accompanying "books" died almost as soon as they arrived. People voting with their pocketbooks still prefer to schlep those unillustrated, dog-eared paperbacks to the beach over any reading material requiring batteries.

This and the following chapters will cover some of the basic principles of graphic design with the goal of enabling all our readers (not just experts) to

- Make their written communications more effective
- Decrease participants' apprehension or fear of the content
- Increase participants' engagement
- Work more smoothly and efficiently with graphic design professionals

BREAKFAST AT TIFFANY'S OR DINNER AT EIGHT? SELECTING THE RIGHT STYLE

The first consideration in any project is how best to meet the project's goals. In the case of eLearning and graphic design this requires establishing the overall tone of the piece. Just as a room is decorated to reflect a certain image (British library, tropical paradise, technology contemporary), eLearning should reflect either the environment and culture of the organization or the program's goals, or both if they are compatible. The design must support the message or it will undermine it.

Robin Williams is a leader in providing graphic design guidance to non-designers. Her books, including *The Non-Designer's Design Book*, *The Non-Designer's Web Book*, and *The Non-Designer's Type Book*, provide a no-nonsense approach to deconstructing the elements of design. Reading them provides virtually anyone with tangible actions they can take to make their projects more visually appealing.

In her book with John Tollett *Design Workshop*, she presents several "looks," each useful for accomplishing different goals, and guidelines as to what gives the pieces that look. Five of the looks particularly relevant to eLearning and their characteristics are described in Table 10.1.

Readers with the luxury of having a graphic designer on the team can use these chapters to open the door to common ground. This introduction to the main principles and concepts of design will help the development process flow more smoothly and facilitate communication. Readers who don't have access to graphic designers will learn how to use simple visual techniques to increase the effectiveness of their eLearning—and all their communications!

Always design a thing by considering it in its next larger context—a chair in a room, a room in a house, a house in an environment, an environment in a city plan.
ELIEL SAARINEN

TABLE 10.1 Five Visual Looks

	Look	Characteristics
Generic	". . . conservative, unimaginative, and boring, a design with no personality. It's probably the least attention-getting look you can design."	Unimaginatively centered alignment A dated typeface (such as Helvetica) Lacks contrast Not enough white space Typewriter apostrophes instead of designer Design doesn't support the message
Corporate	". . . exceptionally neat, organized, and predictable, giving an impression of trust and dependability. If you're not careful this approach can look more like the generic, no-personality approach. But the corporate look is more creative. . . . It's more flexible . . . a company that doesn't get too wild or too far out of the mainstream."	Strong clean lines No superfluous elements Typefaces are not weird or unusual
Visual Wow	". . . grab a reader's attention with a bold image, a stunning photo, or a captivating illustration style."	Oversized, bold, simple graphics Strong contrasts—lots of black and white with small dashes of color
Typographic	"Great type can be eye catching and deliver an emphatic message with just a glance . . . life-savers when you have an unreasonable deadline or an extremely tight budget."	An interesting heading typeface, simple but with a subtle designer quality No graphics Headline is attention getting Classic typeface will look more conservative; a grunge one will look more cutting edge
Trendy	When you want to say, "we're what's hot now."	Whatever is hot

Source: Adapted from Robin Williams and John Tollett, *Design Workshop* (Berkeley, Calif.: Peachpit Press, 2001).

> The secret to effective drama is not how many channels of media can be used, but how well each channel on its own *and each channel working in conjunction with all the others* conjures up an image in the participant's imagination.

Compare the screenshots in Figures 10.3, 10.4, and 10.5 to see the difference in styles. The first (Figure 10.3), from online-learning.com, is corporate. It is well designed and holds the viewer's visual attention. It is neat and predictable, but what distinguishes it from most generic work is the smart design: the way the tutorial is set apart in a sophisticated box (with a blue background) with attractive icons, the clever and subtle navigation system that retracts and expands according to the user's desired path, and the stylish font (rather than a generic Helvetica or Arial).

The next one (Figure 10.4), created for Pfizer by PiCircle, is another example of a corporate look but with a different feel.

The final screenshot (Figure 10.5) also comes from PiCircle and was created to teach project management skills to employees at Caltrans. The

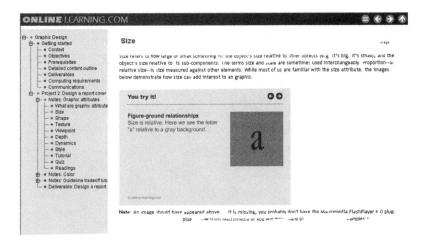

FIGURE 10.3 Online-Learning.com Screenshot

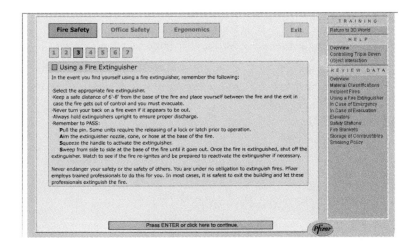

FIGURE 10.4 PiCircle, Inc. Screenshot 1

drawing of the character clearly attracts attention. This is an example of visual wow.

For each of the elements of design we go through in the remainder of the chapter, bear in mind the look you are trying to achieve. Let this look guide your selections. The look we wanted to achieve for this book was a combination of typographic and visual wow (Table 10.1). Our goals were

- To have readers immediately recognize this book is going to be different from all other eLearning ones

FIGURE 10.5   PiCircle, Inc. Screenshot 2

> *Creativity is allowing yourself to make mistakes. Art is knowing which ones to keep.*
>
> **SCOTT ADAMS**

- To reinforce the message that drama is important for learning
- To attract the attention of people just flipping through the book
- To demonstrate that the authors are slightly on the fringes and outside the mainstream

After reading this chapter you can tell us if we accomplished our goals through visual drama.

PICKING THE RIGHT LAYOUT

Layout is how all the elements of a page (text, graphics, navigation elements, other items) are arranged. Functionally, it is the roadmap guiding users through the content. Just as one person might give another exact driving directions, the layout is the designer's way of visually communicating to the user the importance of each element of the content and the desired path through the content. In a landmark study of how a reader's eyes pass over a newspaper page, the Poynter Institute found the following:

1. Readers enter the page through the largest image on the page, usually a photograph.
2. After this, the majority of users look at headlines.
3. Captions under photographs are the third most frequently visited parts of the page.[1]

When the study was repeated with people looking at Web sites instead of newspapers, the findings startled the author of the first study, Mario Garcia. According to Garcia, the results suggest that "many news websites do not use photos properly. . . . Photos are presented in a reduced format, and their impact is lost."

When looking at a news Web site, users followed this path:

1. First their eyes go to text such as brief captions.
2. Then they go back to photos and graphics, often after having mouse-clicked away from the page.
3. Then their eyes skim the text.

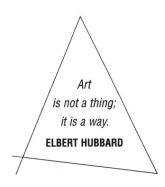

Art is not a thing; it is a way.
ELBERT HUBBARD

The important point is to design the layout of your eLearning to work with the eye's natural tendencies. The layout should provide a *visual hierarchy* that immediately indicates to the participants which content is most important (this should be the most noticeable), which is the second most important (this should be the second most noticeable), and so on.

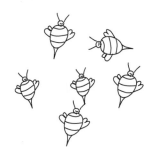

The Sacramento Bee's eLearning module on the environment (See Figure 10.6 on the following page.) has an exceptionally well-designed layout. The eye is immediately drawn first to the photograph, because of its size, location, surrounding white space, and content. The photo establishes an emotional connection with the participant. Next the eye is drawn to the menu for the four chapters. Although it is implied that the participant start at the top and work his way down, the visual similarity of each element as well as the ample white space suggests he could explore the segments in any order. This is an excellent example of a layout designed to both emotionally capture the participant through visual drama and subtly indicate the order of importance of each item. The photo is most important for capturing emotion, followed by each of the chapters with relatively equal weight. The least important is the organization that created the program (see the small logo on the right) and the title.

There are two common ways to design a layout: with a grid or with a sample.

Layout by Grid

A grid is akin to graph paper (with bigger boxes) and serves as a template: each batch of content fits into a designated space in the grid. As a result, once the grid is designed the layout does not need to be entirely recreated when new content is to be added. Like a template, a grid provides consistency, making it easier for the user to navigate and absorb the information because elements are in an expected location and order.

FIGURE 10.6 *Sacramento Bee* Screenshot
Copyright © *Sacramento Bee*

The main difference between a grid and columns is that the content of your pages can span multiple columns. In some cases the content will stay within one column; in others it will span more than one or two columns. Ultimately, the grid provides a backbone to structure the content in a way that is visually appealing.

The most common eLearning grids have either three or four columns. Figure 10.7, a screenshot from Kodak's photo tips Web site, clearly shows a three-column grid in use.

The *Web Style Guide*[2] points out the average user will be able to see only about forty-five square inches without scrolling (the guide calls this the area "above the fold," a term borrowed from newspaper publishing). These dimensions should be your grid boundaries for most eLearning programs. If the program is exclusively browser based, the most important content should be placed in the top forty-five square inches and the less important or supporting materials below that, in effect below the fold.

Layout by Sample

The second way to design the layout is simply to find a layout that is appealing and replicate those aspects that will work with your eLearning or provide the sample to the designer. Look for the elements we discuss in this chapter

Art is not what you see, but what you make others see.

EDGAR DEGAS

FIGURE 10.7 Kodak Screenshot

Copyright © Kodak

and see how they are used. Try to figure out which parts of the layout are most appealing and see how you might play with them to make a design that suits your unique content.

Following is a list of general tips to keep in mind when thinking about style and layout:

- If no designer is on the team, make up placeholders for the following items: (1) blocks of text (that is, the words "This is placeholder text. This is placeholder text" written over and over), (2) headlines, and (3) graphics. Move these different elements around the screen until a design that suits your needs appears.

- Web pages (no matter how big the anticipated participants' monitors may be) should always be designed as if they were single pages and not spreads.

- Personally we find it extremely off-putting to have to scroll horizontally. Unless there is a compelling reason for horizontal scrolling or it is an integral part of a unique and intentional design, make the maximum page width 760 pixels. (To be really safe, designers recommend 800 x 600 pixels.)

Layout Checklist

In their book *Making a Good Layout*, Lori Siebert and Lisa Ballard summarize the three main benefits to be derived from an effective layout:[3]

Figure 10.8 shows how the type of navigation a site makes available to a user relates to the user's perception of the site. The typical training site offers simple page-turning navigation. The next option is a site that has a clear hierarchy starting from a main entry page and then leading down different paths. The most complex type of site, and the one we are suggesting for use with dramatic narrative, has a complex, nonlinear, hyperlinked structure.

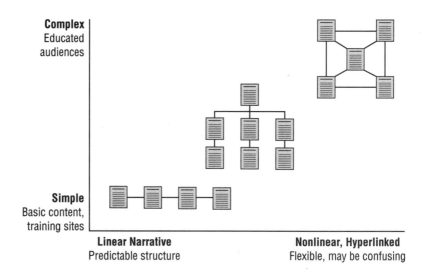

FIGURE 10.8 Types of Navigation in Relation to Audience

Source: Diagram from *Web Style Guide* (www.webstyleguide.com/site/diagrams/html) Copyright © 2002 Lynch and Horton

1. "Works," or achieves stated goal: does what the creator set out to do.
2. Organizes: provides a visual path for readers to follow (including a guide to what is most important and what is least important)
3. Attracts: "grabs your readers' attention and pulls them into your piece."

This is an excellent yardstick against which to measure your visuals. Ask yourself or others questions that get at whether each goal has been accomplished. For example:

- Does my layout _____?
  (Fill in the blank with each goal or objective, being sure to include emotional ones and not just cognitive ones. For example, does the layout explain how to open a car engine? Get the viewer excited about the program? Decrease fear surrounding the new policies?)
- Where is my eye drawn first? Where do I want to look after that? What is the final thing I look at? Does this path match the level of importance of content? Are there too many elements that compete for a viewer's attention?
- If I were walking down a sidewalk or driving down the road and my visual was on a big monitor or billboard, would my eye be drawn to

it over others? After I had seen it ten or twenty times, would it still grab my attention? What happens after it catches my eye? Does it entice me to want to engage on a deeper level?

If you go back and reread our analyses of each of the eight figures in this chapter, you'll see how we presented our answers to these types of questions.

Up Next

We have just scratched the surface of layout and style. These elements make up the frame supporting any house of visual design. The next chapter addresses the first resident that moves into almost any eLearning program's house: type.

NOTES

1. Mario Garcia, *Pure Design* (St. Petersburg, Fla.: Miller Media, 2002).
2. "Design Grids for Web Pages," in *Web Style Guide* (2nd ed.), 2002, http://www.webstyleguide.com/page/grids.html.
3. Lori Siebert and Lisa Ballard, *Making a Good Layout* (Cincinnati, Ohio: North Light Books, 1992).

It is rare for us to encounter a blackboard-style eLearning program that is simultaneously well designed, visually attractive, and instructionally effective. Online-learning.com's classes are miles beyond the rest. The class we took, Graphic Design, was the first class of its type that taught us as much or more than we have learned in a classroom. People whose interest in piqued by this chapter, or who wish to delve further into the topic should sign up for online-learning.com's graphic design class.

JUST THE TYPE

Increasing Impact Through Word Design

NEXT TO LAYOUT, type is the most important feature of most eLearning programs, simply because it is ubiquitous and plentiful. Most eLearning programs use text as the primary means of communicating, which means it accounts for lots and lots of what participants are going to be interacting with. We have yet to run across a program that uses graphics exclusively but can easily find ones that use only text.

A few years ago, discussing text in eLearning might have been a moot point. The Internet was originally designed by physicists to ensure they could keep sending each other those sexy number- and letter-filled documents regardless of what struggles or strife the other 99.9 percent of the planet might be engaged in. The technology wasn't designed to support anything other than the bare necessities: two or three fonts in a few different sizes, with a few pictures only when absolutely essential. Making sure educators could go wild with Comic Sans just wasn't high on the priority list.

In the ensuing years cascading style sheets, Flash, Shockwave, XML, and other advances have knocked down most font-related barriers. Whether the goal is to use an obscure funky font, to place a 250-point "e" dead center, or to make a word stand out by coloring it in an exact Pantone shade, the potential ways to underscore key eLearning messages through type have exploded exponentially.

This basic introduction to type is going to touch on just a few of the many aspects that make up intelligent and attractive text design. We strongly suggest referring to some of the resources listed in the ". . . And

BOOKSHELF BEST BETS

The Non-Designer's Type Book, Robin Williams

Type in Use, Alexander White

The Complete Manual of Typography, James Felici

> *Good design is good business.*
> **THOMAS WATSON JR.**

Even More Reading!" section, as they will go into the topic with more expertise and depth. The aspects we will cover are

- Typeface (font)
- Size
- Case
- Alignment
- Emphasis
- Kerning, tracking, and leading

TYPEFACE

For many people, including ourselves, one of their most exciting computer-related moments came when they discovered how many fun and cool fonts they could use to write letters, posters, cards, and other documents. Typefaces have given people a new tool for putting emotion into their words. Looking at the typeface samples that follow, it is easy to see how each one can put readers into a different frame of mind and can influence their impression of the content.

Renaissance eLearning
(Weidemann Medium)

Renaissance eLearning
(TypoUpright BT)

`Renaissance eLearning`
(Courier)

Renaissance eLearning
(Geometr231)

In a sense, typeface is equated with the personality of the eLearning. Participants will quickly label content as friendly, boring, dull, exciting, mysterious, or sophisticated, basing this initial opinion on the typeface chosen. This can make it tempting to go overboard with a favorite cutesy or approachable font: the current overuse of Comic Sans is the best example of this phenomenon. Ideally, the font should be such a perfect fit for the message it should go unnoticed. If someone says, "Oh, we love the font you used!" it's as bad as if they hated it. The typeface should call attention to the message, not to itself.

There are many perspectives on the "best" screen fonts. Some say sans serif fonts (fonts that do not have little hooks and tails on the letters) are

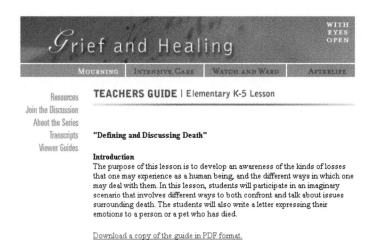

FIGURE 11.1 PBS Screenshot 1

Copyright © Lanker, Inc.

easier to read on a screen and serif fonts (fonts with tails and hooks) are easier to read on paper. Take a look for yourself:

> **Verdana, Arial, and Futura are examples of sans serif fonts, fonts that may be easier to read on a screen. This is set in Futura.**
>
> Georgia, Garamond, and Geometr231 are examples of our favorite serif fonts, fonts that may be easier to read (and that are stylish!) on paper. This is set in Geometr231.

This conventional wisdom is particularly relevant when there is a significant amount of text to be read and when the type is small. For example:

> *Reading small print in a decorative or hard-to-read font is really hard.*
>
> But reading small print in a simple font (such as Arial) is much easier.

This doesn't mean the accent pieces or headlines need to be restricted to generic fonts. Look at Figure 11.1 and notice the way the Public Broadcasting Service used typefaces on a site that provides instructional materials covering death and dying. The body text is in Times New Roman, chosen for legibility. However, an emotional (aka dramatic) ambiance is created by using an unusual typeface for both menus, the title banner, and the subhead. The italic letter in the banner also gives a softer, feminine feel. These elements get the reader's attention and suggest a softer, caring approach.

Contrast this with Figure 11.2, a screenshot from another PBS educational product, this one about World War II artists—soldiers who depicted

FIGURE 11.2 PBS Screenshot 2
Copyright © Lanker, Inc.

scenes of battle and other war-related topics. Again the main content is presented in a generic font, but the heading is a strong, all-uppercase, nonitalicized typeface. It gives off an impression of seriousness bordering almost on harshness. The subhead and menu words balance this out with a rounder, softer touch, but the typeface is still serious.

SIZE

The typical font size for screen reading is between 10 and 12 points. Type size can be used to leverage the principle of contrast: the greater the obvious difference between two items the more they stand out. One of the ways contrast can be wielded effectively is to make headlines or other elements stand apart by making them much bigger than the body font. However, the use of size contrast has to be planned and judicious. The biggest text on the page will be interpreted as the most important and will get the most attention. Use too many large words, and the page will become cluttered or lose impact.

Here are some good guidelines to follow:

1. *Pick the most important information you want to convey.* Write it in a way that communicates quickly and dramatically why the participant should stand up and take notice. In a traditional print medium (such as a newspaper or magazine) this would be called the headline. In eLearning this attention grabber does not necessarily need to be limited, as a headline is, to a summary of the following information.

On the average, five times as many people read the headline as read the body copy. When you have written your headline, you have spent eighty cents out of your dollar.

DAVID OGILVY

Instead it could easily be a word or phrase that is simply memorable and attention getting. If it is one word, make it much larger than the body text but in an interesting way. If it is more than one word, consider making the key one or two words much larger and the other words a size between the sizes of the body text and this "headline."

2. *Pick a piece of information that both summarizes the content to come and attracts attention.* Make sure this subhead contrasts with both the body text and the headline by either using a different typeface or picking a size that is an interesting contrast to the sizes of both the body and the headline. Avoid the temptation to pick a size right in the middle of those two. Instead play with a size slightly larger than that of the body or slightly smaller than that of the head. Another possibility is to make one letter of the subhead very large *and* distinct in some other way (with a different typeface or some form of emphasis) and the rest of the subhead smaller.

3. *Consider what information is merely a sidelight on the main information and make it really small.* Say one element is a comment made by Albert Einstein. Keep his name in the body, but move the quotation elsewhere and put it in 8- or 9-point type. Those who want to hunt it out can, but everyone else can ignore it because it fades into the background. Remember, good design is as much about what you take away as what you keep.

4. *Decide where you might use white space instead of size differences.* A phrase presented in a small typeface and set off all by itself, surrounded by nothing but space (aka white space), can have as big an impact as a phrase set in big type.

5. *Finally, if you are going to use size as a way of creating contrast, you have to go for it.* A headline that's 18 point when the body text is 14? Whoopee! Contrast has to use real differences and can't be done halfway. Make the headline 70 point or 100 point. When you want to create visual drama, size really does matter.

CASE

There are four *cases:*

1. ALL CAPS
2. all lowercase
3. Some Caps
4. SMALL CAPS

WE HAVE YET TO ENCOUNTER AN INSTANCE WHEN A DESIGN BENEFITED FROM THE USE OF ALL CAPS IN BODY TEXT. According to Robin Williams in *The Non-Designer's Design Book*, words in all caps take up twice as much horizontal space, often requiring a reduction in font size, which defeats the purpose of using caps in the first place. All caps also has a socially negative connotation: it's interpreted as meaning the person is shouting. Avoid it whenever possible.

all lowercase used to be a way of writing that reminded people of the poems of e. e. cummings. with the advent of email addresses and urls that are all lowercase, this style has come to be affiliated with content that is trying to give the message of being related to the internet or technology. a final way to use all lowercase is to capture attention the same way black and white captures attention in a color-filled publication—by virtue of being unexpected in a world where the opposite is expected to get attention. the one downside, as you may have noticed, is that it can call attention to itself, which detracts from the message. use it prudently and this style will retain its effectiveness.

There is not much to say about some caps, except this style is the norm. When in doubt, this is the way to go.

The final option, SMALL CAPS is a nice compromise between ALL CAPS (for emphasis) and Some Caps (pedestrian, conventional). As you saw in our list of cases, in the small caps style the first letter of each word is a normal capital letter, and the rest of the letters are also capitalized but they are shorter. SMALL CAPS LENDS AN AIR OF ELEGANCE AND A TOUCH OF UNIQUENESS. It is one of our favorite cases and is a particularly great case to use for titles, headers, and other nonbody content.

ALIGNMENT

We consider *alignment* to apply to two aspects of text. First, it describes the way the sentences in a block of text line up in relation to the page margins.

Left Aligned

This paragraph is left aligned: notice how the text makes a nice neat line down the left side but is jagged on the right. This is how most people expect to see text when they come from cultures that read right to left.

Right Aligned

Now look at this paragraph. Notice how we have aligned it to the right. The nice straight line is on the right, and the text is jagged on the left.

This would almost never be a good choice for body text as it is disconcerting. However, it does make a nice way to set something off. For example:

A quote

A headline

A sidebar

A design element

Center Aligned

Then of course there is the infamous center alignment, in which there is no nice clean line on either side.
This is unquestionably the most amateur and hardest to read for body text which means you should reserve it for items that are traditionally expected to be center aligned, the titles of academic papers, and so on.

The only time
we have seen this used
very effectively was when the
person was using it to make
an interesting design
with the words
themselves.

Justified

Text that is justified has a nice clean line on both sides of the paragraph. We find this to be the easiest to read and most elegant for body text. Justification can be slightly more work as the final words, if there are   not enough of them, can stretch out and be   hard   to   read.

He who works with his hands is a laborer. He who works with his hands and his head is a craftsman. He who works with his hands and his head and his heart is an artist.
ST. FRANCIS OF ASSISI

If you wish to put text in a particular area of the page but don't want to experience some of the ragged-edge downsides discussed earlier, the easy solution is to justify the text, then adjust the margins. As you can see, the result looks much better than text that is just right aligned.

Page Alignment

Most readers will be familiar with the types of alignment just covered. What seems to be less familiar to many people is that objects on a page also have an alignment. This is the balance between all the objects on a page and is synonymous with *layout* for our purposes. The alignment of objects on a page should direct the eye to flow smoothly and effortlessly in hierarchical order, from most to least important. For more details, review our discussion of layout.

EMPHASIS

One of the ways to draw attention to words or indicate one thing is more important than another is to use emphasis: making the words either **bold** or *italic* or **both.** Another technique used on a computer screen is blinking or flashing. We caution again using any of these techniques on screen in eLearning.

In the case of blinking or other flashing movements, they are just plain annoying and distracting. We have yet to see them used well even once. As for bold and italic styling, they should be used with caution as well. Unless the type is large (larger than 20 point), it can be very challenging to read bold or italic words on screen, especially if the basic typeface is hard to read anyway, actually resulting in decreased emphasis.

Another important aspect to take into consideration is the overall balance with the emphasis. Although many may disagree, we feel any program in which more than 5 percent of the words are written with emphasis is poorly designed. There are other ways to graphically indicate importance and highlight important points. Emphasis should be reserved for moments when it adds significantly to understanding or grabs attention. The only exception to this is text used as a graphic touch; for example, a 200-point letter in the background used as an illustration.

KERNING, TRACKING, AND LEADING

The spacing between words, between letters, and between lines affects the overall visual presentation of the content.

When words, letters, or lines are smooshed too close together, they can be hard to read, and the text can appear confusing or intimidating to the participants. Here, words and letters are tightly spaced, and the leading is condensed by one point.

When words and letters are spaced far apart, it also has an effect on the reader.

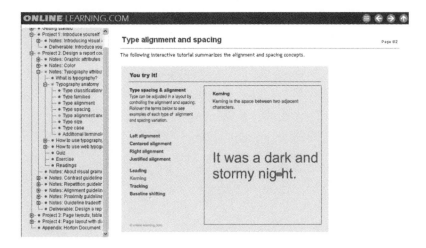

FIGURE 11.3 Online-Learning.com Screenshot 1

In Figure 11.3, online-learning.com's graphic design program illustrates what kerning is. A red marker (the visual element between the letters "g" and "h" in "night") supports the definition above the example: "Kerning is the space between two adjacent characters."

If the user rolls her mouse over "Tracking," that word highlights and the red marker moves to illustrate that word's definition: "Tracking is the space between adjacent characters in entire words, lines or paragraphs" (Figure 11.4).

When the user moves to "Leading," the red marker indicates that "leading is the line spacing, measured from baseline to baseline of adjacent lines of text" (Figure 11.5). An easy way to remember what leading is is to think of the old days when printers used bars of lead to separate the lines of type they were setting. The bars came in different sizes: bigger ones were used when the typeface was larger and smaller ones when the typeface was smaller. Hence the term *leading* to describe line spacing.

These three features of text are critical to both readability and attractiveness. Here are some additional tips about these aspects of typography:

- For body text, in which readability is of primary importance, leading should typically be no less than 120 percent of the font size. In other words, add 20 percent to the point (pt) size of your font. If your font size is 10pt, the leading should be 12pt; if it is 20pt, the

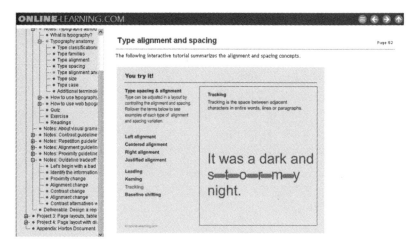

FIGURE 11.4   Online-Learning.com Screenshot 2

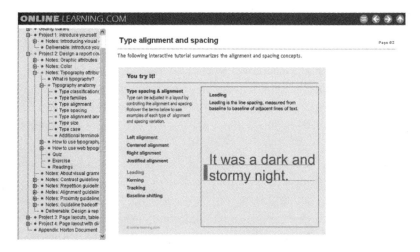

FIGURE 11.5   Online-Learning.com Screenshot 3

leading should be 24pt, and so on. In the *Digital Type Design Guide*,[1] Sean Cavanaugh suggests leading of 130 to 140 percent for sans serif typefaces.

• When text is used to grab attention (in headlines, for example) or for decorative purposes, leading can vary from 120 percent of font size. Try making it smaller (100 percent) to emphasize or 200 percent to appear artistic.

- Most people assume computers are smart enough to automatically select the best kerning and tracking. Although computers are adept at mathematical calculations, thus far their aesthetic skills are not all that well developed. On the one hand, going over the text in your programs to adjust the kerning and tracking can add that *je ne sais quoi* that subtly gives off an impression of quality. On the other hand, sitting around for hours or days putting millimeters between letters and words is not always a smart investment. A possible compromise is to make sure the text elements that stand apart (headlines and other items designed to grab attention) are well balanced and attractive.

Up Next

The elements of design you have learned thus far are building blocks for the topics we address in the next chapter: perspective and color. Both these topics, as well as the universal principles, are overarching facets of design that can determine the emotion, and therefore state of mind, a user feels when approaching a program.

NOTE

1.   Sean Cavanaugh, *Digital Type Design Guide* (Upper Saddle River, N.J.: Macmillan Computer Publishing, 1996).

PUTTING THINGS IN PERSPECTIVE

Using "Camera" Angle to Attract and Involve

IN CHAPTER FIVE we covered narrative perspective—the point of view taken while traveling through a story. Now we are going to talk about visual perspective: the point of view participants take as a result of the angle at which they see things on the screen.

When people see things in real life, they have the option of coming at them from any angle they choose (at least within the limitations on their physical movements—they can't see the other side of the moon without being in a space shuttle but they can see an orange from any angle).

When an image is going to be viewed in two dimensions, the person creating a representation of the object shown in the image (the illustrator, photographer, cameraman, animator, and so forth) needs to make a decision (conscious or otherwise) about the angle from which the audience will see the image. That is, the eLearning participants are put in a specific location relative to the items in the image.

Gunther Kress and Theo Van Leeuwen, authors of *Reading Images*, a seminal work on the semiotics of visual design, have suggested that relationships between people are implied by the different sizes of objects in the image. Peter Sells and Sierra Gonzalez provide this interpretation:

> The physical distance between people defines how much of one participant the other participant can see; the closer you are to a person, the less you can see of their full body. Because social relations influence the distance in which people interact, the size of frame corresponds to a level of social intimacy. Just as a small distance between two people suggests a level

Symbolize and Summarize.
SAUL BASS

of intimacy and a distance of an arm's length suggests a level of formality, a close-up suggests personal interaction while a medium or long shot suggests observation or a distant relationship between viewer and viewed.[1]

That was written to explain how advertisers encourage viewers to engage with their products. It is just as applicable to how eLearning programs affect participants. When the person or object in an image is only partially in view, that suggests a closer, more intimate relationship between that image and the participant. In turn, this communicates a more personal connection and encourages the participant to feel connected to the learning content and experience.

When the person or object is shown in its entirety, that suggests a more distant relationship and makes the participant feel more removed from the content.

CAMERA ANGLE

Another important factor is the angle of the "camera," which in eLearning's case could be a photographer's camera (when an actual photo is used) or a virtual camera (when the image is an animation or illustration).

Horizontal Angle

Kress and Van Leeuwen describe how the horizontal camera angle dictates how much involvement the participant feels with the program and its content. The frontal angle says, "What you see here is part of our world, something we are involved with." The oblique angle says, "What you see here is not a part of our world, this is their world, something we are not involved with."

Vertical Angle

The vertical angle also addresses the type of interaction the participant has with the content. In the following description, *represented participant* means the object shown in the image, and *interactive participant* means the viewer (in this case the person taking the eLearning program):

> If a represented participant is seen from a high angle, then the relation between the interactive participants (. . . the viewer) and the represented participants is depicted as one in which the interactive participant has power over the represented participant—the represented participant is seen from the point of view of power. If the represented participant is seen from a low angle, then the relation between the

FIGURE 12.1 Root Learning Screenshot
Copyright © RootLearning, Inc.

active and represented participants is depicted as one in which the rep-resented participant has power over the interactive participant. If, finally, the picture is at eye level, then the point of view is one of equal-ity and there is no power difference involved.[2]

Stated more simply, show an object so the participants are looking down on the object, and they will feel more empowered and in control. Show the object so the participants are looking up at the object, and they will feel disempowered, out of control. Show the object so the participants face it directly, and the relationship between the object and the partici-pants will feel like one between equals. The following examples show camera angle and object sizing (the elements of perspective described pre-viously) in action.

Consider Figure 12.1, from Root Learning's objective setting program. Notice how your eye sees the entire factory. It looks up at even the lower-most point of the factory. The height of the logo sign relative to the factory (almost the same size) and the large size of the grass patch further give the impression you are standing a good distance away from the factory. This artist put the participants[3] physically far away from and below the objects on the screen. The factory and surrounds are shown from the perspective of a per-son looking up at the complete building. The result of using this perspective is negative. It makes the viewer feel small, less involved, and disempowered. There is no intimacy or involvement implied in this perspective: the eLearning program is fundamentally saying: "We are important; you are not.

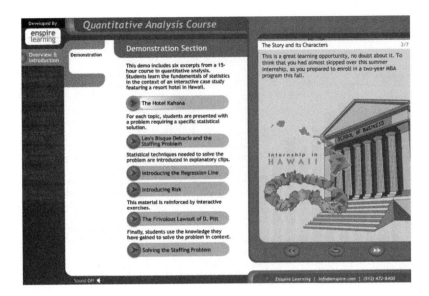

FIGURE 12.2 Enspire Learning, Inc. Screenshot

Source: www.enspire.com

We don't care if you get involved in the content as you will always be an outsider."

Contrast this with the screenshot from Enspire Learning's quantitative analysis program (Figure 12.2). Look at the picture of the building on the right. It too is an intimidating building (neoclassical columns and the large marble steps make it feel solid, traditional, and serious). However, there is a world of difference between the participants' perspectives in this image and the previous one. The vertical angle is still lower than the building but it is only slightly less than equal. Participants glance only slightly upward. The horizontal angle places the building on an oblique. Although this is less inviting than full frontal, because participants see only part of the building, it works to imply they are moving closer to it—approaching it and therefore getting more intimately involved.

Let's view these principles in action when people are the objects in the images.

In Thompson NetG's business etiquette program, each of the 100 or so pages has an image of a person, and these people are all different individuals and all in different positions. In virtually none is the person looking directly at the participant. The people shown in Figures 12.3 and 12.4 are representative.

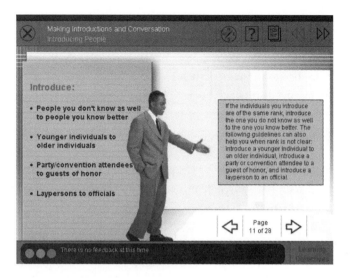

FIGURE 12.3 Thompson NetG Screenshot 1

Copyright © Tower Innovative Learning Solutions, Inc.

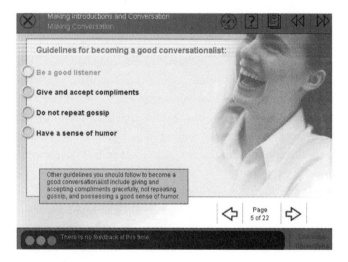

FIGURE 12.4 Thompson NetG Screenshot 2

Copyright © Tower Innovative Learning Solutions, Inc.

In Figure 12.3, the person is standing sideways, offering his hand to no one. It actually looks like he is offering his hand to the text box to his right. Additionally, his size compared to the text around him makes him look like the winner of the honey-I-shrunk-the-eLearning-stock-photo contest. The

The human preference for faces and bodies that are symmetrical presumably reflects selection of the fittest; nonsymmetrical bodies probably are the result of some deficiency in the genes or the maturation process. Humans select for size, color, and appearance. What you are biologically disposed to think of as attractive derives from these considerations. Sure, culture plays a role, so that, for example, some cultures prefer fat people, others thin; but even within those cultures, there is agreement on what is and is not attractive, even if too thin or too fat for specific likes.

DONALD NORMAN

participant's perspective is that of a disconnected person looking down on an ant or other very small character. Any feeling of intimacy between participants and content is minimal because his whole body is showing; he's distant. The horizontal perspective is oblique in a way that says, "You are not really involved in this program." Involvement is implied only by the vertical camera angle: the participant is viewing the man from a slightly elevated angle, giving a feeling of empowerment. Unfortunately, this is not enough to engage the participant.

In Figure 12.4, the woman's face and neck take up almost 30 percent of the entire screen but only part of her face and body are shown. In most instances showing only part of the person would imply intimacy between participants and content. In this case the way she is cropped eliminates the aspects of proximity that foster intimacy (cropping the eyes makes the image eerie instead of intimate). It does not help that she is almost a ghost, transparent and fading. Additionally, showing her from an oblique angle (horizontal) makes the participants feel uninvolved, distant. Again, only the vertical angle implies equality. Participants are seeing her on an equal plane, not from below or above.

In sharp contrast is the Sound Design module from Real: Creative Learning (Figure 12.5). The character is seen in full frontal view, inviting complete engagement (full frontal says, "Come along with me! I am talking directly to you!"). The horizontal angle invites complete involvement and equality. The vertical angle is of empowerment: the character is seen from just the slightest downward glance. Additionally, his body language (arms wide open) displays a universal symbol of acceptance and welcome. This is a perfect illustration of inviting a participant to feel welcome, involved, and engaged.

These contrasting examples demonstrate how the physical placement of graphics can either draw participants deeper into the program—making them feel a part of it, or keep them at an arm's distance. User-centered design requires using perspective in ways that do not alienate or push the participants out but draw them in.

Here are some additional pointers for wielding perspective to make eLearning more personal, engaging, and dramatic:

- Make sure any representations of people or characters are mostly shown as making eye contact with the participants (face forward).
- Try to convey body language that is natural and inclusive.
- Expanding on the previous point, keep the visual perspective consistent with the narrative point of view.

FIGURE 12.5   Real: Creative Learning Screenshot 1

- Unless you are intentionally trying to make the participants feel smaller (for example, instilling fear by using an "evil empire" theme), never make them look up at the entire body of a character or building. Under no circumstances should participants always be looking up at the images; the message they will receive is disempowerment and discouragement.

- Use shadows to make the graphics appear to have depth and dimensionality.

- If you are going to use photographs of real people, choose a few people the participants can relate to and stick with them. Using twenty different people only emphasizes how disconnected the pages are from each other and constantly shifts the users' perspective. Be sure the perspectives are consistent.

- Embrace negative space. White space is empty space, where there are no words or images (but it can have color!). Leaving white space around what you want learners to notice will make the element *pop* to their eye and reduce their sense of being overwhelmed—less clutter is usually better (but not always).

- In Western societies, where people read from left to right, there is a convention of putting the old on the left and the new on the right. For example, a pre–weight loss image will always be on the left and a post one on the right. Unless you are intentionally making a point, stay with this convention.

It is not the voice that commands the story; it is the ear.
ITALO CALVINO

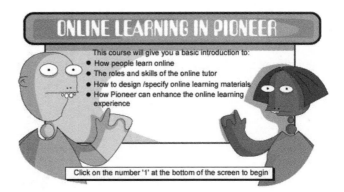

FIGURE 12.6 Real: Creative Learning Screenshot 2

- Show part of a person or building to build intimacy. A good tip is to begin by showing almost the entire image and then show less of the image in subsequent graphics so the participant feels she is approaching the person or building, getting more intimate.

- Never crop out a person's eyes or crop very close to a person's eyes. It is disconcerting and visually displeasing. It can easily break engagement and discourage intimacy. It can even have a disturbing effect.

- Make all elements on the page focus on the most important part. If there are photos of people, try having the people looking at the important text, instead of facing forward, in one screen and then having them look back at the participants in the next.

- Imitate graphically what people would do in real life to draw attention to important elements. An example of this comes from Real: Creative Learning; in Figure 12.6 the characters are pointing to the learning objectives.

- Remove extraneous content if it competes for the eye's attention. Look at Figure 12.7, the PBS site for a program about New York City cabbies. The line of text the program developers most want to attract your attention to is not in the center but off to the left and on the lower part of the screen. The only reason this works is because it is much larger than the rest of the text (and because of intelligent use of color).

The Bottom Line

Show images either from an angle that suggests equality or from one that helps the participants feel intimate, involved, and empowered.

FIGURE 12.7 PBS Screenshot
Copyright © Lanker, Inc.

THE COLOR OF LEARNING

Trying to give the fundamentals of color theory is best left to books printed in color. For that reason we are going to suggest you refer to the materials we recommend here to gain a solid foundation in concepts such as complementary colors, contrast, hue, saturation, and so on.

The resource we recommend above all others is the graphic design class mentioned before (www.online-learning.com). It provides an outstanding, inexpensive, and fast way to gain a good grasp of color fundamentals through both text and experiments. Additionally, online-learning.com provides the entire course as a download so you don't need to be connected to learn.[4] This class is one of our all-time favorite eLearning programs, and its treatment of color is one of the reasons we give it such a high rating.

Also, see these Web sites:

- http://www.worqx.com/color/resources.htm
- http://www.webwhirlers.com/colors/coloursphysics.asp
- http://www.colormatters.com/entercolormatters.html (this site is surprisingly ugly for a color theory site, but the information is excellent)

You can find more resources in the ". . . And Even More Reading!" section.

The one topic that can be introduced without visual representation is people's physiological and psychological response to color. Color is a universal that evokes responses from every sighted person (and many animals).

What is often subject to debate is not whether people respond physiologically to color but to what degree they respond. If people didn't respond physiologically to color, they would not see colors at all. The issue gets muddy when we go beyond whether human optic nerves perceive color and into territory such as how individuals' blood pressure, heart rate, temper, and behaviors are affected by color. Most people agree certain colors will raise blood pressure (red), suppress appetite (blue), and cause eye irritation (yellow).

Other studies in the field of chromodynamics have found numerous other physiological responses to color that are more tenuous. Here are some examples:

- Blue causes people to be more productive.
- People will gamble more and place riskier bets under red light.
- Warm colors (yellows, reds) cause us to feel closer to objects than cool colors (blues).
- Driving a silver car reduces the chance of being in an accident (incidentally, brown increases the chance).
- Being in a yellow room can cause people to lose their temper.

The paint company Glidden has an amusing personality assessment (visit http://www.glidden.com/glbTST_n/NUSGLI/colors/colorpsychology.jsp and click on "Try the Glidden color test") that uses your favorite colors as well as a horoscope based on colors. We did it twice, the first time selecting our genuine preferences, the second the diametric opposite of our preferences. The first time it said we were creative geniuses destined for fame and fortune, the second time that we should go directly to counseling. Clearly it is an accurate judge of character.

We don't buy into these specific theories. However, we do believe color affects mood, behavior, and physiology. People in different cultures make different associations between specific colors and their significance, but all are affected by color.

An integral part of making an eLearning program more effective is selecting colors carefully. If you believe in many of the established theories about how color makes people feel, consult the relevant books to select the colors you will use based upon your desired response (for example, using red as an attention getter). If you are more skeptical or simply want to do a different approach, we advise picking out a few color schemes, testing to see how they appear on many different monitors, and then asking participants to rate their preferences. Many of the resources in the ". . . And Even More Reading!" section will aid in color selection.

UNIVERSAL DESIGN PRINCIPLES

There are some general rules that have come to be accepted by artists and designers over time. We have selected six from various sources to cover here. Many more of equal importance can be found, but we decided these had universal relevance to eLearning and our subject matter.

1. *Adhere to the aesthetic usability principle.*[5] It may seem that making eLearning "pretty" is just a superficial exercise, like putting on

makeup or polishing silver. A nice-to-have that may add to the beauty in the world but won't make one iota of difference to the effectiveness of the learning. There is a universal principle almost as old as the laws of gravity that says something pleasing to the eye is perceived as easier to use than something less attractive. The aesthetic-usability principle basically says things that look more attractive have been shown to "foster positive attitudes . . . [to be] more readily accepted and used over time, [and to] promote creative thinking and problem solving."[6] eLearning with an attractive, appealing look and feel is a need-to-have, not just a nice-to-have. It is particularly critical for deep learning. It can make all the difference when the content requires a commitment of time and psychological adjustment and when the delivery method is unfamiliar or likely to be met with some initial resistance.

> Attractive objects are rated as easier to use than less attractive objects. This holds true across all media, materials, and cultures.

2. *Practice consistency.* A program is easier to use and easier to learn when "similar parts are expressed in similar ways." According to William Lidwell, Kritina Holden, and Jill Butler, two aspects of consistency are under the graphic designer's control: aesthetic and functional. Aesthetic consistency "refers to consistency of style and appearance (e.g. a company logo that uses a consistent font, color, and graphic). . . . [it] enhances recognition, communicates membership, and sets emotional expectations." Functional consistency "refers to consistency of meaning and action (e.g. a traffic light that shows a yellow light before going red) . . . [it] improves usability and learnability by enabling people to leverage existing knowledge about the design functions."[7] Overall consistency can be enhanced by

   - Making sure navigation devices are consistent and identical where appropriate
   - Maintaining a consistent palette of colors throughout the program
   - Maintaining a consistent graphical look and feel throughout the program
   - Using objects, images, or symbols already familiar to (and preferably liked by) participants

3. *Remember the 80/20 rule.* Ah yes, the dreaded this-rule-is-used-all-the-time rule. In this case the principle states that most of the participants will use only 20 percent of the program's functions. This is extremely important in designing eLearning because it means the program should be effective even if only 20 percent of the functions

or features are used. In other words, *all* the program's features should be well designed because each user's 20 percent will be slightly different from every other user's 20 percent.

4. *Take advantage of the Von Restorff effect.*[8] An item or experience that is different from what surrounds it (or preceded it) is more likely to be remembered. Strive to make important or attention-getting elements stand out by making them unique relative to what is around them. Here are some examples of ways this can be done:

   - Use a different typeface, case, size, emphasis, or color.
   - Pick an unusual or unexpected graphic where a traditional one might have been used.
   - Flip colors (if the interface is predominantly blue with a touch of yellow, make the important page predominantly yellow with blue as the minor color).

5. *Make use of proximity.* The principles of Gestalt psychology focus on how the brain processes graphical information. The principle most are familiar with is the completion principle, stating that a partial image is completed in a person's mind (for example, an "O" with a small piece missing is still perceived as an "O"). Another important but less well known principle concerns proximity, stating that the closer items are to each other the more they will appear to be related to each other, and the farther apart items are from each other the less they will be perceived as related. This has important implications for eLearning. Alignment and layout are not just about attractiveness but also about mental grouping. Carefully plan space between items and objects to nonverbally indicate relationships and connections. These cues will subtly facilitate and accelerate learning.

6. *Use the LATCH model for categorizing information.*[9] Richard Saul Wurman, a well-regarded information designer, has developed a system, known by the acronym LATCH, for organizing and presenting information. We have yet to find information that does not work with this model:

   Location: the spatial placement of items relative to one another (for example, geographically or inside a factory)

   Alphabet: arrangement by the alphabetical order of the item's title or name (for example, apples come before zebras)

   Time: arrangement according to the order in which items happen temporally (for example, in 1985 "Loverboy" was the #1 pop hit; in 1987, "With or Without You")

> The difference between top-flight creative men and the hack is the ability to express powerful meanings indirectly.
>
> **VANCE PACKARD**

Category: organization by similarity or relatedness. In Wurman's words, category "can mean different models, types, or even different questions to be answered."[10] Categories can be the things one encounters every day—color, use, number, breed, and so forth—or a new and novel approach. Dylan's, a chic candy store in New York City, categorizes many of its products by color, season, and visual appeal as opposed to traditional sweet merchandising categories.

Hierarchy: organization by magnitude (for example, smallest to biggest, most important to least important)

Up Next

This concludes our treatment of visual design. For more information we suggest you start with our Bookshelf Best Bets and then visit the ". . . And Even More Reading!" section. Part Three, up next, addresses facets of creating an environment in which good dramatic eLearning design can take root, grow, and thrive.

NOTES

1. Peter Sells and Sierra Gonzales, *The Language of Advertising*, http://www.stanford.edu/class/linguist34/index.htm, accessed May 2004.

2. Gunther Kress and Theo Van Leeuwen, *Reading Images* (New York: Routledge, 1996), pp. 135–148.

3. Since these are screenshots from eLearning programs, we have deliberately used the word *participant*. This emphasizes the point that the person is not just a viewer seeing a screenshot (as the reader of this book is doing) but an active learner participating in an experience.

4. With the exception of discussion areas, where users must be online to upload or post messages.

5. All of these principles except the last come from one outstanding reference book: William Lidwell, Kritina Holden, and Jill Butler, *Universal Principles of Design* (Gloucester, Mass.: Rockport, 2003). Everyone involved in design, visual or otherwise, should have this book.

6. Lidwell, Holden, and Butler, *Universal Principles of Design*, p. 18.

7. Lidwell, Holden, and Butler, *Universal Principles of Design*.

8. Hedwig von Restorff, "Analyse von Vorgangen in Spurenfeld I. Uber die Wirkung von Bereichsbilding im Spurenfeld," *Psychologische Forschung*, 1933, *18*, pp. 299–342.

9. Richard Saul Wurman, *Information Anxiety* (Indianapolis: QUE, 2000).

10. Wurman, *Information Anxiety*, p. 41.

SOL ADLER

Executive Director of the 92nd Street YM/WHA

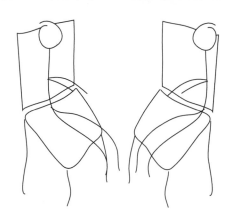

ON THE 92ND STREET Y'S CREATIVE PROCESS . . .

I guess in some ways I look at the Y or even in the world in general as a major corporation that deals with the issue of pure research, practical research, and day-to-day improvement of their products. In a well-balanced corporation, they try to do all those things.

They recognize the value of having a group doing things most of the corporation can't understand. It is well beyond the current capabilities of what the corporation could bring to market. However, they know somewhere in there is some spark of genius that could change the world or change their bottom line.

Then there is the practical or applied research. In any good company you take your product and say however wonderful it is, tomorrow we'll make it a little bit better.

We don't have the ability to do pure research, but our equivalent is to do more esoteric things. For example, we commission artists on a regular basis. You have no idea what's going to come out after the end of that commission, but that's my favorite part. You pick an artist in whom you have faith and confidence that he or she can both expand himself or herself and then maybe expand the genre. Some people might not like the end result, but that's not the point.

Another example is this renegade from the ballet world. She showed up and spent twelve years here developing modern dance. That was Martha Graham. She was unhappy with the restrictions of the ballet world and wanted to express herself somewhat differently. We gave her a home here. For twelve years she choreographed and performed until they became the Martha Graham Company and moved on. We have done that many times.

What we have learned from all these experiences is how to not only nurture the artist but how to nurture the child, the adult, the people in the health fitness center [that is, each program, even if it is directed at one particular patron group of the 92nd Street Y, spills over into teaching the Y how to make all the other programs for all other patron groups better as well].

ON THE 92ND STREET Y'S PEOPLE . . .

About ten years ago there was a woman who was commissioned by the Mellon Foundation to do a study on the educational programs that were attached to major orchestras. At the time we had an orchestra and an educational program, the New York Chamber Symphony. She went to all the big orchestras, the New York Philharmonic, the Chicago, the Saint Louis, and so on, and she said, "Your educational program is one of the top, why, do you think?"

My first reaction was that we have a great staff, but then I stopped myself and said that it is not just that. If you run the educational program at the New York Philharmonic, however well it is run, you are still the appendage, the main show is the Philharmonic. But if you run the music educational program at the 92nd Street Y, you are sitting around your table with a diverse group of colleagues. They are the social worker who runs the after-school programs, the educators who run the nursery school, the health and fitness center director who has a master's in exercise physiology, and so on. . . . I went through all the different disciplines that we bring around the table on a daily basis and realized our orchestra education director is learning from this diverse group of people on a daily basis. Where are you going to get that?

The child psychologist is saying those instruments and the music sounds a little too sophisticated for a six-year-old. The social worker says, "I have a number of families that I would like to get involved with you, because they can use that program in the issues that they are dealing with." This translates into this incredible energy and vibrancy that is almost a majestic enrichment of that program.

I guess the other part of creativity is that it needs to be supported in every way it can be. The trick here is to combine the business of the entity with the business of allowing that creativity to come to the world. My whole job is to enable the people around me to do what they do best. When I hear angst from someone, saying our bureaucracy or our procedures aren't allowing them to get what they need, it troubles me. It means my job is not being done as well as they are doing their job. I have to get that stuff out of the way for them, I have to make it so that they can come to the fore and create.

ON THE 92ND STREET Y'S RESULTS . . .

People from North America and around the world look to us and say, "What have you got?"

They know whatever it is it is going to be interesting. They may not want it and it may not be for them for whatever reason, but they know it will be of high quality and they can trust it and sell it to their audience. They know it will be delivered and delivered professionally. That is really the basis of eLearning or any other type of learning. It's having a reputation of quality that is critical. It is the reason people will keep coming back.

PART 3
COMING ATTRACTIONS

Fertile Ground

Paradigm shifts are like avalanches: they happen only when critical mass has been reached. In the first part of this book we suggested force is gathering behind the idea that creativity is a valued economic driver to be supported and fostered.

The first three chapters of *Renaissance eLearning* provided the context in which we see this new use of eLearning residing, in the Creative Economy, where applying knowledge in new and unusual ways is an economic driver. This is the larger, macro environment in which the people and organizations are sitting.

Part Two, "Lights, Camera, eLearning!" came at this situation from an application angle. The camera zoomed in to focus on dramatic techniques and emotion, just one of the many approaches through which you can develop eLearning programs that simultaneously leverage and develop creativity.

Part Three, "Fertile Ground," has the camera pulling out again to focus your attention halfway between the first and second parts of the book, on the immediate environment. This is the micro world, in which individuals operate in groups and larger environmental forces exert their influence. It is more predictable and subject to influence than the macro environment but is infinitely less manageable than the individual, application world.

It is at this level that the rubber meets the road, so to speak. In order for you to successfully use eLearning to drive results in the Creative Economy, the micro system has to be properly aligned and supportive. Whenever a new paradigm is introduced, taking steps to get the people and processes that have the potential to facilitate or hinder success is a smart move.

We approach this feat from three angles. First, getting the right people on board (Chapter Thirteen). Next, we suggest ways research that is done every minute of every day can be harnessed to achieve better results (Chapter Fourteen). We close the section with ideas on how to encourage people to constantly examine their beliefs—and their beliefs about their beliefs(!) (Chapter Fifteen). The goal of all three approaches is to foster development of an environment that is more fertile for ideas, idea suggestion, idea development, and mistakes. It is only when all three of these levels that require your attention are properly aligned that innovation can become a long-term key strategic asset.

TOPICS IN PART 3

**WHAT IS THE
CREATIVITY
ETHERNET?**

**IDENTIFYING
CREATIVITY ETHERNET
FREQUENT FLIERS**

**FINDING CREATIVITY
ETHERNET
FREQUENT FLIERS**

**TIPS FOR WIN-WIN
RELATIONS WITH
"CREATIVES"**

**NEW RESEARCH
PARADIGM**

**STEPS IN THE
RESEARCH PROCESS**

PRIMARY RESEARCH
COLLECTION IDEAS
Page 234

SECONDARY RESEARCH
COLLECTION IDEAS
Page 243

RELIABILITY
CONTINUUM
Page 246

SKEPTIC'S
TOOLKIT
Page 250

INTEGRATIVE
THINKING AND
INNOVATION
Page 261

DEFINING
REFLECTIVE
THINKING
Page 263

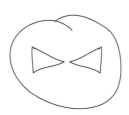

FOSTERING
REFLECTIVE
THINKING
Page 265

THE CREATIVITY ETHERNET

Thinking Outside the Recruiting Box

THE WORLD'S BIGGEST CREATIVITY TRADE SHOW!

EVERY AUGUST eight "festivals" take place concurrently in Edinburgh, Scotland: the Edinburgh international festival, the book festival, the military tattoo, and the fringe are the main ones. This doesn't count the hundreds of other events that have sprung up around them—art exhibits, university classes, walking tours, and so on. Here are just a few of the events that took place during the festivals over the years, representative of the 2,000+ taking place. They are just a small indication of how the whole city exists outside the mainstream during this time.

- A comedian who performs his act in his Toyota while driving you around the city
- Susan Sontag discussing the Iraq war in the context of how photographs shape society
- Two men doing origami with their penises
- A film on the Indian equivalent of the Mafia

We are sure on any given day New York City (Sam's hometown) probably has the same number and quality of events as happen on a typical festival day. So what pulls a self-confessed Manhattan snob back to Edinburgh every single August? It is not the chilly climate and rain. Instead it is the ineffable life and energy that flows through the small town as a result of the swell of nearly one million creative and curious over-the-top types that fills every pub, street, theater, park, and bed for thirty days. A reporter for the

BOOKSHELF BEST BETS

Confessions of an Advertising Man,
David Ogilvy

Why Are You Creative?
Hermann Vaske

"Business and Ethical Expectations for Professional Designers,"
American Institute of Graphic Arts (AIGA)

Handbook of Creativity,
Robert J. Sternberg (ed.)

Scotsman accurately pegged it when he called Edinburgh in August the world's biggest arts trade show.

This energetic magic is like creative spillover. Unless you wear blinders and earplugs all day every day (or you are really super closed minded and set in your ways) you are bound to experience epiphanies, aha moments, or at the least, new insights.

You are bound to have new ideas and to reevaluate old ways.

It's simply a side effect of being exposed to so many new ideas and concepts in such an immersive, intense way. It would be virtually impossible for the creativity in the ether not to rub off on anyone in the vicinity.

Like language, it's something you can't help but pick up if you are immersed in the environment where it is spoken. Welcome to a superhub of the creativity ethernet.

> *An artist is not paid for his labor but for his vision.*
> **JAMES McNEILL WHISTLER**

THE CREATIVITY ETHERNET

Robin Goldman, an amazing marketing writer who has a special talent for finding just the right word or phrase to pin down a complex concept, has coined the phrase *creativity ethernet* to describe a connection between all the ideas, talents, and people floating around in the world. It is definitely real, but like the Internet or that creative energy we described earlier, it is at once both very tangible and approachable and completely ineffable and remote.

When you tap into this ethernet you have the opportunity to harness the power of every single person on it. You have the opportunity to open doors, be more innovative, create solutions that more closely meet customer needs, are more in touch with the cutting edge of society, and get much higher quality work for a fraction of the price.

From an eLearning and corporate perspective the most important aspect of this ethernet are the tangible results: the innovations or changes that contribute to a better bottom line, society, or organization. But the only way to tap these results is either to be very immersed in the ethernet yourself or to dip into the immersion vicariously, by connecting with people who are an integral part of it. We refer to the latter as CEFFs, creativity ethernet frequent fliers.

ROOT LEARNING

The directors of Root Learning do not hesitate even a second when asked what enables them to be so successful: the diversity of knowledge brought to their table by people from varied backgrounds outside the mainstream.

Tom Crawford and Jim Haudan started thinking about people who play fantasy games. Fantasy baseball, football, and so forth. It struck them as odd that these same people who are absolutely entranced and engaged by these complex worlds during play were completely and totally disengaged and disconnected from the realities of the businesses they worked for. The question became a simple one for them: "How can you create that level of engagement and that level of connectivity from the employee to the biz and to the marketplace and make it fun and meaningful and relevant?"

They knew they need look no further than their own staff. Because they seek out and hire the fringe people ("we find the people who can bring things to the table that other organizations would hire or look for"), they knew the answer was just a matter of getting everyone together on the picnic tables outside the office and giving the question over to them.

As a result of having a diverse group of fringe professionals (among them a former toy designer, genetic counselor, newspaper illustrator, and school principal), they are able to "harness the knowledge that a company doing all the research in the world couldn't get." As a further result their offerings are not only award winners that are widely acclaimed as exceptional but have been used by ten million-plus people working in a considerable portion of the world's leading corporations, including GM, Pfizer, and Coca-Cola.

There is much to be gained from leveraging the insights, energy, and talents of these people (the CEFFs):

- Dramatic increases in exposure to new ideas.
- Development of constantly fresh and innovative solutions and offerings.
- Opportunities to scoop up new ideas and innovations for very little money.
- As in Edinburgh, chances to experience the rub-off effect. Being around people who spend their days looking at the world differently will almost certainly inspire others to do the same.

The main reason to connect with the CEFFs is that the farther away you are from a supernode, the harder it is to harness these benefits.

This chapter will show you how to harness the power of this creativity ethernet without having to change your own organization drastically. Just as

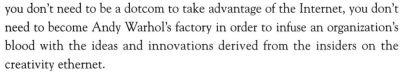

In the long history of humankind (and animalkind, too) those who learned to collaborate and improvise most effectively have prevailed.

CHARLES DARWIN

you don't need to be a dotcom to take advantage of the Internet, you don't need to become Andy Warhol's factory in order to infuse an organization's blood with the ideas and innovations derived from the insiders on the creativity ethernet.

We will begin by describing what the creativity ethernet is, who its frequent flyers are, and why you and CEFFs can be of mutual benefit to each other. Next, we will show how to find and screen CEFFs to make sure you get people who best meet your needs. We will then provide some ideas to help people work together with minimal friction. We will conclude with a chapter resource: a listing of many additional ways to find the creative people you need.

WHAT IS THE CREATIVITY ETHERNET?

The creativity ethernet shares characteristics of the Internet (a virtual world) and the "real" world. In its essence it is the connection between all the creative people, places, things, thoughts, and events present in the world. If you think of it as being Internet-like, it becomes easier to understand. Here are some of its characteristics, viewed through the Internet metaphor:

- It is a network that has "visible" aspects. Just as the avenue to entry for the Internet is to log on or launch a browser, you can tap into this world by participating in a creative event, using the product of a creative moment, or transforming your own creativity into a work product.

- It is a network made up of people, and people are the most significant part of the network. The messages and content may be communicated in any one of a zillion different ways—wires, airwaves, smoke signals, back of envelopes, Web sites, and so on. But ultimately each of these is a medium, and in this case the medium is definitely *not* as important as the message.

- It is too large and disparate to be completely known or controlled by any one person or individual—or even by many.

- On a fundamental level, every chunk of its information has the exact same prominence and importance as every other chunk. However, the filters and conventions people place on top of even the most basic unit of communication establish a hierarchy of value.

Here are a few other important aspects of the creativity ethernet:

- It is organic.
- Finances do not make the network go round. In fact, the network's delicate balance can easily be knocked off center when money takes center stage, displacing the other motivations—fun, curiosity, recognition.

- There is little or no filtering or censorship. The gross, unpleasant, unpopular, and unwelcome have just as much opportunity and right to exist as anything else.
- The barriers to entry and exit are low; the two requirements are intention and effort.

People often encounter two barriers when attempting to leverage the creativity ethernet (CE)—the first, logistical; the second, psychological. Logistically, it can be challenging to find people who are frequent flyers of the CE. It is not as though they advertise in the Yellow Pages or wear logo shirts. The first part of this chapter will address strategies to locate and meet them.

The second barrier, psychological, is harder to recognize and describe. Some people have a fear of anything not deemed "normal," "ordinary," or "regular." What this really means is anything outside the mainstream. As a person or idea gets further from the mainstream, that person or idea seems more and more threatening to other people's choices. We all feel this way to a certain extent, but some people find the fringe more scary or threatening than others.

The final part of this chapter is a list of ways of working together that can benefit anyone working with CEFFs. However, it will be of most use to those people who may have fears or issues about people and ideas outside the mainstream.

WHO ARE THE CEFFS?

On the whole CEFFs are not any more creative or intelligent than any other group. However, they tend to have a closer alignment than others between work and play. Often they will do what they do at work over the weekend, except it will be for pleasure not money. Some will spend more time doing "art for art's sake" (so to speak) because it is their priority.

To summarize . . .

There is a great man who makes every man feel small. But the real great man is the man who makes every man feel great.
C. K. CHESTERTON

CEFFs are the people who deliberately and regularly cultivate their role as a part of the creation, dissemination, and use of ideas, creativity, and society outside the mainstream.

BRAINPOP

Yves Saada of BrainPOP finds it simple to identify those creative people who will add to the success of the organization. They are the ones who are engaged, actively involved, and busy. Specifically, he has a weekend warrior litmus test (our term, not his).

When he speaks of his coworkers and the people who contribute to the BrainPOP site's richness, he describes a group who "do things on weekends." For example, the director in charge of his movies is out making her own films on weekends. He routinely finds out about interesting goings-on about town by discussing what people are doing or have done over the weekend. While he might not want to do exactly what they find interesting, the point is they engage in activities that stimulate their brains. They don't just sit home and watch TV for forty-eight hours.

Saada believes the success of BrainPOP is largely due to having an engaged, interested group of people contributing to the product.

Identifying CEFFs

CEFFs are often considered the fringe element by people in the mainstream. They don't fit into any one profile or discipline or area of interest. The only thing that unites them is that they all belong to the category of nonbelongers.

We asked the president of the International Association of Graphic Designers what his biggest challenge was in creating an eLearning and mentorship program for members of his organization. He didn't miss a beat, "Trying to run an association of nonbelongers." He explained the inherent challenge of trying to figure out what solution could possibly work for a group of people who have practically made nonconformity a religion.

The same barrier is present for people who try to find CEFFs. Nonbelongers do not label themselves in ways that make them easy to locate and recognize. They don't join associations, visibly affiliate with recognizable institutions or organizations, or use standard job titles. Even when they do mainstream activities they tend to approach them from nontraditional angles: for example, going to school as nonmatriculated students and informally interning.

The only real way to discern if someone is a CEFF is to spend time with him or her. The people who on the surface may look like nonconformists or in touch with the fringe may actually be following a current trend to be on the fringe. Remember back when only Goths wore dark nail polish? A few years later a certain set of Manhattan's upper crust soon appropriated it as the in style. Then there are those who may be doing interesting things but with an entirely different agenda. One of our parents tells a story of attending meetings for a particular religious group when he was younger not because he liked the ideology but because "it was a great way to pick up women."

Even the term *nonconformist* can be tricky. We define *nonconformists* as people who are outside the mainstream, where *mainstream* is a relative term. For us, a nonconformist could easily be the right-wing conservative wearing a suit and tie where the majority are multipierced punks wearing black leather, spikes, and dyed black hair.

We present ideas in this chapter to help you begin to identify fringe people. Your instincts and intelligence will take you the rest of the way.

> *No great artist ever sees things as they really are. If he did, he would cease to be an artist.*
> **OSCAR WILDE**

Characteristics

There are certain characteristics that when looked at in combination with others can indicate a person is a CEFF. Here are a few of the many:

- Less "safe" lifestyle
- More likely to live in a city or in a less affluent part of town
- Risk seeker
- Outward appearance gives impression of nonconformity
- Very tolerant toward other people

Before you delve into finding CEFFs it is important to clearly understand what you and a CEFF have to offer each other. Managing expectations will get any relationship off on the right foot.

WHAT CAN YOU AND A CEFF OFFER EACH OTHER?

The amount of benefit that can be derived from the creative ethernet is dependent on (1) how closely aligned the nature of your organization is to the nature of the CE and (2) how receptive you and your organization are to the aspects of the CE that are different from what is familiar or comfortable to you.

If the relationship can be managed properly, there can be an excellent fit between organizations and CEFFs because each has what the other needs and wants. If you work in a typical organization, you can offer one or more of these highly desired assets:

> *A team effort is a lot of people doing what I say.*
> **MICHAEL WINNER**

- Access to capital
- Legitimacy, credibility
- Structure
- Organization, planning
- Market development expertise (converting people's ideas into viable services and products)
- Networking with people of influence
- Potential for greater public and corporate recognition
- Select business skill competencies

> *No one should drive a hard bargain with an artist.*
> **LUDWIG VAN BEETHOVEN**

In short, you and CEFFs each have something compelling and powerful to offer the other. We hope you now agree you need to leverage the frequent flyers of the creative ethernet. The next questions to be answered are how to find them and how to work with them once you've got them in your sights.

On a final note, the following suggestions will help you recruit both people who may want to work for your company and people who will want a less traditional arrangement. However, the main emphasis of the chapter is on the latter, as this seems to be the more frequent and beneficial relationship.

LOCATE THEM

We mentioned above that the only characteristic you can count on is CEFFs' lack of desiring to be grouped into one group. Although they may share some similar characteristics, often the most common one is the desire not to share things in common. And yet, even though each one of us is an individual, we are all also social animals. We need to be with other people at least for part of our lives, as a wolf needs to belong to a pack. Even isolated loners (think of J. D. Salinger, for example) have a close group of friends. This means finding these people may be more difficult than finding people who eagerly embrace mainstream groups—so it may not be too hard to find members of ASTD but much more difficult to find people who are fostering the learning of others through electronic means but do not define themselves as people in the education or training industry.

There are no hard and fast rules for doing this right. This is one of those "problems" (as we mention in our chapter on reflection time) that has no right or wrong or better or worse solution—just a solution that works for you or one that doesn't. Based on our own experience and extensive interviews, here are the suggested ways to go about finding CEFFs. The overarching best practice cited by eLearning professionals time and again was to go where the people you want to find are rather than expecting them to come to you or to find you in the places you like to frequent.

Through an Ad

When you are trying to reach people by posting an ad, your first instinct is often to go to the mainstream places—the local paper, monster.com, and so on. These communities are easy to find and mainstream, which is why everyone thinks of them first. Unfortunately, this is exactly what robs them of any effectiveness. And they have two additional limitations. The first is the narrow categories of the ads. If you want someone to fill a position that is traditional or easy to describe, great. But it is hard for these structures to accommodate ads that are less clear-cut or are focused on nontraditional relationships. When was the last time you looked in the help wanted section to find a mentor? a firm to merge with or acquire? a temporary position? What if the position you are advertising is vice president of playing? Would you list that under education? sports? entertainment? The second downside is the lack of screening. Getting 100 responses most of which fit your needs well is far better than getting thousands most of which have virtually no connection to your request. These communities result in a deluge of responses, many of which seem to come from outer space.

The exact place you put your ad will depend on the exact profile you are seeking. Because specific locations change so often, it is not feasible for us to give you a directory matching general profiles to locations. Here are some general places to start:

- Local alternative newspapers or similar publications
- Smaller or funkier recruiting agencies
- Web sites targeted at people on the fringe that display classified-type ads
- Email newsletters targeted at people on the fringe that include classifieds

Through Your Network

As we will discuss in Chapter Fourteen, the key to finding what you need is often taking that first step: finding the anchorperson or resource who will then connect you to a much bigger world previously not readily accessible. Go through your Rolodex, look through your photo albums, call up friends and family, find someone who fits the profile of someone you think has a closer connection to the CE than you. Leverage that person by asking some or all of the following questions:

> Back when this author, Samantha, was single, my friends and I used to avoid bars like the plague, preferring to do sports, take classes, and go to dinner parties—and of course meet people through work. We figured we were most likely to find compatible partners at places we went because they enjoyed being there—not because there were single people there. Since we hated to drink and do the kinds of activities people do in bars, it simply didn't make sense to try to find someone in a bar because presumably people in bars were there because they enjoyed the experience.

- If you were looking for someone who is intimately involved in sharing ideas, regularly delving into her imagination, and being intellectually curious, where would you go?
- Where do such people hang out?
- How would you approach them?
- Do you know anyone who fits this description as much as or more than you?

Through a Physical Location

As nice as it is to try to reach these people indirectly, sometimes you just have to put on your innovation shoes and go out to find them. The kinds of places to look are locations where CEFFs are likely to go, hang out, or work. It is not that the location has only those types of people. It is that the concentration of CEFFs is likely to be higher than in other destinations. Not everyone who is in a Starbucks is drinking coffee, but there are likely to be more coffee drinkers in Starbucks than in a bar or theater.

Here are some places to try:

- Public spaces (parks, open-air events, trails, gardens, lunchtime hangouts; in some foreign countries, places like piazzas and zocalos)
- Hot spots around university campuses
- Places that are currently trendy
- Airports and flights to particular locations
- Waiters and waitresses in creative parts of town
- Cafés and coffeehouses that are not big chains
- Pubs in select countries
- Nightclubs that cater to the more edgy crowd
- Participatory exercise events (biking, walking, running)
- Alternative theaters
- Fringe conferences and events
- Other places where nonconformists tend to go and congregate
- Events and activities that require thinking and attract people who are intellectually curious
- Redevelopment zones in cities—especially near housing and hangouts
- Places that are known for tolerance and acceptance of others
- Places where debates (for example, public hearings on controversial issues) take place
- Events put on by associations that are on the fringe (for example,

PETA [People for the Ethical Treatment of Animals], ACLU [American Civil Liberties Union])

- Think tanks for liberal-minded people
- Stores that sell less mainstream goods (for example, organic farmer's markets, S&M clothing shops)
- Alternative music, art, and entertainment venues
- Places like the Maverick club in London, where the norm is people who disagree with each other (these places arose as a response to gentleman's clubs, where people by nature share the same outlook)
- And they all go to Edinburgh in August . . .

SCREENING

Finding a group of people is different from finding an individual. By following some of the advice in the prior section you will be getting warmer. However, any group has variability, and any one individual may or may not be able to make a significant contribution to your organization. Now we get to the micro level, where you are seeking to sift through the masses to find those few who will meet your needs.

The following is advice culled from the people who are creating outstanding eLearning.

> *Hire people who are better than you are, then leave them to get on with it. Look for people who will aim for the remarkable, who will not settle for the routine.*
> **DAVID OGILVY**

Get the Interested Ones

Frank Pignatelli and Kirk Ramsey have X-ray vision. They can tell in less than two minutes whether someone is right for their organization, learndirect. They simply ask her to talk about herself and her interests. If the first two minutes are filled with what she thinks Pignatelli and Ramsey want to hear, she will be shown to the door.

If the picture she paints is of an interesting and involved person, the door opens wide. The actual interests are not important, nor is having a common interest. What counts is that the person be active intellectually, and so on.

Their reasoning is that interested people will bring something to the table that cannot be grown or developed in people who are not interested. These people will naturally develop eLearning that is more effective and engaging because they will be drawing from the exponentially larger base of ideas, insights, tools, and resources than a person who has a smaller circle of interests.

How do you tell if someone is interested? According to Yves Saada of BrainPOP, one of the best ways to find out quickly is to ask about life outside the office (treading only in legal areas of course). Here are some suggestions:

- Ask what she did over the weekend.
- Ask what she would do if she won the lottery and never had to work again.
- See if she has strong opinions and perspectives.
- Look for an area in which she has deep experience and passion—for example, is she widely read? A film buff? An expert on a particular person's life? Able to explain complicated or intricate scientific phenomena or events?
- See if she can readily discuss a wide variety of topics.

Storytellers

Everyone can tell a good story about something. People may not tell stories about what you think is interesting, but again, the goal is not to share passions but to have them! No matter how inarticulate or nonverbal people are, they will be able to spin a tale about something that is near and dear to their hearts, souls, or minds. The work for you is to find that topic that lights their fire.

Deep and Wide Networks

People who are engaged and interested tend to spend much of their time sharing ideas and being exposed to others. Their mental Rolodexes will read like a page from a jack-of-all-trades magazine. Whatever topic is broached they will likely know someone in that area who can be of assistance.

In some cases you will learn this just from talking to the person. In others you have to set the situation up correctly, as most people don't readily offer their friends or colleagues to strangers. Consider these ways to have a conversation that gets at this information:

- Create a hypothetical scenario. Make up a situation that is close to your own, in which you are looking for a group of people made up of those likely to positively influence your current projects: an artist if you are doing multimedia, an academic if you are looking for research to support your work, a project manager, a person who speaks many languages if you are looking to translate or localize, and so on. When you bring this up in the course of the conversation, does the other person indicate she might know some people or does she say she can't think of anyone?
- Ask about leisure-time activities. Finding out what others do in their free time will often indicate what kinds of people are in their networks.

- Ask others to send an email to their distribution lists offering whatever opportunity or assets you can provide.
- Deliberately start a conversation about the six-degrees-of-separation concept. See if others have ever been in an interesting "I knew someone who knew someone who knew someone" situation. Listen to how they say the people were connected together. If any of the areas seem relevant, probe about other people they might know in that sphere of life.

MANAGING CREATIVE PEOPLE?

Anyone who uses the words *manage* and *creatives* in the same sentence is getting off on the wrong foot. As David Ogilvy points out, getting the most from creatives involves getting stuff out of their way, not getting in their way. Creatives can be no more managed than the weather or world peace can be managed.

CEFFs are a river. People who manage to work with them successfully are riverbanks. Over time CEFFs can be gently guided and channeled in a certain direction. In exchange, you will receive the nutrients and hydration to help you grow and thrive. There will be times of flood when they will overwhelm you. And times of drought when they will not provide enough interaction or innovation. However, like investors in relation to the stock market or riverbanks in relation to rivers, you will find that seeking long-term success while accepting short-term fluctuations is the only way to achieve and sustain mutually beneficial, symbiotic relationships.

Here are some best practices derived from our own experience and our interviews:

- *Become at least minimally versed in the creative's field.* In any area of life, people appreciate when others make the effort to meet them halfway. Most people will forgive many faults in a person who is making a genuine attempt to do something nice or respectful of another person. If you are not well versed in the field or area in which the creatives around you work, surf the Web for a few minutes, glance at a book, ask a tapped-in friend, take a quick class, watch a PBS special, whatever! Just do something that will give you enough basic information about their area of expertise to show you have made an effort.
- *Provide clear direction upfront.* Managing expectations at the outset does not guarantee a smooth relationship. There have been numerous

> *I have come to the conclusion that the top man has one principal responsibility: to provide an atmosphere in which creative mavericks can do useful work.*
> **DAVID OGILVY**

times when we repeatedly explained the amount and quality of the work in both writing and verbally and an overenthusiastic creative still allowed himself to get carried away. He took on more than he could handle and both sides wound up disappointed.

Nevertheless, having expectations clearly laid out—always in writing!—will minimize these situations and lessen the aftermath when they do occur. Even when the creative feels like a soul mate, resist the urge to gloss over any aspect of the requirements. Additionally, ask the person to repeat back to you in her own words what the expectations are of her, to make sure her understanding of terms and concepts is the same as yours.

- *Avoid dress codes and other superficial restrictions.* Sure, if you are a surgeon or an astronaut a strict dress code is warranted. But if the person is going to sit in his cubicle all day staring at a monitor or if he is running around connecting wires and jiggling parts, do you really care whether he wears jeans or khakis? A dress code (or a manager who makes fun of others' dress styles) is one of the least recognized but most frequent reasons that creative people seek greener pastures and clients.

- *Develop clear deliverables and timelines, leave the rest to them.* Not only do creatives not like babysitters or micromanagers, their work suffers when they are operating in that environment. At the outset do a detailed chart of what is to be provided when. Then leave them to their own devices. If the schedule starts to slip because of them, either you have the wrong creative working on the project, your schedule was unrealistic, or a problem has arisen. It is your job to find and remove whatever that obstacle is, within reason. Contrary to popular belief, the majority of creatives when left to their own devices and given clear and reasonable expectations, will deliver. Additionally, creatives often get work done in ways that are nontraditional. We have worked with people who went shopping, went Rollerblading, and took cooking classes as part of creating their deliverables. When they felt stuck, they would "self-medicate" by doing something physical or entertaining, and inevitably the deliverable would land on the right desk and be met with great acclaim. Hovering over them will only hinder their creative process and delay results.

- *Build in reviews before the point of no return.* If you have never worked with a particular person before or if the project has high visibility,

There are very few men of genius in advertising agencies. But we need all we can find. Almost without exception they are disagreeable. Don't destroy them. They lay golden eggs.
DAVID OGILVY

build in several opportunities to review whatever work has been done early on. For example, if the person is writing a script, do not make the rough draft the first consultation moment. Ask for the outline of ideas, then the concepts, and so on. This enables drastic changes to be made with little anger or resentment. Once the rough draft is written (or the animation finished, or the design created, and so forth) the creative will resent having to redo the entire effort because you didn't build in earlier checkpoints.

- *Make it clear the project is about meeting the client's needs, not the creative's needs.* Creatives often take on tasks because they are a challenge. But there are instances where a project is just a project, with due respect to Freud. The creative might not want to stop until she's written something worthy of a Pulitzer Prize or drawn something Walt Disney would come back from the dead just to marvel at. The client just wants it to be on time and to meet the "pretty good" criterion. Make it clear when speccing the project that the ultimate judge is the client and that the person must be willing to put her own desires and feelings about the client's judgment or taste aside.

- *The carrot is mightier than the stick.* Creatives are their own worst enemy. It is not uncommon for the punishment they regularly give themselves (often in the form of silent verbal abuse and frustration at not being perfect) to be much harsher than anything you could dole out. Which is just one of the many many reasons why they do not respond to external punishments. The best strategy for fostering a long-term positive relationship is to continually use rewards. Several of the other suggestions in this section detail rewards that will be highly effective with creatives (for example, time to be creative, help in promoting their nonwork creative products, and so on).

- *Provide concrete evidence upfront that your views are legitimate and that your conclusions result from serious thought and not just an opinion.* The easiest way to lose credibility—and increase frustration— when dealing with a creative is to act as if your feedback is off the cuff or derived from ignorance. The person who sees a drawing or hears a presentation or looks at a storyboard and immediately dismisses it with little more than "it's just wrong" as an explanation is undermining his own power. This does not mean your feedback can't be instinctive or intuitive. That will be respected as long as it is presented in a way that indicates you went through a genuine process of thinking about the other person's work and why you want it changed.

- *Don't penalize creatives for your lack of planning or change of strategy.* Suppose you go into a store and buy a blue suit for a wedding. The next day you find out it is going to be a black-tie event. Would you go back to the store and demand they give you a tuxedo without your spending any more money on it and without returning the blue suit? No way. The fastest way to burn bridges and lose talent is to consider this acceptable behavior on your part. All too often creatives are asked to make modifications to the work they have already done because the client has had a change of heart or strategy. This is no more acceptable (without additional pay) than demanding that Bloomingdale's give you that tuxedo—unless of course you worked with the creatives to build multiple strategy and direction changes into the initial budget.

- *Encourage creatives not to take style differences personally.* There is *nothing* more frustrating to us than having a person who is extremely talented break down in tears because the client or department or whatever didn't like her ideas or execution. In so many cases it is just an example of people with different tastes, not talents.

- *Provide lots of room for reflection and musing.* As we described earlier, few creative leaps are made without some time away from the "lab." People need to have time away from anything that remotely reminds them of the questions they are dealing with in order to come up with genuinely creative solutions. The best method is to provide creatives with the freedom to get out of the work context without guilt or repercussions. If this is not possible, as it often isn't, at the very least provide spaces within the workplace where people can go to get away from it all. We really don't think the latter is the better option, so aim for the time away from the office if at all possible.

- *Focus on the challenge, not the money.* Money is a necessity but it is often not the principal force motivating creatives. If it was, do you think they'd be trying to make a living from their creativity? Repeatedly pointing out how a particular project will push their current level of competency or experience or thirst for challenge to a higher level (as long as it is true) is a better approach than waving dollar bills.

- *Inspire them: give them opportunities to stretch their creative legs.* Stimulation is to creatives what a fix is to drug addicts. Providing challenges of increasing intensity is a sure way to reinforce loyalty. Ideally, give them projects you aren't quite sure they can handle (but have a backup plan and make sure the challenge is not too far beyond their current abilities). If day-to-day tasks can't be made any more interesting, find other projects they might not normally undertake that you are willing to fund or support them in doing. In the long run this will pay off richly in decreased costs, increased loyalty, and better quality work.

- *Help them with their passion.* As much as they may love the work they are doing for you, chances are there is another passion they would rather be fulfilling. For those who are actively pursuing those passions (for example, filmmaking, writing, making works of art, acting, computer programming), take a proactive step to demonstrate how much you believe in them. Find ways to promote the activities they are doing for their passion. For instance, enter them in contests, encourage them to attend relevant industry events, help them to get increased media attention, and so on.

- *Share them: if you find someone good, pass him or her along.* These people will not only get a fresh perspective, they will be increasingly loyal to you.

- *Build traditions.* At the Learning Company in the early years, the vice president of marketing would walk around on Fridays giving every employee a logo item. Sometimes it was a pen, a shirt, or a mug. When the company was taken over the first thing people cited when they discussed low morale was no longer having "Diana's Fridays." At another organization, every Thursday at 5:30 the employees would gather for the "martini cart"—an airline drink cart going from desk to desk handing out drinks until everyone congregated together to celebrate the week. Creatives are especially fond of sincere traditions. Activities that foster bonding, on an alternative, voluntary attendance basis, are a key part of keeping a creatives' space lively and stimulating.

- *Fund extra courses or things they would never be able to afford.* Find out some of the "if I won the lottery" fantasies your creatives hold. Pick a subject they would enjoy learning more about and splurge! Sending them to a class they could not afford on their own (or would be unlikely to enroll in) reinforces your appreciation of their talents at the same time as it recharges their creative juices. You both win in the end.

- *Cut them off*. What? Now that you've found these great people, we're suggesting you fire them? Not exactly. People that get too comfortable in a routine might not get as many opportunities to expose themselves to fresh ideas or new innovations. Providing sabbaticals, requiring involuntary job swaps, or yes, placing term limits on certain positions or roles can combat complacency and attract people who are more interested in staying fresh.

- *And finally, never ever make them go to boring, stupid meetings!*

RESOURCE: CASTING CALL

In addition to the places discussed earlier in this chapter, the following are good places to look for talent to help you create more dramatic eLearning. Oftentimes simply sending a fax or email, posting a notice on a bulletin board, posting an opening on a Web site, or calling a program head will result in finding a deluge of talented people. Many of these creatives don't look for work through traditional channels so this is a good way to tap into an otherwise inaccessible resource.

Places to Start Looking for Graphic Designers

- Temporary agencies, such as Aquent (http://www.aquent.com), M Squared (http://www.msquared.com), The Creative Group (http://www.creativegroup.com)
- American Institute of Graphic Arts (AIGA) designer finder Web site (http://www.aiga.org), Graphic Artists Guild job Web site (http://www.gag.org/jobline/index.html)
- Communication Arts job Web site (http://www.creativehotlist.com), *HOW* magazine's Web site (http://www.howdesign.com/jobs), Coroflot (http://www.coroflot.com)
- Craigslist for your local area (http://www.craigslist.org/about/cities.html)
- Alumni and college career centers in your area, especially those for University of California at Los Angeles (UCLA), New York University (NYU), Parsons School of Design, Fashion Institute of Technology, Cooper-Hewitt, Rhode Island School of Design, and other major design universities
- Conferences, such as HOW design conference, SIGGRAPH, Success by Design

If each of us hires people who are smaller than we are, we shall become a company of dwarfs. But if each of us hires people who are bigger than we are, we shall become a company of giants.

DAVID OGILVY

Places to Start Looking for Scriptwriters

- Introductory screenwriting classes and workshops, such as Robert McKee's courses (which are very popular), the Screenwriting Conference in Santa Fe
- Mediabistro.com
- Postings on bulletin boards (virtual and real) in places where prospective writers go
- Classified ads in magazines and publications related to film, such as *Variety, Backstage, Creative Screenwriting, Hollywood Reporter, Screentalk*
- Associations, such as American Screenwriters Association, American Film Institute, Screenwriters Guild of America, Writers Guild of America
- Film festivals, especially lesser known ones
- Schools teaching film and media, such as UCLA, NYU, New York Film Academy
- Online Web sites, such as http://www.scriptmag.com/index.php (the site of *scr(i)pt* magazine), http://tvandradiojobs.com, http://lostremote.com, http://tvjobs.com, http://tvspy.com

Places to Start Looking for Playwrights and Novelists

- Publications, such as *Playbill, Writer's Digest, Publishers Weekly, Poets & Writers, American Theatre, Backstage, Editor & Publisher*
- Schools, such as Yale
- Writers' retreats and workshops, such as Dorset Colony for writers, Iowa Writers' Workshop
- Associations, such as American Society of Journalists and Writers, Authors Guild, Dramatists Guild
- Online sites, such as Craigslist, Mediabistro, http://writejobs.com; also social networking sites such as Ryze, Spoke, ZeroDegrees, Plaxo, http://freelancewriting.com, http://freelancers.com
- Small theater artist-in-residence programs

Up Next

In this chapter we have just scratched the surface of finding and harnessing the power of creatives in a way that will work within the constraints of any organization. Our next area of focus is how to harness the power of the research that is done every day, but whose contribution goes unrecognized, to achieve better results.

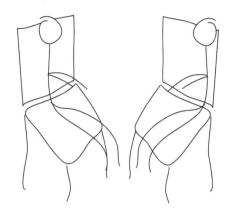

YVES SAADA

Founder of BrainPOP

ON THE GESTATION OF THE IDEA
AND HOW IT CAME TO BE . . .

Dr. Abram Khadar wanted to create tools for kids with asthma, to help explain the basics. For example, when it is very dusty or very hot outside that you should not go out. He wanted to give a few tips that would very significantly improve their condition.

He decided to create a CD-ROM to explain asthma to kids. Because there was no distribution network, the CD-ROM didn't work from a business perspective. This CD-ROM didn't go anywhere, but testing it with families we saw that they really enjoyed some portions of it. We realized they wanted snippets rather than the whole CD-ROM, [which] is usually like fifteen, twenty, fifty hours of content. Who is going to stay in front of his computer that long? They want to pay attention for like four or five minutes. This gave us the idea to create a five-minute multimedia experience. This led to us creating these health-related movies and putting them up on the Internet.

The kids loved it. They really look at it. They love repetition. In order to really understand a topic they are going to replay and replay it. You want to tell a story ten times before they really get it—the same way they love to watch the same series on TV ten times—and that's why it is very important that when you look at series like *Blue Clues* on Nickelodeon, they repeat the same thing all week long, mostly for kids that are three to five years old. We tried to create these short movies explaining complex health concepts to kids in about five minutes that they could just play again and again. We put them on the Internet in 1999; Yahoo nominated us for best site of the year. This really generated a lot of traffic.

People asked us to create stuff about science and other school topics. All of a sudden it went from families watching BrainPOP to the teachers using BrainPOP at school.

This was a successful accident. We immediately saw potential in schools. From there, we started to build a library of science content. We started with the movies then created content to work with the movies: activities that kids could do with their teachers. For example, there is an experiment page, a build the "X" lab rat, a comic with Cassie and Rita, two Californian kids. One is geeky and one is silly. The important thing is they are talking about personal issues with a connection to the topic. For example, if we do a movie about the solar system we talk about astrology. We started to get many awards and more and more Web sites connected to our site.

That was when we started to work on distribution deals. In 2000, we signed distribution deals with Yahoo and AOL which took us to the next level in terms of our traffic and credibility.

We never got venture capital money. We were looking for different things in terms of business model. Advertising didn't work, so we focused on trimming costs, because each time you watch a movie it costs us money. We looked at how we could get money. At this point the Internet started to crash. So we decided to try having people pay for our content.

We really thought it amazing that people wanted to pay for it. We started a family subscription price and a school subscription price. We didn't do any marketing; we didn't have any money for it. It all came from word of mouth, and the reason we are still doing well today is word of mouth. The only marketing expenditures we had are a bit of PR and educational conference costs to show BrainPOP to school administrators and teachers.

In schools they use it in one of two ways. One is a computer lab, and the other one is one computer in a class with a big screen all the kids see. The teacher might say, "We are going to talk about the solar system . . . so first let's watch a BrainPOP movie about the solar system and use it as an introduction to the concept." The movie is shown and then the teacher might say, "Turn to page 68. Saturn blah blah. Now close your book." She will then divide the class into two teams, go back to BrainPOP, and do the quiz. That is typical.

ON BRAINPOP'S CREATIVE PROCESS . . .

Interestingly, most of our movies are produced for nine- to fourteen-year-olds. But not one week goes by that a nursing or medical school doesn't buy a subscription. Perhaps this is because we have to explain to people who are eight years old [so] we have learned quickly that our expertise is being able to explain the difficult concepts in a very simple way in three minutes, and it is a challenge when you think about it. How do you explain the solar system or lightning in three minutes?

The way that we write our scripts, our movie, that is the really hard part, because you must have the right tone. You can't be too patriarchal or have too babyish a tone.

We get about ten to fifteen thousand emails each month from kids asking questions. Some are about homework but many are about personal issues. "I don't like to share my room with my little sister," or, "I don't like the new boyfriend of my mother," things like that.

The kids need to trust our characters. They may know it is a cartoon character, but they also know this character answers each child personally. That helps us tweak the tone, because the minute we do something that kids don't like, even the same day, we will get tons of emails objecting to it. That is a beautiful thing about the Internet, instant feedback. Also, since it is all digital, it is very easy to change it.

We don't want to replace the parents; we don't want to replace teachers. We try to encourage kids to go to their teacher or ask their parents about stuff. We are not a doctor and we are not their parents. We try to be very factual, not opinionated. Our specialty is trying to explain difficult concepts with facts. . . .

Writing the movie is really what we are good at. The way a script is going to be written will dictate how good the eLearning is. Our director of content is great because on weekends she is doing short movies. She lives this; it is not just her job. We also talk about it as a group. Every person feels they are really providing useful material for kids to learn. It is just amazing to see the impact that we have on our kids.

ON BRAINPOP'S PEOPLE . . .

Our content director was really supervising the writing and our creative director was supervising all of the animation from the beginning. They put a lot of themselves into the style of the content. One of our reasons for success is a mix of people that are very young. Both of our directors are twenty-five. They are not corrupted because this is basically their first jobs.

They have pure and original imaginations. The site has a fresh tone because their approach is very fresh. A fresh tone and attitude is critical in a creative business. When you have seen things in other places there is a tendency to apply lessons learned in those other start-ups or corporations. For example, everyday I do things that I have learned at Mattel or Microsoft or in other start-ups, which may be good on the business side. But on the creative side it's important to have a fresh outlook and approach.

It is hard to find people like that.

We look for people who understand kids. If they have a sibling of the same age that we are targeting that's good. Understanding kids is the number one priority. We also look for a certain freshness, coolness. As I mentioned before, if the person on weekends goes to movies or makes movies, they are into what we are doing here and they will talk about what they do outside work at work, which makes our movies and site better. We definitely have some people who are a little more intellectual, more interesting, more curious, more traveled. They are from around the world, and they themselves are really interested in learning.

For example, our creative director is American, but he is from Hawaii, of Japanese decent. Our comp director, she often goes to this place in Brooklyn where they have these mega Trivial Pursuit contests. It's really about sharing knowledge.

We have a very informal structure and can take many more risks than you can at a large company. I saw something that I didn't like on our Web site. I told the woman in charge before I left for lunch I'd like it changed. I know that before I get back this afternoon it is going to be changed. That can't happen at Mattel or some giant company. We are very informal and verbal. We don't have memos going around. It's a very informal structure.

ON RESULTS . . .

Kids that have difficulties at school email us and tell us they now understand concepts, understand science, understand math! You have changed the way this kid feels about school. Maybe before he wasn't verbal in school. But now he is. If you can change this one aspect of the kid's life it impacts not only what they are learning. . . . later it will impact what they will become. It will impact their social approach to school, to interacting with their teachers, other kids, and things like that. That is a huge motivation for all of us. We feel we are doing some good things and that has really improved both the kids and helped a teacher.

ON THE IMPORTANCE OF DRAMA AND METAPHOR . . .

In most of our movies, we explain things by metaphor. It is a really critical part of the writing process. For example, when we explain multiplication . . . we put Tim and Moby into the bathroom putting up tile. If you put four tiles like this and three tiles like that it is twelve. You need to accompany it with visual explanation. It is really a little accelerator, a little booster to make it easier when they first encounter a concept. We really use it as a tool to explain a concept, and characters are very important also. When we talk about the assets of a company, for us our major assets are our characters: Tim, Moby, and the gang.

DIGGING DEEPER DAILY

Leveraging Everyday Research

 Fast Forward *If you already believe the research paradigm people in eLearning are currently operating under is outdated, elitist, and unwieldy, skip to the section titled "The Research Process," later in this chapter.*

If you already know how to do research but would like a quick checklist for evaluating the soundness of research, go to "Resource 2: The Skeptic's Toolkit," at the end of the chapter.

If you don't want to learn more about how to do research but do want to see the least and the most reliable sources of research, go to "Resource 1: Reliability Continuum," near the end of the chapter.

> A desk is a dangerous place from which to watch the world.
>
> **JOHN LE CARRÉ**

INVESTORS OF YORE handed their money over to stockbrokers, pension fund managers, and other financial "experts" because conventional wisdom said the market was too risky and complex for the layperson. Experts perpetuated the model that they were the only people qualified to tackle such a risky undertaking, using a convincing smoke-and-mirrors show (including confusing jargon, complex formulas, and elaborate graphs). Many people, living under this spell, either avoided investing or invested only through professionals, for the following reasons:

- They were intimidated. As a result they didn't feel competent to master such a complex situation.
- There was a requisite high financial investment.
- They thought a large chunk of time would need to be dedicated to investment management.

BOOKSHELF BEST BETS

How to Lie with Statistics, Darrell Huff

How to Lie with Charts, Gerald Everett Jones

A Mathematician Reads the Newspaper, or, Innumeracy, John Allen Paulos

Diagnosing Organizations, Michael I. Harrison

Online Competitive Intelligence, Helen Burwell, Carl R. Ernst, and Michael Sankey

Many of the books in Sage Publications' Applied Social Research Methods series

- They thought investing was well beyond the reach of the average guy or gal.
- They saw investing as technically challenging. (How could people place purchases? sell? get quotes?)

Dear George—Is there any point in management gurus during a recession? PW, Oxford

. . . The trouble with management consultants is that the vast majority are idiots who can't get a proper job—that's why they're gurus (a title my dictionary says often is facetious). Their abilities tend to rely on making money in rising markets, which is something any fool can do. In falling markets they should be avoided at all costs—although that may mean that the sharpest among them will charge you to stay away from your business.

George Pitcher[1]

Charles Schwab, E*Trade, and others did a Toto. They pulled the curtain back and revealed this "wizard" for what it really was: nothing more than a bunch of fraudulent average Joes whose main expertise was putting on a well-rehearsed act. They introduced an alternative investing reality in which individuals were empowered with both the tools and the self-confidence to manage their own portfolios.

It is a paradigm that has stuck. In 1980, thirty million U.S. residents invested their own money. By 2002, that number had more than tripled to eighty-four million.[2] Not surprisingly, once subject to competition many of these experts didn't do any better than individuals. Some even did much worse, whether through honesty, incompetence, corruption, greed, or fraud!

This is an appropriate metaphor for conducting research in the learning and training context. A group of experts has appropriated data collection, analysis, and dissemination by waving the intimidation flag. Like investors twenty-five years ago, anyone serious about developing eLearning today is led to believe the right way of doing it requires following a complex, challenging, resource-intensive, technically demanding process. In other words, don't try this at home.

The only exception comes when an individual attempts to take on this risky and complicated undertaking with acknowledgment of others' expertise. As long as she stays within the narrow confines of the experts' cookbooks, formulas, or rigid models—which of course were learned by buying their publications, attending their seminars, or going to their conference sessions—all is well. Only then can the average Jane or Joe possibly hope to get results even half as good as those of the experts.

If you board the wrong train it is no use running along the corridor in the other direction.

DIETRICH BONHOEFFER

We have all bought into this myth. Research analysts who put out forecasts, surveys, and other reports; consultants who provide opinions and suggestions for a price; professors who sit on industry boards—all are revered in an almost cultlike way. Their results are considered at the very least above critique and at the most almost sacred. Deep down inside, people really believe these gurus can do something they themselves are not competent to do.

We know because until recently we were just as much under the sway of these Svengalis as anyone else—perhaps more so.

> *Status quo is Latin for the mess we're in.*
> **JEVE MOORMAN**

Just as the gatekeeper investment paradigm does not work in the Internet age, this paradigm is ill suited to the Knowledge and Creative Economies. Here are six reasons why this old model needs to change:

1. It offers a fundamentally adversarial relationship. This model is characterized by an underlying adversarial relationship between the client and the person performing the research. For example, in Allison Rossett's book *First Things Fast*, she suggests responding to clients who claim there is no time for analysis by
   - "Acknowledging their complaint"
   - "Selling your strategy"
   - "Describing your analysis 'game plan'"[3]

   Notice how the language implies the client must have a problem.

2. It is essentially negative, always asking how to solve a problem, fill a gap. In the new economy people need to turn this on its head and ask, What can be done to enhance people even more than they already are? What will make people take a positive perspective instead of remedying problems, see opportunities to enhance, and further develop what is being done right?

3. It is too separatist. Even the most minor needs assessments, forecasting processes, and other analysis techniques outline a group of discrete (as in separate) activities. In this day and age this is not only archaic, it is impossible. Even if the stakeholders and resource providers give researchers the luxury of extensive time and budget, the competitors, society, or the world at large will not.

4. It is disempowering. Instead of proclaiming and rejoicing in every individual's ability to do research, it promotes exclusivity and expertise.

> *Don't be too certain of learning the past from the lips of the present. Beware of the most honest broker. Remember that what you are told is really threefold: shaped by the teller, reshaped by the listener, concealed from both by the dead man of the tale.*
> **VLADIMIR NABOKOV**

Only people who have studied, practiced, and been ordained are qualified to do it. Only proprietary processes keep the huddled masses out.

5. It lacks rewards for coloring outside the lines. People are not rewarded for taking creative approaches that are not already described or condoned by the experts. Again, this goes back to the idea that a critical part of the creativity that drives economic success is finding problems no one has recognized before, not just solving problems others have discovered. The current paradigm does not value this part of creativity in research.

6. It assumes the participant and the researcher are different entities. Traditional needs assessments consistently state the goal is to find the gap between the learner's current state and the desired state. Implicit in this model is the assumption that a person who will not be participating in the learning is determining what learning needs to take place. This is the antithesis of self-directed learning.

> The shepherd always tries to persuade the sheep that their interests and his own are the same.
> **STENDHAL**

DON'T THROW THE BABY OUT WITH THE BATH WATER

In general we have seen little redeeming value in industry research experts. Many of the people who run awards ceremonies, evaluate vendors, sell industry forecasts, consult, or tour the speaker's circuit are so invested in maintaining the status quo it seems to impair their self-proclaimed objectivity and makes them resistant to looking for ways to change currently popular ideas (because these are often their own ideas!).

With that said, there are some people who have been labeled gurus who deserve respect for changing with the times and encouraging others to do so. Two examples are Jane Massey and Allison Rossett. Because this chapter is about research, we will address just the latter.

Rossett's needs assessment model and books have been widely adopted and used.[4] You'll notice in other parts of this chapter that we don't completely buy into her model. However, the difference between her stance in 1987 and her current position indicates she has not only changed with the times, she has eagerly and actively ushered them in. In 1987, she defined training needs assessment as "systematic study that incorporates data and opinions from varied sources in order to create, install, and evaluate educational . . . products and services."[5] The connotation of this statement is that assessment

Is a discrete activity, separate from the day-to-day work of an organization

Needs to be purposeful and methodic

Takes place predominantly at the start of a training program

Requires objectivity

Is done only to ascertain training products

However, the research chapter of her 2001 book, *Beyond the Podium,* reflects a significant shift toward the paradigm that is much better suited to the Creative Economy. Specifically, she greatly enlarges the scope of an assessment, suggests it be seamlessly integrated into the organization's daily activities, and emphasizes the continuous nature of the process: "continuous and virtual engagement with customers, so that products, services, and systems are tailored to match emergent needs and priorities. . . . The challenge for professionals, then, is to be both responsive and anticipatory, immediate and perpetual . . . to recognize that it is critical to already have some handle on the global staff's strengths and weaknesses, even before asking . . . and be continuously updating their intelligence. . . ."[6]

Much progress still needs to take place before the new research paradigm can be declared ubiquitous (see our definition later in the chapter for more details). However, Rossett's new approach reflects how a person with a vested interest in continuing the status quo can choose not to and instead be in favor of pushing for a new and better way.

We hope this chapter will be one small step toward bringing about the eLearning world's ideological equivalent of what happened when Schwab and others arrived on the investment scene. We want to encourage people to herald in a new paradigm of research for training. One in which democracy and empowerment are the norm. Here are some of the main principles of this new paradigm we envision:

> *Opportunities are never lost. They are simply taken by others.*
> **ANONYMOUS**

1. *Empowerment of individuals.* Every individual has the talent to do the requisite research to drive outstanding business results through eLearning. If individuals feel the need to develop additional skills, these can be honed through experience, self-study, apprenticeship, observation, or other learning methods.

2. *Seamless integration of research and activities.* Research activities are seamlessly integrated into the day-to-day operations of the organization. Needs assessments, mini–needs assessments, and even rapid needs assessments conducted exclusively by training professionals are all just the same product packaged differently. Today's economy requires an entirely different approach: like breathing, circulating blood, thinking about and doing other bodily functions, research activities need to be constantly and seamlessly performed in conjunction with all other activities.

3. *Intuition and emotion as an integral part of research.* Intuition and emotion are critical to accurate data collection. Most data collection scriptures emphasize the importance of objectivity and quantification.

If you can't put a number on it or observe it, it should be excised from the findings. However, as the saying goes, "Figures don't lie, but liars figure." Emotion is always going to come into research, so we say better to leverage it than ignore it.

4. *Complementary outsourcing, not replacement outsourcing.* Hiring outsiders to do research should be done only when time is short or the desire to do one's own research doesn't exist.

5. *Avoidance of incestuous research.* Research purchased from people whose existence is almost exclusively dependent on the health of the eLearning industry should be regarded with skepticism and avoided whenever possible.

6. *Use of an open source model.* A paradigm in which experts dictate what is and isn't done is fundamentally incompatible with an environment in which anyone is able to freely share information with others—such as the Internet. The increasing proliferation of free tools and reports (or reports for a minimal cost—say under $30) and the ability of anyone to almost effortlessly post his or her own content is already starting to change the face of research. In the five years since we first posted our eLearning readiness assessment, free for anyone's use, over five million people have used it, elaborated on or changed it, and created similar assessments. We, in turn, have expanded well beyond the boundaries and borders of what the experts dictated was the right way to do things, simply by connecting with the work of others. A prime example of this is our chapter on heutagogy, a concept that we discovered largely through our peer network.

The first part of this chapter reconceptualizes two common aspects of research: the definition and the steps. We reposition each to deliberately move away from the ideology characterized by the limitations we listed earlier and toward one that embodies more democratic empowerment principles.

The second part presents a collection of alternative ideas for finding the information you need. To best serve our readers we decided to keep this section really practical. So the ideas reflect the spirit of the new paradigm, but they are set within the framework and context of a traditional research project. The same old primary and secondary data collection techniques are supported but in alternative ways. There is an entire world beyond this.

We also call your attention to two important chapter resources at the end of the chapter. The first is a reliability continuum. We map all of the sources you could use for research according to how reliable and trustworthy they are.

The second item is our skeptic's toolkit. This is a combination X-ray machine and reliability litmus test for those times when you use external research products or resources. It describes what to look for and look out for. Any person performing research with nothing to hide will eagerly and willingly share the information you need to assess the validity of her findings.

I CAN'T DEFINE IT, BUT I'LL KNOW IT WHEN I SEE IT: DEFINING RESEARCH

In the sidebar "Don't Throw the Baby Out with the Bath Water," we briefly focused on the definition of one aspect of research, needs assessment, and how Allison Rossett has helped herald a new paradigm. This paradigm broadens the focus from the narrow target of training needs to a wider systems view of organizational needs.

This is a step in the right direction of reconceptualizing research for the Creative Economy. Now more progress needs to be made. Specifically, it's time to reposition the process in order to start changing the metaphor people currently operate under (reminder: the metaphor we are seeking to change is one where experts control the process and accurate results).

Research is . . .

Constantly mining the intuitions, emotions, data, and opinions surrounding you in order to take steps that will increase the success of the organization and society.

This definition encourages people to see a paradigm characterized by the following (in addition to what we spotlighted in the sidebar "Don't Throw the Baby Out with the Bath Water"):

- *Inclusivity.* Anyone and everyone is included as practitioners and researchers. No distinction (and therefore no division) is made between experts, professionals, trainers and learners, laypeople, and other participants and subjects.

- *Empowerment.* Not only can anyone do it, learners and participants are expected to take responsibility for a large part of the assessment.

- *Emotion.* The touchy-feely stuff that already always comes into play when people collect data is given a seat at the table and made explicit as a contributor—even respected!

- *Seamlessness.* The research people already intuitively perform (along with additional deliberate techniques) becomes a part of the regular day-to-day workings of the organization and beyond.

- *Awareness of environment.* It expands the scope of results from the small view of a department or organization to include the greater surrounding community (think Whole Foods).
- *Cooperativeness.* Instead of the adversarial positioning currently adopted (for example, needing to "sell" a sponsor on the validity of the research), this definition reflects a system where everyone is on the same side, working together toward a common goal.
- *Optimism.* Most low-level research definitions focus on either gap analysis or problem solving. Our definition implies the research is being done to get better, without making any judgments about where the individuals or organization may be already. If your organization does not have problems (or doesn't wish to address them) "focusing on problem areas"[7] will only work against you.

We expect readers to respond with the pragmatic argument: "Sounds great but it's so unrealistic! How can we possibly figure out what the needs are of our organization if we have this ephemeral process?" One answer is that we have provided help in the rest of this chapter. All the content and suggestions included germinate from this ideology and are designed to help herald this new paradigm.

> Contentment: The smother of invention.
> **ETHEL MUMFORD**

Another answer, equally valid, is that we don't have an answer for you. As we have stated numerous times, our goal with this book is not to give you some form of "cookbook" with fleshed out step by steps or a boxed cake mix that you just add water to and stir. What we want to do is encourage a change in mindset, in metaphor. Some people exposed to the information here will get aha moments or at the least new ideas. Of these people, some will expand upon or create tools that reflect a slightly different paradigm. These will be the people who will help their organizations leverage the economic power of creativity. But each person will need to find his or her own way.

On a tangible level, here is just one example of how simply framing something differently can entirely change results. Assume you go to a manager to do a presentation on doing research for eLearning. You might use the definition Rossett suggests and describe the process using her outline in the book *Beyond the Podium*. This includes suggestions such as:

- "Focusing on problem areas"
- "Defining future desirable state"
- "[T]he question is *why*. Why are reviews flawed?"
- "What will the professional do about the situation now?"

Alternately, you might use our definition and focus on

- Finding opportunities to remain outstanding and grow with the times
- Capitalizing on the research everyone is already doing, with minimal extra costs or time
- Building ways of rewarding anyone who supplies valuable suggestions (which are accompanied by research results) about any topic—with extra support for covering their own development
- Demonstrating how intuition has contributed to the organization's success already and how to heighten recognition of translating intuition into data others can use
- Showing how the research results can generate revenue in and of themselves (for example, when used as part of the marketing and public relations efforts)

In the first instance the sponsors or stakeholders will react as they have always reacted, and you will be forced to react as you have always reacted—finding better ways to sell the idea, to defend your position, and so on. We know because we have been there.

In the latter instance the listener is more likely to see the research as an opportunity and not a threat. Once again we know this because this is the approach we now take, and it has been successful each time. For example, we recently did some research under this paradigm with one of the world's largest banks. It was an organization that would have resisted research under the old paradigm. We proposed something similar to the options we just listed. Not only did we get the contract, in the long run we wound up providing the research to five of the top seven financial services firms, each of whom used it to make a profit for themselves as well as to garner positive publicity.

The brain is a wonderful organ; it starts working the moment you get up in the morning and doesn't stop until you get into the office.
ROBERT FROST

THE RESEARCH PROCESS

Some research firms such as IDC, Gartner, and Accenture want you to feel baffled or intimidated, or both, by their research process (aka *methodology*). Others, such as the small guru research shops, seem to cloak their methodologies by failing to post them in any public forum—including their Web site.[8]

The purpose of all the elaborate charts, graphs, and lengthy explanations (or lack thereof) is to give off the impression that this is some mysterious or complex process, to make the average person feel this other group has the

Like other occult techniques of divination, the statistical method has a private jargon deliberately contrived to obscure its methods from non-practitioners.
G. O. ASHLEY

tools and techniques to accomplish what she never could. Most important, the purpose is to elevate the firm and its work so far above anyone else that the work will appear bulletproof and therefore not subject to scrutiny. The tagline for many of these firms could easily be, "How dare you question our work or results!"

In reality, research is not about a secret or proprietary process. It is also not guaranteed. (Which of the big research firms predicted the attacks of September 11, 2001, and their aftermath?) Anyone (yes, you read that right), anyone can do research. We'll even be so bold as to take our statement one step further: we all do research already.

Have you ever bought a house? a car? picked a vacation spot? found a unique gift for a partner or spouse? found a new job? troubleshot a computer problem? determined which school to send your kids to? voted for a cause or a candidate? Everyone does research and most people do it really really well. They just do it so naturally they rarely think much about it. They don't ask how what they do everyday can be carried over into their professional lives.

In this section we are going to deconstruct and demystify the research process. Typically this is broken down into steps. We despise this artificial construction—describing research in this way is the antithesis of doing it. Every minute of every day people are doing each step concurrently. Sometimes they skip steps (for instance, there are some people who never formulate a problem but stumble across a solution, others who work only from the data they already have and never collect more). Sometimes people get a hunch but have no data to support it.

Instead, we have grouped what most people put into steps into activities. There are five activities that people do every day that constitute research. Because it can be so hard to nail down when each takes place and how they feed each other, we decided a better way of describing them is to simply list the activities, not to group them in any form of hierarchy.

The following sections will provide some ideas on how to make the most of each type of activity.

Knowledge does not keep any better than fish.
ALFRED NORTH WHITEHEAD

Activity 1: Formulate or Define the Problem (Formulate the Goal)

Better information starts with defining the problem realistically and accurately. This is the main topic covered in Chapter Fifteen, on reflective thinking. We just touch on it briefly here. Generally, two things get in the way of proper formulation:

1. The natural human tendency to see oneself and the situations one is in through old familiar and comfortable glasses

2. Insufficient use of intuition and sensitivity skills

The best illustration of the first hurdle to be overcome comes from Wayne Hodgins. He attributes the demise of the iceman to an inaccurate assessment of job function. Icemen framed their role as the people who deliver ice. When ice was no longer needed they became obsolete. If they had seen themselves as the people who keep food cold they might have become founders or executives of Frigidaire or Sub-Zero (or Viking!).

Often 90 percent of problem resolution is all about reframing the problem. A perfect example is presented by Yvonne Brown of learndirect scotland. Once the organization had achieved its goal of being self-supporting, after three years of government start-up funds, the goal was to brand learndirect as a player in the global education market. Unfortunately, the legacy of its first few years as a quasi-government agency meant its image was still as a Scottish government matchmaker, setting up learners with learning providers.

Some framed the problem as a quantity issue: if the organization only got more publicity and went to more conferences it would achieve its goal. Although this might help, Brown saw the situation differently. She framed the problem as one of quality, not quantity. The question became how can we develop our own learning material that demonstrates we are not just match-makers but also fountainheads of knowledge, creativity, and solutions. This reframing enabled learndirect to take a guerrilla approach that would have an impact well beyond what its budget and resources would allow were the organization to use that more traditional quantity approach to public relations.

The second hurdle, insufficient use of intuition and sensitivity, is more difficult to overcome—not because people don't have those qualities or because some have more than others but because for so many years many people have been taught to suppress their instincts and intuitions, to subsume them in favor of scientific or what-you-can-see approaches. Chapter Fifteen is designed to help you get in better touch with your inner instincts and intuition so we will not go into that here. You can also find more sources in the ". . . And Even More Reading!" section later in this book.

One cannot evaluate an innovation by asking potential customers for their views. This requires people to imagine something they have no experience with. Their answers, historically, have been notoriously bad. People have said they would really like some products that then failed in the marketplace. Similarly, they have said they were simply not interested in products that went on to become huge market successes.

DONALD NORMAN

Getting more adept at framing the research question will prevent opportunities from slipping through your fingers and landing in someone else's hands.

Activity 2: Select Research Methods and Sources for Data Collection

There are only two ways to collect data: primary research and secondary research.

Primary research is the academic term that describes going straight to the horse's mouth. You're collecting information and opinions from people directly by interviewing them, listening to them in focus groups, observing them, and so on. Typically this is raw data that you need to sift through and organize. Another way of doing primary research, all too often overlooked, is to *be* your target market!

RESEARCH AT BRAINPOP

Yves Saada believes he has the perfect formula for research and a whole lot of reviewers, judges, teachers, parents, and kids agree. Does he have the time or money to commission a study on his audience or trends? Even if he did, the world of teens and preteens is so dynamic that by the end of the study the information would be obsolete. Instead he relies on two guerrilla methods to keep his finger constantly on the pulse of his audience.

First, he maintains a staff that can relate to BrainPOP's audience. Many are twenty somethings or even younger people who are in touch with popular culture and trends. The director who makes BrainPOP's movies is twenty-five and the other key director of the company is also twenty-five. She ensures the right tone, style, and content is created. Too parental or authoritative and it will be shut out. Too artificial or passé and it will be mocked. In order to be effective and reach the audience the director and other staff need only do what they already do: remember what it was like for them six years before and stay close to people that age now.

Second, Saada has made feedback such an integral part of the offering that from the customer perspective it is simply "community." Saada repeatedly emphasizes how the community keeps the product alive and successful. He has developed characters that kids, parents, and teachers interact with every day through email. Through this system, Saada is able to capture critical data about trends, preferences, concerns, and other things in a kid's world that will subsequently influence the product and community. For example, a child might email to ask advice about getting rid of a new brother or sister; another might follow up with some questions that weren't answered in the video.

All in all Saada has created an economical way for research to be so integrated into every facet of the organization that it does not require any additional effort or time. It is simply done as part of the course of daily events.

Secondary research is any information obtained from a middleperson, someone who has interpreted the raw data of another person. The surest way to identify second-hand research is see whether it contains opinions and messages that are aggregated from more than one person. A second hint is that the content is coherent and well organized. Some examples of secondary research are

- Academic papers
- Articles in journals, magazines, on the Web, and so forth

- Research reports called "analyst's findings," "benchmarking reports," and so on
- Books (like this one!)

If you are going the secondary research route, you will still carry out the activities discussed here, but you will be analyzing another researcher's work, not raw data.

Activity 3: Collect Data

Some data are better than others. The most helpful data have some of these characteristics: they

- Are more accurate
- Are more reliable
- Have more information
- Cost less money
- Take less time
- Are more respected

The less helpful data are less accurate and reliable, have less information, cost more money, take more time, and are less respected. As a result they are basically the opposite of what is listed above and don't shed as much light as desired on the question you are trying to answer.

In this activity the astute and effective eLearning professional is looking for any and all information that could be helpful. Keeping eyes and ears open in all places at all times will help greatly. Intuition, experience, and being in the right place at the right time will go a long way.

KEEPING EYES AND EARS OPEN

Two interviewees (who wish to remain anonymous) told us these data collection stories:

Scooping the competition. One told us about information gathering through public transportation. He works for the eLearning division of a bank and regularly rides the train between two cities. He was sitting next to a group of men who, he quickly learned, worked for a competitor. They were talking among each other, loud enough for other passengers to hear, about a new offering to be introduced in a few months. The bank employee immediately contacted the right person at his bank, resulting in its being able to match the offering.

Flying high. Another person was eager to get new clients. She called a prospect from a prominent airline to see if there was any interest. The prospect revealed detailed plans of a similar offering the prospect's airline was going to be bringing out imminently. The person seeking new clients then phoned the major competitor, explaining what the first airline was about to do and providing a quick way for the competitor to beat that offering.

Activity 4: Analyze Data

"Figures don't lie, but liars figure." Few remarks do a better job of summing up this research activity. In this activity the data that have been collected are sorted to find patterns and indicators that become the foundation of future decisions and actions.

Like Zyklon B gas or a screwdriver, data themselves are neutral. Alas, few researchers are. So data are typically analyzed through the refraction of the glasses that a particular researcher may not even realize he or she is wearing.

Activity 5: Select a Proper Course of Action (Supporting Evidence in Hand)

After the data are collected and analyzed a case is made for a course of action.

ALTERNATIVE DATA COLLECTION IDEAS

Now that we have covered the basics, we are going to describe how eLearning professionals can accomplish these activities in a guerrilla way. We have divided our tips on data collection into primary and secondary collection.

Primary Data Collection

The best reason for doing primary research is the greater likelihood of accuracy. In both primary and secondary research there is always the possibility the research participants will present inaccurate information (often unintentionally). However, in secondary research this initial problem is compounded by the biases of the person analyzing or organizing the raw data.

There can be numerous barriers to doing your own primary research, not the least of which are recruiting a large sample size, creating the questions to be asked, and taking the time to crunch the data. One of the biggest barriers for business to business (b2b) eLearning firms can be the limited customer base. If you have only 100 target customers, how do you get primary data from them and sell to them at the same time? Here are our top ways to do your own primary data collection while minimizing these barriers.

1. *Recruit consumers for focus groups or interviews nontraditionally.* There is little people prefer to do more than give their opinion on something. Throw in some money and you'll make some people ecstatic. If you are seeking consumer input, focus groups are a great way to go,

but the trick is to find the people you really want, not addicts who make a living learning how to "play" the people conducting the group. In other words, you want to try to get people who are genuinely in your target market, not just looking to make an income from focus groups. Just as when you are seeking people who are regulars on the creativity ethernet (Chapter Thirteen), you will have the best chance of success if you go where these people play. Here are some places to look:

- Post paper flyers in the places your target market hangs out.
- Post electronic notices on discussion boards and classifieds on relevant Web sites. (For example, do you want people who travel? Post notices on sites with bulletin boards for people who travel. Want younger, more computer savvy people? Post on Craigslist or another community-based site. Want seniors? Use the AARP site.)
- Pay for ads in very small local newspapers or newsletters that focus on your special interest or geography.
- Chat with people who are buying products or services similar to or in competition with your own, and if they seem desirable, ask them to join your focus group.

2. *For b2b focus groups: move the mountain to Mohammed.*
   - Place ads in newsletters of special interest to local industry groups.
   - Carry a card around with you at all times explaining who you are, the type of research you do, and the logistics of participating. Hand one out whenever you meet someone who might be interested in participating, or take his card and enter him into your database of possible subjects.
   - Run focus groups during industry events where the people you seek will be in attendance.
   - Develop a pilot program or tester forum in which a regular group of people participate who have agreed to provide feedback in exchange for some benefit (getting the product earlier, cheaper, with more features, and so forth).

3. *Use Web conferencing to conduct focus groups and interviews.* If your target market is computer savvy and has computers, which seems logical for eLearning professionals, Web conferencing systems can be your best friend. In addition to the obvious benefits, they offer

- Anonymity (if desired)
- Ability to span distances
- Ability to effortlessly introduce multimedia
- Ability to record for sharing and posterity

One thing that needs to be managed is focus: make it clear at the outset that other applications running on the person's desktop and other distractions (phone, kids, and so on) must be avoided. This is an excellent solution for corporate focus groups or interviews because the participants are likely to have ready access to fast connections and the technology.

4. *On-the-spot interviews: using handheld devices and wifi laptops.* We all spend so much time focusing on how to use technology for learning that we sometimes forget some applications that are right in front of us. The proliferation of wireless networks that connect to small mobile devices (PDAs, laptops, and such) means that data can be obtained on the fly at a moment's notice. Suppose you are standing in line at a supermarket or attending a meeting. You see someone who looks like a good person to interview. Whip out your handheld (with access to any of the zillions of mobile networks) and have the prospect try out your offering. Or ask the person some questions and immediately feed the answers into a database at your site. Or find a way to solve a problem the person is having by searching through your systems (capturing the problem for later collation, of course). At the very least, conduct an interview then and there. Offer the person an on-the-spot incentive: show him you are emailing him a coupon for the product of his choice or a date with a Swedish supermodel (just checking to see if you are still awake).

5. *Form your own listserv.* For several years our research firm, Research Dog, ran a listserv called Digging Deeper. We asked about 500 members, including thought leaders such as Wayne Hodgins and Eilif Trondsen, to share their perspectives on controversial eLearning issues about once a month. It was a great way to both encourage and provoke people into giving information about the true convictions and beliefs they hold that influence eLearning. A skillful moderator will be able to constantly pull a fresh stream of information from members and keep them engaged, as long as she is not afraid to cut through the bull and call people to task.

6. *Become a journalist.* If you have the skills and persistence to become a regular contributor to a *real* magazine (we're not talking about writ-

ing one or two articles for *T+D* or *Training* magazine, we mean
Newsweek, Time, Forbes, and the like), this will open doors to interviewing people who otherwise would not give you the time of day.
You'd be surprised how many CEOs will open their doors and their
phone lines to a person who is interviewing them for *Newsweek* or
the *Wall Street Journal.* Of course for many people this is unrealistic.
If you simply lack the writing skills, you can hire a firm like ours to
do the writing. If you have priorities other than getting articles in big
newspapers and don't want to hire anyone to help you with that
effort, create your own publication, one that is not just a shabby
excuse for a marketing piece. Make it something people *outside* the
industry will really want to read and pay for. If you make it a
respected piece, you will (down the road) gain entrée to people who
might otherwise be off limits.

7. *Give back more than you take.* In the eLearning world the beta testing
concept is somewhat unfeasible because companies have more to
lose than to gain. From their perspective, being given the privilege
of testing out your system before the kinks are worked out can be just
as appealing as getting a free car before the new braking technology
has been tested. Unlike the consumer market, where people are willing to go to great lengths to save $39.95, in the b2b market, organi-
zations need to invest so much time and energy just to get to the
point of deciding to test your system, let alone the effort of playing
with a buggy computer program, that it is simply not worth the hassle.

Turn this on its head by providing something your subjects want and
perhaps haven't gotten anywhere else. Only you know what that is,
but here are two best practices you can draw from: We were doing a
project for one of the world's largest banks that required constant
benchmarking of what other financial service firms were doing to
develop their employees, with and without eLearning. We might
have been able to go to the competitors once or twice without
revealing the real agenda, but this would be both unethical and
uncomfortable. Instead, we formed a benchmarking forum that
attracted top human resource professionals (vice presidents and
above) from the world's biggest banks. As part of the membership we
required they make themselves available to answer questions about
two hours per month and attend a quarterly two-day benchmarking
summit where they would get to meet their peers. In exchange they
would be provided with an executive summary of the findings for

I saw the angel in the marble and carved until I set him free.
MICHELANGELO

each topic examined and the option was available to purchase the full report. These clients got all the information they desired, our integrity was maintained, and members received a valuable service well worth their time.

8. *Change the spin entirely.* If you want to stay in tune with the needs and wants of one particular group over a long period of time (five or ten years), the best way to get the information you need is to approach data collection from a different perspective. Instead of seeing it as extracting information, look at it as providing members of a special interest forum with content that will engage them. Like the suggestion made in item 7, this gives more than it takes. Perhaps your target market is employees who love to play multiplayer computer games or vendors who enjoy going to the gym or doing Pilates or senior executives who golf.

Whatever the interest, provide an arena in which it can be discussed and done. Include some of the following components: a full expenses-paid day of enjoyment, an email listserv, magazine subscriptions, amenities such as beer or soft drinks and food, and other activities and materials that promote dialoguing and interaction. At the right times, interject some questions relevant to your product in an appropriate and seamless way. If this is done skillfully it will simply come across as a conversation. If done incorrectly it risks being seen as an interrogation or an inappropriate intrusion into private areas. This is not the right forum for detailed product or service questions that have nothing to do with the activity at hand. However, it is a great opportunity to get a handle on other research topics that should be equally of interest to you. For example, with the senior executives, ask what they see as the top priorities for their organization over the next year, what the biggest issues dogging their firms now are, and so on. For employees, ask what could be done to ensure they are able to do their job better, what types of learning have been worth their time over the last year, which types were a waste and why, and so on.

9. *Hire students to do forecasting for you.* As a general rule, we despise forecasting. If anyone could genuinely do it well, he or she wouldn't be selling it to you as a service (when was the last time Warren Buffett offered you his stock picking services?). Still, just as there will always be people who read horoscopes, there are some businesspeople who really really want to know what the future will hold. One

option is to pay $5,000 to get a report (be sure you get a guarantee of getting your money back if the data do not prove accurate). A better choice is to contact people in the economics, sociology, or even statistics department of a good university. See if they can point you to a few graduate students who are known for their ability to do forecasting and who know the area you are interested in. You can hire them on a project basis to do a forecast for you, and it is likely to be more accurate and less costly than anything obtained from the establishment. As an added bonus, it will become your property to share with as many people as you wish in any way you want (did someone say marketing vehicle?).

10. *Send out a query to places other than those in your target market.* Services such as Profnet enable you to email a group of experts who have voluntarily signed up to receive emails from people who need experts to quote in publications. Most recipients will not be eLearning professionals, which is a great advantage if you are looking for experts or authorities outside the field.

11. *Always use critical incident methodology.* If you are not sure what this is or how to use it, look at the ". . . And Even More Reading" section.

12. *Offer substantial case studies and anecdotes.* Remember the last time you saw one of those TV charity appeals showing emaciated kids with flies on their mouths and desperation in their eyes? Think how much more impact this had on you than all the statistics put together on child poverty or hunger. Numbers persuade but people convey. When you are doing your research look out for those case studies that will tell an emotionally charged story. For every cold statistic have at least one or two of these real-world people examples in your back pocket.

13. *Make your market research methods transparent to others.* The more your research is open to scrutiny, the more likely people are to believe your results. Even if they wind up not agreeing with your findings, your reputation for integrity and good intentions will remain intact. If you have a reason to shroud your methods in secrecy, your audience and critics have good reason to question not only your results and skills but also your honesty.

Secondary Data Collection

For gregarious extroverts, primary research is about as good as it gets. For people who prefer the comfort and safety of an Internet connection and a search engine, secondary research is just so much easier. The only drawback is accuracy. As we have repeatedly emphasized, there are people out there who have a vested interest in keeping their positions and power. This can result in deliberately or inadvertently biased findings.

A prerequisite is to become an educated consumer. Naivete and innocence are what allow many gurus and experts to keep prices high and integrity low. One step in the right direction is to use a few of the techniques in our skeptic's toolkit (presented later in this chapter) when evaluating and assessing secondary research. In addition, consider these approaches:

1. *Use anchor terms.* For any topic, be it spelunking or eLearning, certain keywords will open doors. We call them *anchor terms* because finding the right word sets off a chain reaction: it sends you down multiple paths, each of which leads to multiple other paths. Let's look at a great example. If you do a search on eLearning via Google your first-page results will include an eLearning magazine, two eLearning organizations, and macromedia. If you search on "online learning" (with quotation marks), the first page has on it several vendors, a learning disabilities site, and a gateway to curriculum resources. These are two very different paths. When we followed the first one by clicking on www.europa.eu, which is the Web site for the EU's education initiatives, we could then follow the trail to more European resources, links, and so forth. When we followed the second path by clicking on www.online-learning.com, we were led to one of the organizations discussed in this book—a Canadian vendor who does not have further links. In this case both paths would open doors but very different ones. It is important to try many combinations until you find the right word to open the magic door.

2. *Get ahead of the curve.* Of all the benefits of the Internet and connectivity, one of the best is the ability to be a filter feeder. One little proactive effort on your part will reap multiple results. Do your research to find the organizations that specialize in doing research on eLearning, lifelong learning, productivity, or whatever. See how many of them have email lists you can sign up for, either as an average person or as a PR recipient, and sign up! Without having to constantly scan hundreds of Web sites you'll be the first to know about important findings—way before magazines or conferences have gotten them on the radar screen.

3. *Use industry analyst libraries.* Maybe it's just us, but spending $5,000 on a generic industry report that may or may not answer some of our

basic questions seems insane. A better option is to visit the libraries of big analyst firms. You aren't allowed to bring more than a pencil and paper and they don't have any copy machines. But in a few hours you'll be able to find the nuggets you need to beef up that presentation. If you really do need that whole report desperately and can't afford it, try putting out a query on a relevant listserv to buy it used.

4. *Receive industry analyst press releases.* Another way to get just the high-level facts without spending money on reports is to sign up for email notifications and press releases from those same research agencies. They will give the big-picture statistics you might be eager to cite in reports and may even alert you to new information you didn't seek out.

5. *Dig through the archives of your own organization's files.* When I, Sam, worked at the Learning Company, I once spent two days reorganizing my manager's office. This manager had been in the education industry for over twenty-five years. I found hundreds (literally) of extremely valuable research reports and studies. Many of them were important for providing historical context. However, an equal number had findings that were timeless: information about pedagogy, andragogy, and heutagogy. Your own organization may be sitting on a gold mine of secondary research data. If you are in a large organization or if there has been a great deal of turnover, it is critical to send out emails and dig around looking for anything that might affect current activities.

6. *Get a library card from major universities and cities.* Few of us can afford access to major online research databases such as Lexis-Nexis, Proquest, and Abi-Inform on our own. However, these and other data repositories are readily available through many major libraries. Many licensing agreements restrict access to on-site library patrons. However, many others (and that number is growing) are accessible from home for people who hold cards from the subscriber library. It is easy enough to get a library card from your local public library, but chances are, even if you live in a major city (as we do in New York), there are many databases not licensed for home use through the local institution. Here are a few ways to get home access to major databases.

- Join the alumni association of your alma mater if the school library has good remote database access. Often, for a small additional fee, you will also be entitled to an alumni library card that is valid for a year.

- Sign up for a super cheap extension class at a major university when enrollment includes a library card (assuming the library has stellar home access).

7. *Conduct citation searches.* One of the best ways to uncover academic research you might not otherwise find is to use a process called citation search. There are databases that do a form of reverse look-up. Once you have the author or title of a paper that is relevant and interesting, you can type the name of the author or the paper into the citation search program. The results will be a list of all the other papers by other researchers that cite that particular paper or that author. The real beauty of this is that in the case of a paper it will find only researchers and work that build on that original paper (because it is obviously impossible for a work that predates the paper to cite it).

8. *Become a board member or leader of local organizations.* It is difficult for the average professional to become a board member to the large research organizations—for example, the Organization for Economic Cooperation and Development (OECD). However, it is relatively easy to become one for a smaller organization that might have access to research. Local American Society for Training and Development (ASTD), Society for Human Resource Management (SHRM), and International Society for Performance Improvement (IPSI) groups are prime examples.

9. *Affiliate with a student.* Students often get access to important information for free or for a minimal fee. Hire an intern to do research a few hours a week. Task the student with keeping current on the research that is out there and presenting the "Reader's Digest" version to you once a week or month.

RESOURCE 1: RELIABILITY CONTINUUM

There are seven sources that can provide you with raw data or prepackaged research results. We have mapped them on a continuum from most to least reliable.

Most Reliable

PASSIONATE ABOUT RESEARCH (RESEARCH PROFESSIONALS)

The first source consists of research experts who are in the research business and not tied to any particular industry. Typically they do research because they really enjoy doing it and decided to follow that path as a career out of passion (as evidenced by the low salaries they typically get). They may be experts in quantitative analysis, focus groups, questionnaires, anthropology, and so on. This is the group of people who are least vested in providing you with a rosy picture. They will get paid no matter what the results and often their future relationship with you is directly tied to how accurate their results prove to be.

YOUR TAX DOLLARS AT WORK

It never fails to amaze us how many people do not take full benefit of the masses of information their tax dollars (and the tax dollars from other nations' citizens) have purchased. For English speakers, the United States, Canada, United Kingdom, and EU are treasure troves of information virtually free for the asking.

There are also quasi-governmental not-for-profits whose research methods are rigorous, whose survival is not dependent on the health of any one industry or country, and who have a history of presenting balanced information (that is, negative as well as positive information). We will cover getting the most from these sources in our skeptic's toolkit.

Middle-of-the-Road Reliable

FELLOW eLEARNING TRAVELERS

Other people in the industry who are in a position similar to your own can be a rich source of information. At first glance most people dismiss this source because it is "the competition." People shy away, fearing others will be unwilling to relinquish information or don't have anything more valuable to contribute than what they already know (à la the conference-circuiters). In our skeptic's toolkit we'll show you how to circumvent these barriers and find fresh voices, such as members of Eilif Trondsen's SRI eLearning forum in Menlo Park.

INVESTORS

Talk is cheap. Analysts in investment houses (such as Merrill Lynch and Hambrecht) are paid whether or not their predictions and analyses prove true. They have little to lose and much to gain by coming out with regular proclamations of industry trends, health, and players. In contrast, actual venture capitalists put their money where their mouth is. They very very carefully consider where to place their own money and why they are doing it. As such, they are one of the most valuable sources of industry information, particularly about trends and rankings.

PARENTHETICAL PROFESSIONALS

Professionals who already have much information about your product and service, gathered as a by-product of other work they did for the organization, can be sponges of information waiting to be squeezed. For example, when we develop marketing collateral we gather massive amounts of data on how a company is viewed by its customers, vendors, the press, and others. And yet it is a rare day when people in the client organization ever ask us about data of use beyond the immediate task.

Least Reliable

INDUSTRY ANALYSTS

When someone's career depends, even indirectly, on positive growth in eLearning, his integrity immediately comes into question. Sure, there are some reliable and objective industry analysts out there. But if your salary was tied to getting more and more people to read reports about a particular industry, which means you need to not only drum up attention for that industry but also attract more people to the industry, how quickly would you publicize your honest view that the market size or a particular firm in that industry is in the toilet?

SNAKE OIL AND STRONG ARMING

The first quotation in this chapter just about sums up our opinion of people who put out the industry guru shingle. Alas, this book presents the opinions of people making exceptional eLearning, not just ours. Opinions about gurus' value or lack thereof are so strong and plentiful that we have supplied a chapter resource dedicated to them (see "Resource 2: The Skeptic's Toolkit").

RESEARCH SOURCES ARE WHERE YOU FIND THEM

As a child, I often dreamt of more interesting ways that subjects could be taught to me. Years later when I became a teacher I ended up gazing at the same conundrum from a different perspective. Froguts is the result of these daydreams, where fascination and ecology are intertwined.

Here's a very simple example that emphasizes the wide circle of research sources that most people are not aware of until they fall into it. Richard Hill relived his former feelings of boredom with school subject matter when he visited his daughter's school science fair. Determined to do something about it, he created a free online interactive frog dissection program (www.froguts.com). This is one of the instances where eLearning was able to exceed by a long shot what can be done in real life. The kids can do the same dissection step over and over, take quizzes along the way, gain an understanding of the entire life cycle of a frog from tadpole to mature frog, and learn how the different organs work together.

As expected, his dissection eLearning did make it more engaging for school kids.

What he didn't anticipate was how his small free program would affect not only his financial status but the greater society (and frogs!). One of the first unanticipated impacts was the number of students who began refusing to do live dissections. Students around the country in high schools have led a movement that has resulted in eight states creating opt-out policies for kids who don't want to dissect real animals on the basis that there are viable computer options available. This has gotten the attention of animal rights organizations who have created an infrastructure (including toll-free numbers, literature, legal assistance, and moral support) to promote the use of eLearning dissections in place of real ones. Many of these organizations publicize Hill's site, generating more awareness and users for froguts, which of course leads to greater recognition for Hill.

His site has won the esteem and praise of numerous groups, including a prestigious Childnet award from Cable & Wireless. The number of visitors has far exceeded his expectations, 100,000 as of last count several months ago.

This recognition has allowed Hill to expand his "hobby" into a business that will sell eLearning dissection modules for a wide range of animals (no humans in the works yet). In essence his customer base includes the politicians, animal rights organizations, parents, lawyers, and protestors who supported the antidissection students and increased the popularity of his offering. Of course another beneficiary, perhaps the target market with the greatest investment in his success, consists of the millions of frogs that are not being killed for dissections.

Chances are, even if he had done deliberate market research he would never have considered these groups as part of his target market. And yet it is them and not his original one that have laid the track on which his success train will travel. They have established the froguts "brand."

RESOURCE 2: THE SKEPTIC'S TOOLKIT

In *Fiddler on the Roof*, a young boy living in a shtetl (a Jewish community in Russia) asks the rabbi whether there is an appropriate blessing for the tsar. The rabbi replies with this witty prayer, which reveals his ambivalent feelings: "Why of course my son. May God bless and keep the Tsar . . . far away from us."

That about sums up how people in the eLearning industry feel about eLearning's self-proclaimed experts and gurus. From a distance, they are perceived as adding value by raising awareness of eLearning among people outside the fold. From close range they are seen, at best, as adding almost no value, and at worst, carelessly bringing about, albeit indirectly, negative repercussions.

A majority of the people we interviewed said industry gurus were "irrelevant" to their work. Some criticized them for being too focused on making money. Many Europeans found it distasteful that U.S.-based gurus "think the whole world is just like America." Several cited examples where gurus offended. In one instance an entire room of people who paid to have a guru come and speak thought that he blatantly disrespected the importance of tradition and evolutionary change to their organization. Another person recounted how a guru almost instigated a fistfight when this person vocally and publicly disagreed with his "expert." Still another cited a specific instance where the guru's work cost a particular group much time and money. The most common complaint was of waste. Several people recounted tales of a guru's plan being scrapped after an expensive implementation. The main reason cited was that the guru didn't really understand the cultures, systems, and constraints of organizations.

It will benefit you to evaluate any gurus or vendors through the filter of the following skeptic's toolkit whenever you are looking for one of the following kinds of research:

- Prepackaged reports, typically covering
    Company or product comparisons
    Stock movements
    Market forecasts
- Conferences
    Running conferences for buyers
    Speaking at conferences
- Consulting
    Strategic planning

Vendor selection

Business development

Positioning

Product development

- Investing

Encouraging public investment

Underwriting IPOs

Any consultant, guru, or researcher who has integrity will have no qualms about sharing methods, findings, references, or previous projects with you (albeit it may have to be done without revealing clients' names to you). In fact the really good ones will welcome the conversation.

Developing a skeptic's eye will ensure the research you rely on is worth the investment (be it emotional, temporal, or financial) you put into it. The following seven techniques constitute an X-ray machine to help you scrutinize both people and their research results. Over time using these methods will become second nature. And once again we urge you to be wary of giving money or time to people who make excuses instead of sharing relevant methodological information.

1. *Find out who funds the study.* It's not as if researchers are immune to monetary gravity. When the funder wants certain results it is almost impossible not to come to conclusions that in some way support the funding body's agenda. Samantha's favorite example of this appeared about fourteen months after she gave birth to our very happy, healthy baby, who was born three weeks after her due date, despite not flossing every day. An ad in a popular newspaper declared: "Women with periodontal disease are three times as likely to give birth to a premature child." Not surprisingly the study was funded by Crest. Either the researcher who did this study is a total moron (possible), or he or she decided not to present the real cause and effect in the ad because it wouldn't suit Crest's agenda. Making a simple intellectual leap, who are the women who are most likely to suffer periodontal disease or any other disease that is untreated? Poor women and women who don't have access to regular, affordable medical care. So, although the numbers are no doubt accurate, it's like saying milk promotes criminal behavior because 80 percent of prisoners drink milk.

2. *Find out the sample size.* If we told you four out of five people think Samantha is a complete genius of a higher magnitude than Einstein,

Even if you can't find a source of demonstratable bias, allow yourself some skepticism about the results as long as there is a possibility of bias somewhere. There always is.

DARRYL HUFF

Beethoven, and Martha Graham put together, would it be more convincing if the sample size was five million people or if it was Samantha's husband, daughter, best friend, and parents? So very often people pull this trick on the unsuspecting. Before you are bowled over by the seemingly overwhelming support or approval a firm or study has, peel back the layers of how many people provided input. Ignore what is "statistically significant" and see if the logic rings true. It is fine for a sample size of 100 to love your eLearning customer service program if you have 200 customer service people. It is not so great if you have 10,000 people.

3. *Find out the sample demographics.* Continuing from toolkit item 2, the perspective of the people who are being asked for information will make all the difference to the validity of the findings for your purposes. Suppose you are trying to sell eLearning to small businesses with fewer than fifty people or to not-for-profits. In order to sculpt your future offerings you read through a report that segments the market for eLearning by offering and market size opportunity. Wow! Seventy-two percent of the market is going to be in learning management systems. Before you add funds to that division while killing some of your other offerings, it would be wise to find out whether the numbers for your target market lead to the same conclusion.

4. *Find out what is at stake for the sample.* The more the sample has at stake, the more accurate the research. For example, the head of IVIMeds is spearheading a large initiative, with the cooperation of several other prominent schools, to create an online medical school. When he held a meeting to discuss the virtual medical school, he didn't ask the thirty-eight attending medical school deans to rate the system. He asked them to fund it. He didn't just want their mouths, he wanted their money put where their mouths were. When all thirty-eight provided a generous £40,000—despite serious budget cutbacks—he got the accurate feedback he needed. When you look at the methodology, find out what was at risk for the participants. Did they already own any of the eLearning being studied? Did they have to publicly state their opinions or was the survey or interview anonymous? What would they have to lose by lying? is really the question you want to uncover. The more they would have to lose by lying, the more you can figure the data is accurate. One exception to this rule is people who have so much at stake that they will deliberately color the research in order to promote their own advancement.

5. *Get the original research tools.* One of the benefits of relying on academic research is that it is a relatively transparent process. Because of the internal critique process, most reports will include all the original instruments used with the sample population. Any questionnaires, tally sheets, or guidelines will be in an appendix for all to see. Sources closer to the "less reliable" part of our reliability continuum justify hiding these original materials by calling them part of their intellectual property and trade secrets. As a result it is almost impossible to examine the validity of their results as they relate to the raw data.

6. *Look for the researcher's pattern of bias.* Everyone has biases. Although people may or may not admit it, these biases affect every minute of every day because they are the filter through which people see the world. The best researchers can do is work hard to overcome this natural human tendency by being as conscious of their subjectivity as possible and by involving others in the data collection and critique process. In order to ascertain which researchers might be more in keeping with your standard of reliability, you'll need to track them over time:

   - Try to find the work they have done in the past. Read through it and see if any patterns emerge. Do they have a preference for one technology over another? Do they ignore mistakes they made in the past, or do they openly reconcile them? Do they concede humbly not knowing whether their findings are accurate, or do they brazenly declare them to be the word of G-d?

   - Look into their personal lives. Where do they contribute money? Which associations do they belong to? Which companies do they consult for, if any? What do the people in the industry or former employees say about them?

7. *Decide on standards before you read the report.* When you see the conclusions that have been drawn, ask yourself what would justify these results. If 38 percent of people agreed? If the sample size was 5,000? If the study was done over seven years? Whatever your criteria are, write them down somewhere and then see if the study meets your own bar of rigor.

Up Next

The final chapter in Part Three brings us full circle. We began the book by looking at the large societal movement towards creativity as an economic driver. In Chapter Fifteen, "I Think About What I Think, Therefore I Am" we provide ideas on how you personally can contribute to making the environment riper for innovation and become more creative in a way that winds up adding to the economy and society.

NOTES

1. George Pitcher, *Business Life*, Aug. 2003.

2. The Securities Industry Administration, "Key Trends in the Securities Industry," Nov. 3, 2003, http://www.sia.com/research/html/key_industry_trends_.html.

3. Allison Rossett, "Customers: Responding to," http://www.josseybass.com/legacy/rossett/rossett/respond/customer1.htm, accessed May 2004.

4. Rossett's activities and credentials make her a candidate for being a member of the old guard. In addition to writing the book on needs assessment (both literally and figuratively), she appears at most relevant conferences, is a member of two Halls of Fame (Human Resources Development and *Training* magazine), is a regular editor of American Society for Training and Development books on eLearning and performance analysis, and is a winner of the International Society of Performance Improvement's Instructional Communications award. She is also a professor in educational technology at San Diego State University.

5. Allison Rossett, *Training Needs Assessment* (Englewood Cliffs, N.J.: Educational Technology, 1987).

6. Allison Rossett and Kendra Sheldon, *Beyond the Podium* (San Francisco: Jossey-Bass/Pfeiffer, 2001), p. 34.

7. Rossett and Sheldon, *Beyond the Podium*, p. 39.

8. For example, a scan of the Web site of one self-proclaimed guru who regularly puts out reports did not find any explanation of his methodology, nor does the site allow people to freely download sections of his reports, which may or may not describe his methodology.

JIM HAUDAN AND TOM CRAWFORD

CEO and Director of eLearning,
respectively, of Root Learning

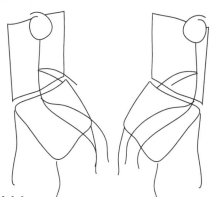

ON THE GESTATION OF THE IDEA FOR ROOT LEARNING . . .

We were strategic planners and trend futurists who would go to organizations to paint a picture of a business landscape that is radically changing. We would try to get people to see the opportunities so they could ride the waves of change, rather than being decimated by them.

We thought, "If you could see what we see you wouldn't be doing what you're doing." This was true at the executive level and through the ranks of an enterprise. We got excited because it was as if we were in a hot-air balloon and could see all these forces, possibilities, before they become obvious, while they are still exciting, while they are your ally and not enemy.

We would go off to executive retreats and become the *provocateurs* of their strategic planning sessions. Then it was put in a gold binder with gold corners, put on a shelf, and nothing changed. You would come back six months later and it was stillborn.This prompted us to begin to really think about how to get people in the thick of it—to see how they specifically could capitalize on the opportunities brought about by the changes in the environment.

We asked two basic questions: What do people need to understand, and how do people learn? Those questions were driven by the Grand Canyon we saw between the leaders, who could see what needed to be done but didn't do it everyday, and the doers, who had their hands on change but didn't have a clue what needed to be done.

The answers to those questions became very focused on critical business systems, because many of the challenges people faced had to be understood at a systemic level.

We saw it as . . . a book with multiple chapters. The chapters included

- The big picture of the enterprise
- The economic situation of the enterprise
- The customer value being delivered by the enterprise
- The core processes of the enterprise
- And the strategic direction of the enterprise

If you were to understand these things, you'd understand why it is important to change, what is of greatest value to customers, how to deliver that value, where to head, and so on. Those things would become important to everyone and there would be a common language. We believe the execution of a good strategy is not about the learning speed of the brightest few, but the understanding speed of the slowest many.

We became focused on having a direct line of sight from the marketplace to each individual. Which led us to ask, How do you understand those five elements and how do you understand them quickly?

Most people think their leader is very screwed up, very flavor-of-the-month. That is because every week or month their leader passes just one piece of a 400-piece jigsaw puzzle across the table. This week they get a piece on total quality, another week it's on balanced scorecard, the next on learning organization, reengineering, and so on.

They want to say back to their leaders, "Get back to me when these pieces that don't have any hope of connecting are going to connect. Until then I'll just keep doing what I'm doing."

Our approach was to say, "Why don't you show me the cover of that jigsaw puzzle box with the whole picture. When I get all these little pieces I will be able to see that there is a place for water and sky, for rocks and trees, and that it all does fit together."

Let's say a company said their strategy was to cut costs like hell and to innovate wherever they can. By going through this learning map process you could realize the CEO isn't actually talking from both sides of his mouth. You could find out it's not indecision. You could find out that, really, we do need to find a way to cut costs in these specific areas, and we do need to innovate and take risks and spend money in these other areas, and they do very much fit together in the same mouth.

ON THE IMPORTANCE OF DRAMA AND METAPHOR . . .

Three years ago our customers asked how we could leverage some of the new technology and the learning created through our methodology. Many people came at eLearning from a cost perspective. Sure it could do that. But we came at it believing e-learning could do something much more important, it could bring whatever system that we've laid on the table to life. In other words, we could show the cause and effect, the movements of that system in real time. People could immediately see how their interactions changed the system. You can begin to start to see not only the beginning and the end, but also the interplay. This is how the flat learning maps became full-blown simulations of systems.

The best way to understand a system is through visualization, that's one of the ways the brain works. We can give you a zillion examples of how a picture or a metaphor accelerates our ability to think and act in systems and to see how pieces of a system fit together. We started developing these physical things called learning maps. They are custom, large tabletop drawings that show the critical business systems and allow people to see how all the pieces fit together and the essential *drama* of that system.

The engine to navigate that system became a dialogue to compare and contrast, examine, contemplate, reflect, and apply all the answers to the problems that were inherent within that system or the opportunity.

We found a way for this process to be a dynamic session held with a small group. Groups of six to eight people would get around the learning maps (those table-sized maps) and go through a process of dialoguing and interaction. This was a way to very quickly enable people with all learning styles to understand complex content in about an hour or less. The process involved self-discovery and the energy and excitement of how we learn.

This learning map process took strategies that weren't understandable and found a way to create a common language around the business so everybody would get in the game.

The passion driving us was the idea that all this human capital was dormant because 98 percent of the people weren't in the game. If they were they could drastically change the results.

People can't learn anything new if it's not attached to something they already know. It's critical to find what is relevant to the learner, what will allow him or her to connect new concepts to what they already know so that they really get it.

Whether the metaphor is a ship or a train or a tornado or the Grand Canyon or whatever, it is a way to create something that is friendly, familiar. We are introducing unfriendly and complex concepts by using metaphor. It is through that that people begin to embrace the unknown, which is really what learning is all about.

One thing that has always been fascinating to us is that teachers put blame on the learner when people don't learn. We have a totally different perspective. You can't learn unless you're interested; so we think the medium and the provider need to provide a way to capture that interest. Metaphors and humor and story, all those things, stick.

The deliverable we created to take this learning map to the next level was the learning map module. It uses a visual metaphor, dialogue questions, and learning exercises to really create a common framework and roadmap of a particular complex topic. This makes it digestible for many people.

ON RESULTS . . .

Over ten million people have gone through these processes. Organizations like UPS had 700,000 people. Deutsche Bank, in Germany, shut down the bank for the whole day and everybody went through the process. At Charles Schwab, 32,000 people went through it in thirty-two different global sites. Pfizer has gone through it.

After having engaged ten million people in many languages and many countries, there has not been a time it hasn't been a tremendous tool. There hasn't been one time it didn't help transform people from feeling a sense of victimization or disillusionment to one of insightful urgency about their ability to contribute.

ON THEIR CREATIVE PROCESS AND PEOPLE . . .

We've got a lot of great people in house. We gathered people around the picnic table in the back of the building, sat down for three hours, and said, "Okay. We've got to solve this problem. We need to do *this* for individuals online. Let's spend our time figuring out everything we know, everything we've ever heard. . . ."

We've got people with a lot of experience. We've got teachers, principals, instructional designers, artists, and MBAs. All those people got around the table, threw out ideas of things they've seen and heard throughout their careers on ways to engage people and different alternatives. We looked at teenagers playing with a gamebox, addicted to it, and asked, "What's in that box that is so intriguing?" Most of our team have young kids, under six, and they love to play games. So we bought games and played games. Backyard Baseball. Backyard Soccer. SimCity. All these other complex video games that have managed to be simple enough for a three-year-old to figure out. We asked what made this interface so simple? Why is it that people are learning so well through those games? We read lots of books. We talked to lots of smart people.

Then we asked, What do we do? We just started applying those basic learning design principles in an online environment. We really came from a person perspective, not a technology one. We wanted to know things like who's your audience, what do you want them to know, what do they already know, where are they at, tell us about their whole background, tell us about the topic you want to learn about, and so on. All of those kinds of things come long before the technology. Then the technology is really just a delivery mechanism.

We have very diverse people. One of our artists was a toy designer in a previous life. Another was a newspaper illustrator, a principal, a counselor. Our people came from all over. Those different experiences feed in to what we have going on. They're bringing their thoughts and experiences to the company, which creates a unique, rich blend of results that all the research in the world can't compare to. Our competitors are playing with the same games, but they're not coming to the same conclusions.

I THINK ABOUT WHAT I THINK, THEREFORE I AM

The Benefits of Navel Gazing

FAST FORWARD *If you believe questioning assumptions, beliefs, and arguments is critical to developing a creative environment, skip to the section of this chapter titled "Reflective Thinking," (p. 263).*

If you already understand and agree with the value of reflective thinking and just want some ideas on how it may be better encouraged, skip to the section titled "Hang a Mirror," (p. 265).

ROSABETH MOSS KANTER, the Harvard Business School professor with a well-deserved reputation for promoting innovation among large organizations, did a landmark study on corporations. She examined the most successful "progressive" companies (those most innovative on a number of dimensions) and found they all had one thing in common. They all exhibited a culture of integrative thinking, "the willingness to move beyond received wisdom, to combine ideas from unconnected sources, to embrace change as an opportunity to test limits."[1]

Reflective thinking is a crucial underpinning of integrative thinking. This chapter will address why it is important and how to leverage it both within your organization and for clients through eLearning.

This is important because reflective thinking has become much more important in today's workplace. It is not so much that innovation has taken center stage and pushed other activities off the stage. Rather it is that the responsibilities and activities of a larger number of people require innovation, as indicated by Kanter's study.

> *I roamed the countryside searching for answers to things I did not understand.*
>
> **LEONARDO DA VINCI**

All workers (from the mailperson to the CEO) are increasingly being asked to perform functions that require reflective thinking, to

- Reengineer processes, procedures, and physical configurations.

- Create new business models to replace outdated or less effective ones.

- Develop programs that decrease errors, accidents, and returns.

- Invent or modify products and services that give the organization a competitive advantage.

Here are some examples:

- Almost all employees are now expected to make decisions that have a larger impact on the organization than decisions at their levels did in previous eras.

- Data are more readily available from more sources, and frequently the recipient plays a larger role than before in determining what is or isn't credible and supporting that position.

- Authority has become more fluid, requiring people who prefer following a "leader" to constantly reevaluate exactly which person to follow for a particular skill, task, or project.

- Tasks and roles are becoming more complex, requiring more decision-making skills that take into account adjustments to prior judgments.

- It is harder to differentiate your products and services, giving the edge to people who can make and support a more convincing (well thought out, considered) argument than the competition can muster.

- Defying authority has become more mainstream.

All of this points to the underlying issue of problem complexity. Problems that have one right solution or that are structured so that people take a particular mental path to come to a particular predetermined solution are increasingly rare in the workplace. Consider the simple example of car repair.

Forty years ago a car mechanic working on a car with a defective bulb could find and fix the problem in minutes. In contrast, a friend has been bringing her 1990 Jaguar to the dealership for fourteen years and the mechanics still can't figure out why the computer constantly says "bulb out" and "coolant low" when neither is the case.

Accompanying the increasing percentage of workplace problems that are more complex, like car repair, is the increasing number of people who are facing complex problems. For example, fifty years ago managers may have been the only ones expected to find ways to increase productivity. Today, ensuring the success of six sigma and Total Quality Management initiatives is a responsibility placed on the shoulders of almost all employees.

Multiply this increasing number of complex problems by the increasing number of people dealing with complex problems, and you get a workplace in which easy answers are rare. In fact, for more and more problems, there is often no solution because there is no objective way to measure success.

In the future, for a widening group of people, success will mean who can make the most persuasive argument derived from the most logical and thoroughly thought-out reflection process. Not who is right according to an absolute standard. Having more people making better decisions based on thinking back about how their prior thoughts and actions did or didn't bring about desired results will benefit both the individual and the organization.

This spells an increased challenge for eLearning. Simplistic eLearning that addresses simplistic problems or favors simplistic answers does virtually nothing to prepare people for the complexity of the real world. To help people wrestle with this workplace, to help them develop integrative thinking, requires sophisticated eLearning. Self-reflection, critical thinking, alternate pathways, and complexity (and sometimes an answer structure that goes beyond simple right or wrong responses) characterize the eLearning that will have maximum impact on results.

Creating and evaluating this sophisticated eLearning requires a solid understanding of reflective thinking and awareness of reflective thinking techniques. The next section presents a very brief overview of reflective thinking. The final section presents some techniques that can be added to most eLearning programs to increase proficiency in reflective thinking.

REFLECTIVE THINKING

We define *reflective thinking* as John Dewey did in what has remained to this day the seminal work in this area, *How We Think*: **"Active, persistent, and careful consideration of any belief or supposed form of knowledge in the light of the grounds that support it and the further conclusions to which it tends."**[2]

At first glance most people mistake reflective thinking for learning or critical thinking because these endeavors share many similar components. All involve

- Making inferences
- Making generalizations
- Analogies
- Making discriminations
- Making evaluations
- Feeling
- Remembering
- Solving problems[3]

The main difference, as pointed out by Edward Cell, is that all involve assessing one's prejudices, distortions, and provincialisms, but only reflective

COMPLEXITY OF PROBLEMS: MORALE AT THE LEARNING COMPANY
The Learning Company was taken over by Softkey in a hostile takeover. It was clear to virtually everyone that morale among employees was in the toilet. Numerous attempts were made to resolve the crisis before it affected product schedules, quality, and so on. Not only could no one agree which strategy to take, different interpretations of success appeared. Not surprisingly, the people who led the hostile takeover declared the end of the morale problem with much fanfare as a baffled and disenfranchised employee pool sat silently. Apparently those taking over had hired a consulting firm to do some kind of study, which came back with the good news. Surprise.

thinking involves actually *correcting* distortions in one's reasoning and attitudes.[4]

> *A moment's insight is sometimes worth a lifetime's experience.*
> **OLIVER WENDELL HOLMES**

Reflective thinking is a goal-oriented behavior. Individuals engage in it for a specific purpose: to reassess their prior learning to determine whether the approach they are taking or are about to take is the right one for a new situation. It is just as focused on carving out a better way of approaching things in the future as it is on finding a solution to the presenting symptoms.

What distinguishes reflective thinking from the skills taught in most problem-solving classes is the level of depth. Typical problem-solving classes will focus on acquiring and weighing data on a number of variables in order to determine which decision will most closely meet the requirements.

Reflective thinking takes a step back and examines the very nature of knowing. It is a deliberate, focused, intense activity in which individuals carefully ponder not only the problem itself but the fundamental way problems are solved.

There are times when reflective thinking is of less value:

- The problem is highly technical.
- The answer is known by the experts.
- The issue presents very little ambiguity.
- The issue has only one stakeholder.
- The decision maker has decided what to do.

In other words, it's a waste of time to use reflective thinking to address issues meeting these criteria. However, reflective thinking is the right approach to take when, as we mentioned at the opening of the chapter, problems are complex and may either not have an easy answer or may not have any "right" answer at all.

There is always an opportunity to help participants develop their reflective-thinking muscles regardless of the actual learning subject matter. As long as participants will be expected to make decisions and judgments in their lives, particularly if they exist in a complex world, reflective learning should be put in the "must have" column of the specifications. eLearning makes it easy to do this without much additional effort.

Here are some techniques and activities that can weave reflective thinking into any eLearning program.

Robert Greenberg is responsible for the interactive university part of Kaplan, one of the world's largest test preparation companies. He recognizes the important role of reflection in developing and improving the content. He builds this into his management process in many ways. One of the things he does demonstrates how we all perform some degree of reflective thinking without noticing it. He works with his team at meetings to develop lists of what has happened and what needs to be done. This encourages people, in a nonintrusive and basic way, to reflect on what they have been doing, how they have been spending their time, how they have been setting their priorities, and how their actions have not matched their stated priorities.

HANG A MIRROR: IDEAS FOR FOSTERING REFLECTIVE THINKING THROUGH eLEARNING

1. *Get people off guard. Put them in an unfamiliar setting and situation.* One of the reasons why travel is the best educational experience is that being in new situations and meeting new people encourages you to challenge your own thoughts and assumptions. If you encounter someone who is eating dinner in a five star restaurant with her dog under the table when you live in a culture where dogs are not allowed to be in eateries, you question whether dogs are really a health hazard. When people need to actually think how to do the basic things they take for granted at home, the ball is set in motion. The process of having people question the basic way they do things has been initiated. This opens the door to questioning deeply held beliefs, assumptions, and methods.

2. *Incorporate questions that challenge an individual's internal status quo:*
   - Why am I doing this in this way?
   - Why have I always done this in this way?
   - Would my results be any different if I did it differently?
   - What stops me from regularly questioning my own thoughts and actions?
   - What could I fit into my already existing life that would encourage reflective thinking on a day-to-day basis?

Glasgow's learning program, Real, contains an eLearning course that is unparalleled in its effective use of reflective thinking. The goal is to encourage users to reframe how they look at their own beliefs, attitudes, and actions as these beliefs relate to learning and employment. The entire curriculum uses an optimistic, encouraging tone to drive home the point that people have more assets and talents than they realize. It clearly places responsibility on the user to learn how to reflect in order to gain the self-esteem and insight to continually draw from his or her wealth of assets.

One example is a module called "How clever are you?" (*clever* in the sense of intelligent and innovative, not coy or manipulative). The module begins by encouraging users to reframe this question about their abilities:

"We should change the question in our minds from 'How clever are you?' to 'How are you clever?'"

It continues by expanding people's conception of intelligence to include assets such as emotional and social intelligences. And ends by asking users questions to encourage self-reflection:

Ask yourself:

- Am I really quite clever?
- Is there something I'm really good at?
- Why have I not developed this further?

3. *Incorporate questions that challenge individuals' beliefs about their organizational status quo:*

- Why is the organization like this?
- How did it come to be like this?
- What role do I play in perpetuating positive parts of the organization?
- What role do I play in perpetuating less positive aspects?

4. *Get the participation of people with widely differing viewpoints.* Most people spend their time running in social and professional circles, surrounded by people who share similar views and beliefs. Put a voice with a widely differing perspective into the program. If the topic is leadership for investment bankers, get socialists to give their point of view; if it's cutting-edge engineering for software developers, let them hear the thoughts of a Luddite or a senior citizen who doesn't use a computer, and so on.

5. *Continually have people reassess exactly what problem they are working on.* Problems change. Encourage people to continually take a step back and look at what they are working on. Is it still the same beast, or has a different one silently taken its place?

6. *Provide opportunities for people to develop and test their own theories.* People should balance their acceptance of other people's theories, facts, and forecasts with their own ideas. Develop projects and environments where they are able not only to test other points of view and critique them but to build their own from scratch. For example,

I wrote somewhere once that the third-rate mind was only happy when it was thinking with the majority, the second-rate mind was only happy when it was thinking with the minority, and the first-rate mind was only happy when it was thinking.

A. A. MILNE

a simulation (sim) allows people to play with their own ideas but only in the context others have set for them. If people are to test their own ideas and theories, the sim should allow them to build their own sim, beyond what the original creator may have envisioned. Or do a role play in which, instead of being handed predefined roles, individuals create their own.

That is what learning is. You suddenly understand something you've understood all your life, but in a new way.
DORIS LESSING

7. *Start from the learner's experience base, not the expert's knowledge base.* Reflective thinking is more about the how and why of the learner, not about the what of the expert. While the thinking might take place in the context of learning something new, the first thing to be addressed must be how the participant views himself or herself, and his or her behaviors.

Who says reflection time has to be boring or challenging. Daniel Bernardi wants to encourage students to think and to think about what they think about. Because he is a teacher of new media studies, he gets the privilege of having one barrier knocked down for him: motivation.

Daniel's students are eager to begin the process of introspection because they don't realize they are doing it. Rather than explicitly saying, "We are going to look at how you form arguments, question assumptions, and change actions," he asks questions about media presentations that have that end result but go about it differently, making use of the fact that most people like to give opinions and like to critique popular culture.

He asks such things as

- What did you like about this media example?
- How do you think society is affected by this?
- What does this tell you about the writer [or actor or society, and so forth]?
- What do you think the writer [or actor and so forth] was thinking?
- What would you do differently?

In ways like this he builds reflective thinking into both his classroom instruction and his eLearning.

8. *Build a learning journal into the process.* A learning journal is a diary that focuses on the thoughts, feelings, beliefs, and actions involved in the learning process. Create a private space (or encourage people to keep a hard-copy diary if privacy on a network is an issue) for people to jot down thoughts and feelings only they have access to. Create guidelines and sample entries. Incorporate questions (such as those in items 2 and 3 of this list) that are meant to be answered in the learning journal in your curriculum. If possible, provide a forum in which

people share parts of their learning journals. Particularly encourage thoughts about their process. For example, if the student says, "I really didn't like the teacher," encourage introspection about this feeling: "What is it about yourself that doesn't make you a good fit with this teacher?" or, "What type of person or student might really like this teacher?"

9. *Make a tight connection between insights and performance.* Having insights (the result of effective reflective thinking) means little if they do not get translated into action. Do whatever possible to reinforce and encourage changes in thoughts and actions that result in benefits for the organization. If you don't support people's changed behavior, don't bother encouraging reflective thinking. People who do it will simply think their way out of your stifling organization.

10. *Make the tacit or implicit explicit.* Encourage people to notice and discuss the assumption and beliefs they take for granted. Why does a company need to have first-mover advantage? What examples can you come up with to illustrate that first-mover advantage has not spelled success in the long run? What is more important: coming up with a higher-quality offering later or a lower-quality one sooner? Why? Are there instances where the opposite of your response is true? When?

11. *Encourage people to examine their own self-doubts.* We have all been subject to moments when we filter our thoughts or ideas through the self-doubt-o'matic. You elect not to say or do something because it's stupid or pointless or it would never work out anyway or someone has probably already done it. This is not some self-help book that is going to encourage you to turn off those voices or to encourage others to do so. For all we know, the voices may be quite right. Rather, encourage people to recognize and analyze their filters. By discovering the how and why of the machine they will at the least understand how it is influencing their lives and decisions. At the most, they will be able to share control with it.

12. *Ask people to interpret the truth and the evidence used to support it.* Every day, people who work are confronted by opinions masquerading as "truths." Becoming a lifelong learner will make you more employable and get you a better job. Getting projects done under budget and on time will advance your career. eLearning will revolutionize the way people learn. Some opinions may be true at a certain moment in time, some not. But the goal is to get learners to

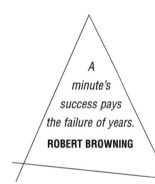

A minute's success pays the failure of years.
ROBERT BROWNING

interpret these truths by questioning them in light of the evidence used to support them. What makes these truths true? What makes the evidence count?

13. Ask people to *use critical incident methodology instead of hypotheticals* (this works best in a group setting). Have people recount a specific incident from the past in a way that makes it come alive for them. The retelling should include when and where it happened, the people involved, and the reason the event was significant. Focus on finding

    - The discrepancies between people's experiences then and what they feel now
    - The distortions, contradictions, oversimplifications, inaccuracies, and ambiguities in the tale[5]
    - The underlying assumptions, ideologies, or beliefs

14. *Ask participants to compose a structured biography, an "about me" document.* Even the most adept writers seem to stumble when creating a resume or bio. How can you reduce the complexity that is a human being into three paragraphs? And yet, creating a bio is one of the best opportunities to reflect on oneself in light of a particular perspective. Create a filter, related to the eLearning content or the instructional goals, through which people will write their bios.

15. *Have participants carry out metaphor analysis.* Have people do what we have described in several techniques here (for example, *critical incident methodology*), using the metaphors the person creates as the gateway. For example, let's assume a person frequently uses cooking as a metaphor. Probe to find out why the metaphor seems relevant for that person. Listen or read carefully for other metaphors embedded in the description. When a person says, "This company is like a restaurant," perhaps he also uses phrases like "too many cooks in the kitchen," "well-oiled machine," "pot about to boil over," or "five stars." What insights does his language give about his feelings and assumptions about the company? Point these out to the person and have him try this kind of analysis for himself or with others.

16. *Draw diagrams such as concept maps, MindMaps, and flow charts.*[6] Discuss the relationships between the ideas:

    - What is missing? What has been intentionally omitted?
    - Are there many cross-ties? Should there be more?

> *"The truth shall make you free" means that, given the right conditions, the human soul will find that tentative truth which is best for itself. . . . Every step in personal development is through original inference and its practical application. No human being can find the truth for another.*
>
> **FRANCIS W. PARKER**

*We shall never cease
from exploration*

*And the end of
all our exploring*

*Will be to arrive
where we started*

*And know the place
for the first time.*

T. S. ELIOT

- Are all the relationships represented, or are there others that have not been considered?
- What themes emerge and why?
- Are there cause-and-effect relationships?

NOTES

1. Rosabeth Moss Kanter, *The Change Masters* (New York: Free Press, 1985), p. 27.

2. John Dewey, *How We Think* (Chicago: Henry Regnery, 1933), p. 9. Although the term *reflective thinking* has since been replaced by the currently more popular term *critical thinking*, Dewey's definition is still the industry standard, and the one we will use.

3. Jack Mezirow and Associates, *Fostering Critical Reflection in Adulthood* (San Francisco: Jossey-Bass, 1990), p. 5.

4. Edward Cell, *Learning to Learn from Experience* (Albany: State University of New York Press, 1984).

5. Jack Mezirow and Associates, *Fostering Critical Reflection in Adulthood*, p. 181.

6. Jack Mezirow and Associates, *Fostering Critical Reflection in Adulthood*, p. 181.

16

THAT'S A WRAP!

Truth Is a Pathless Land

You may remember the story of how the devil and a friend of his were walking down the street, when they saw ahead of them a man stoop down and pick up something from the ground, look at it, and put it away in his pocket.

The friend said to the devil, "What did that man pick up?"

"He picked up a piece of Truth," said the devil.

"That is a very bad business for you, then," said his friend.

"Oh, not at all," the devil replied. "I am going to help him organize it."

—Krishnamurti, head of the Order of the Star, on the day he disbanded it

KRISHNAMURTI DISBANDED HIS organization almost as soon as he was made head of it. For him, there could be no other way. He believed spiritual organizations only hinder the acquisition of truth because belief and truth exist only on an individual level. For every single individual, belief and truth are entirely different, and therefore there can be no one true path to either. Organizations by their very nature require members to agree on certain mores, norms, and paths, which quickly become adopted as truths. Because on the group level there are no right or wrong paths to truth, it is a fundamental impossibility that any organization or group can lead any person to the right path. "The minute you follow someone you cease to follow the truth."

We are in deep agreement with Krishnamurti. We believe there is no one right way to do anything and each person has to carve out his or her own path.

If we had just one goal for this book, it would be that all the techniques and best practices inspire readers to look beyond the menus and recipes they are given by experts, gurus, associations, clients, professors, authors, and so

> [Knowledge] is the small part of ignorance that we arrange and classify.
> **AMBROSE BIERCE**

> There is no safety in numbers or in anything else.
> **JAMES THURBER**

> When you try to formalize or socialize creative activity, the only sure result is commercial constipation. . . . The good ideas are all hammered out in agony by individuals, not spewed out by groups.
> **CHARLES BROWDER**

> *Much of the messy advertising you see on television today is the product of committees. Committees can criticize advertisements, but they should never be allowed to create them.*
>
> **DAVID OGILVY**

> *My way is not the way of learned men. These sublime truths my pupils will not learn from me; they will . . . discover them of themselves. . . . My whole task will consist in aiding them to unfold, to develop their own ideas.*
>
> **JOSEPH NEEF**

> *If they give you ruled paper, write the other way.*
>
> **JUAN RAMÓN JIMÉNEZ**

forth, and instead make up their own meals.

Some readers, typically the ones who ascribe to the-organization-as-vehicle-of-truth belief system, may see this book as disjointed and contradictory. At first glance, it may seem to lack a clear simple theme that is readily grasped and easily reproduced. To the people who want a menu, our ingredient list may appear confusing and inadequate and overwhelming. There are no comprehensive case studies that shed light on every facet of what a particular group or individual has done.

This is intentional, as we follow a more organic belief about eLearning, business, and society. In fact, what characterizes both the Creative Economy and heutagogy is the organic process. The Creative Economy requires people to trust in those scary intangibles they are so often trying to organize and plan—intuition, faith, gut instinct, improvisation. Heutagogy requires the "teacher" to completely relinquish control and the learner to believe in the process, without trying to codify or force it.

If we followed the typical formula it would be a betrayal of our belief in the principles underlying these movements. At no point did we teach you anything nor did we ever take on the role of teacher. Nor did we proclaim our expertise or certainty in there being only one way.

Instead we were gardeners. We scattered thousands of seeds into your garden. Some of them will be picked up, nurtured, and tended to in a way that is uniquely yours. Others will be disregarded, written off, and so on. In both cases, you will be a learner who will own your own experience and create your own path. We are just one of the many gardeners in the industry and in the much larger human ecosystem.

Instead of closing this book with a rehash of what has already been said, we decided to do something more worthy of your time: point to other gardeners who may provide other seeds to our readers. But before we do, we will offer an observation made by Mark Twain that we hope inspires you to keep gathering seeds:

> Twenty years from now, you will be more disappointed by the things you didn't do . . . than by the ones you did do.
>
> So throw off the bowlines.
> Sail away from safe harbor.
> Catch the trade winds in your sails.
> Explore. Dream. Discover.

MORE ON THE CREATIVE ECONOMY

*Evidence of the Shift to
the Creative Economy*

SOME OF THE EVIDENCE for the shift to the Creative Economy is ethnographic—anecdotal conclusions we have formed through projects with thousands of people over the past three years. The rest is hard data.[1]

- There is an unprecedented increase[2] in the number of people and organizations that are directing resources toward creative activities.

- A wider variety of creative behaviors and activities are being valued as economic contributors.

- People in the traditional creative industries are accounting for a larger percentage of the wealth and growth in the economy:

  In the United Kingdom. "The creative and media industries in the UK generate revenues of around £112.5 billion and employ more than 1.3 million people, which is 5% of the total employed workforce. Exports contribute around £10.3 billion to the balance of trade, and the industries account for over 5% of GDP. The value of the creative industries to UK gross domestic product is therefore greater than the contribution of any of the UK's manufacturing industry. In the year 1997–98, output grew by 16%, compared to under 6% for the economy as a whole."[3]

  In the United States. The people who make a living from creativity make up 30 percent of the U.S. workforce (38.3 million people). The creative industries contribute $960 billion to the U.S. economy.[4]

In the rest of the world. The creative industries contribute $2.24 trillion to the world economy.[5]

- More organizations are being formed to focus on creative industries and the Creative Economy: see, for example:

    http://creative-economy.org/index2.html

    http://www.nycfuture.org

- Organizational areas whose profitability rests fundamentally in the hands of big "C" creativity[6] are seeing increased investment and respect.

- The number of patents granted in the United States has increased exponentially; from 1950 to 1999, it tripled from 43,000 to 150,000.

- Governments are putting significant resources into development of creative cities and towns: see, for example:

    New England: http://www.nefa.org/pubs

    Memphis: http://www.creativeclass.org/acrobat/manifesto.pdf

    Tampa Bay: http://www.creativetampabay.com/creative_learning.php

    Providence: http://mailman.intermedia.net/

    Edinburgh: http://www.creative-edinburgh.com

- Consultants who focus on creativity are gaining the edge over those who are pitching knowledge management and performance improvement.

- An increasing number of popular press outlets are writing articles expressing the tenets of the Creative Economy: see, for example:

    Business Week: http://creative-economy.org/index2.html

    New York Times: http://www.creativeclass.org/nyt6.shtml

    Washington Post: http://www.postwritersgroup.com/archives/peir0609.htm

- More executives, CEOs, and other stakeholders are taking cold calls or responding to emails when the caller clearly demonstrates he or she has a new idea of value to the organization. More are verbalizing the "invisible value" of creativity as an economic force contributing to the organization's bottom line.

- An increasing number of organizations are relying on individuals to sculpt their own positions and manage their own skills and knowledge.

- More governments and organizations are beginning to calculate the contribution to the economy of creative industries as a separate segment and statistic.

- A number of organizations are starting to put on conferences and host meetings or roundtables where the economic contribution of creativity is the main topic. See, for example, the First World Creative Forum (worldcreativeforum.com).

NOTES

1. The focus and scope of this book requires us to only scratch the surface of the Creative Economy. We suggest that those who wish to learn more go directly to the source. Several people whose ideas are represented in this resource have achieved significant results through championing the Creative Economy. In the United Kingdom, where the Creative Economy was first labeled and investigated, start with thinkers such as Charles Landry, Tom Bentley, and Stuart Cosgrove. Their efforts have resulted directly in the successful creation of institutes, infrastructure, government policies, conferences, funding, business initiatives, start-up ventures, academic projects, and particularly relevant for the topic at hand, learning programs. In the United States, Richard Florida and the Center for Urban Futures are good starting points.

2. The increase is unprecedented in modern times. Increases during the Italian Renaissance and some other historical eras could easily match or exceed the increase in the current era.

3. U.K. Department for Culture, Media, and Sport, *Creative Industries Mapping Document* (U.K. Department for Culture, Media, and Sport, 2000).

4. Richard Florida, *The Rise of the Creative Class* (New York: Basic Books, 2002). Florida draws these data from John Howkins, *The Creative Economy* (New York: Penguin Books, 2002).

5. U.K. Department for Culture, Media, and Sport, *Creative Industries Mapping Document*.

6. Just a reminder: if you didn't read the sections in Chapter Two that address the difference between little "c" and big "C" creativity, we suggest doing that now.

. . . AND EVEN MORE READING!

BOTH THE TREES sacrificed to print this book and our publisher encouraged us to keep the print version of this resources section brief. Here you will find just a few additional materials for each chapter from Chapter Two through Chapter Fifteen. They are all in addition to the books listed in the "Bookshelf Best Bets" at the start of most chapters.

Go online to our Web site at itours.org/renaissanceelearning.htm for the equivalent of over forty pages of additional resources.

Chapter Two: The Creative Economy Is Coming!

Amabile, T. *The Social Psychology of Creativity*. New York: Springer-Verlag, 1983.

De Bono, Edward. *Serious Creativity*. New York: HarperBusiness, 1992.

De Bono, Edward. *Parallel Thinking*. New York: Penguin Books, 1994.

Ekvall, G., and Y. Tangeberg-Andersson. "Working Climate and Creativity: A Study of an Innovative Newspaper Office." *Journal of Creative Behavior*, 1986, *20*, 215–225.

Fontenot, N. A. "Effects of Training in Creativity and Creative Problem Finding upon Business People." *Journal of Social Psychology*, 1992, *133*(1), 11–22.

Isaksen, S. G., K. B. Dorval, and D. J. Treffinger. *Creative Approaches to Problem Solving*. (Rev. ed.) Buffalo, N.Y.: The Creative Problem Solving Group-Buffalo, 1993.

Osborn, Alex F. *Applied Imagination*. New York: Scribner's, 1957.

Smith, B. L. "Interpersonal Behaviors That Damage the Productivity of Creative Problem-Solving Groups." *Journal of Creative Behavior*, 1993, *27*(3), 171–187.

Chapter Three: From Andragogy to Heutagogy

Hase, Stewart. "From Andragogy to Heutagogy," http://ultibase.rmit.edu.au/Articles/dec00/hase2.htm.

Hase, Stewart. "Heutagogy and Developing Capable People and Capable Workplaces: Strategies for Dealing with Complexity." Paper presented at the Work and Learning Network (WLN) Conference, Sept. 2003, University of Alberta.

Palloff, R. M., and K. Pratt. *The Virtual Student: A Profile and Guide to Working with Online Learners*. San Francisco: Jossey-Bass, 2003.

Thissen, Frank. *Inventing a New Way of Learning? Constructive Fundamentals of a Multimedia Teaching Methodology*, http://www.frank-thissen.de/lt97e.pdf.

Chapter Four: Lights, Camera, eLearning!

Antonacopoulou, Elena P., and Yiannis Gabriel. "Emotion, Learning and Organizational Change: Towards an Integration of Psychoanalytic and Other Perspectives." *Journal of Organizational Change Management*, 2001, 14(5), 435–451.

Astleitner, H. "Designing Emotionally Sound Instruction: The FEASP-Approach." *Instructional Science*, 2000, *28*, 169–198.

Astleitner, Hermann, and Detlev Leutner. "Designing Instructional Technology from an Emotional Perspective." *Journal of Research on Computing in Education*, Summer 2000, *32*(4), 497–510.

Buckles, Mary Ann. "Interactive Fiction: The Computer Storygame 'Adventure'." Ph.D. thesis, University of California at San Diego, 1985.

Dirkx, J. "The Power of Feelings: Emotion, Imagination, and the Construction of Meaning in Adult Learning." In Sharan Merriam (ed.), *The New Update on Adult Learning Theory. New Directions for Adult and Continuing Education*, no. 89. San Francisco: Jossey-Bass, 2001.

Freytag, Gustav. *The Technique of the Drama*. New York: Johnson Reprints, 1968. (Originally published in 1863)

Goleman, Daniel. *Emotional Intelligence*. New York: Bantam Books, 1995.

Hayes Roth, Barbara. "Character-Based Interactive Story Systems." *IEEE Intelligent Systems and Their Applications*, 1998, *13*(6), 12–15.

Martinez, M. "Key Design Considerations for Personalized Learning on the Web." *Educational Technology and Society*, 2001, 4(1), 26–40.

Murray, Janet Horowitz. *Hamlet on the Holodeck: The Future of Narrative in Cyberspace*. New York: Free Press, 1997.

O'Regan, Kerry. "Emotion and eLearning." *Journal of Asynchronous Learning Networks*, Sept. 2003, http://www.sloan-c.org/publications/jaln/v7n3/v7n3_oregan.asp.

Salovey, Peter, and John D. Mayer. "Emotional Intelligence." *Imagination, Cognition and Personality*, 1990, 9(3), 185–211.

Chapter Five: As Seen on TV

Bickham, Jack M. *Setting (Elements of Fiction Writing)*. Cincinnati: Writer's Digest Books, 2000.

Denning, Stephen. *The Springboard: How Storytelling Ignites Action in Knowledge-Era Organizations*. Oxford, U.K.: Butterworth-Heinemann, 2000.

Maguire, Jack. *The Power of Personal Storytelling: Spinning Tales to Connect with Others*. New York: Putnam, 1998.

Stevenson, Doug. *Never Be Boring Again: Make Your Business Presentations Capture Attention, Inspire Action, and Produce Results*. Colorado Springs, Colo.: Cornelia Press, 2003.

Thompson, Kristin. *Storytelling in the New Hollywood: Understanding Classical Narrative Technique*. Cambridge, Mass.: Harvard University Press, 1999.

Chapter Six: Action!

Campbell, Joseph. *The Hero with a Thousand Faces*. Princeton, N.J.: Princeton University Press, 1972.

Frey, James N. *How to Write a Damn Good Novel: A Step-by-Step No Nonsense Guide to Dramatic Storytelling*. New York: St. Martin's Press, 1987.

Lerch, Jennifer. *500 Ways to Beat the Hollywood Script Reader: Writing the Screenplay the Reader Will Recommend*. New York: Fireside Books, 1999.

Seger, Linda. *Making a Good Writer Great: A Creativity Workbook for Screenwriters*. Los Angeles: Silman-James Press, 1999.

Chapter Seven: What a Character!

Horton, Andrew. *Writing the Character-Centered Screenplay*. Berkeley: University of California Press, 2000.

Kress, Nancy. *Dynamic Characters: How to Create Personalities That Keep Readers Captivated*. Cincinnati: Writer's Digest Books, 1998.

Seger, Linda. *Creating Unforgettable Characters*. New York: Owl Books, 1990.

Stein, Sol. *Six Points About Character, Plot, and Dialogue You Wish You'd Have Known Yesterday*. At http://www.right-writing.com/published-novel-sixpoints.html, accessed July 12, 2004.

Wood, Monica. *Description (Elements of Fiction Writing)*. Cincinnati: Writer's Digest Books, 1999.

Chapter Eight: Are You Talkin' to Me?

Ballon, Rachel. *Breathing Life into Your Characters*. Cincinnati: Writer's Digest Books, 2003.

Chiarella, Tom. *Writing Dialogue*. Ohio: Story Press Books, 1998.

Pattison, Pat. *Writing Better Lyrics*. Cincinnati: Writer's Digest Books, 2001.

Chapter Nine: It Was a Dark and Stormy Night . . .

Fiske, Robert Hartwell. *Thesaurus of Alternatives to Worn-Out Words and Phrases*. Cincinnati: F & W Publications, 1994.

Glazier, Stephen. *Random House Word Menu: New and Essential Companion to the Dictionary*. New York: Random House, 1998.

McClanahan, Rebecca. *Word Painting: A Guide to Writing More Descriptively*. Cincinnati: Writer's Digest Books, 1999.

Chapter Ten: Visually Arresting

Berger, John. *Ways of Seeing*. New York: Penguin Books, 1972.

Hurlburt, Allen. *Grid: A Modular System for the Design and Production of Newspapers, Magazines, and Books*. Hoboken, N.J.: John Wiley and Sons, 1982.

Krause, Jim. *Idea Index: Graphic Effects and Typographic Treatments*. Cincinnati: North Light Books, 2000.

Krug, Steve. *Don't Make Me Think: A Common Sense Approach to Web Usability*. Indianapolis: New Riders Publishing, 2000.

Laurel, Brenda. *The Art of Human-Computer Interface Design*. Boston: Addison-Wesley, 1990.

Muller-Brockmann, Josef. *Grid Systems in Graphic Design*. Santa Monica, Calif.: R.A.M. Publications, 1996.

Nielsen, Jakob, and Marie Tahir. *Homepage Usability: 50 Websites Deconstructed*. Indianapolis: New Riders Publishing, 2001.

Chapter Eleven: Just the Type

Bringhurst, Robert. *The Elements of Typographic Style*. Point Roberts, Wash.: Hartley and Marks, 2002.

Spiekermann, Erik, and E. M. Ginger. *Stop Stealing Sheep & Find Out How Type Works*. (2nd ed.) Boston: Addison-Wesley, 1993.

Chapter Twelve: Putting Things in Perspective

Elkins, James. *The Object Stares Back: On the Nature of Seeing*. New York: Simon and Schuster, 1996.

Elkins, James. *The Poetics of Perspective*. Ithaca, N.Y.: Cornell University Press, 1996.

Elkins, James. *How to Use Your Eyes*. New York: Routledge, 2000.

Kemp, Martin. *The Science of Art: Optical Themes in Western Art from Brunelleschi to Seurat*. New Haven, Conn.: Yale University Press, 1992.

Metzger, Philip W. *Perspective Without Pain*. Duluth, Minn.: Northern Lights Books, 1992.

Norling, Ernest. *Perspective Made Easy*. Mineola, N.Y.: Dover, 1999.

Panofsky, Erwin, and Christopher S. Wood. *Perspective as Symbolic Form*. Brooklyn, N.Y.: Zone Books, 1997.

Chapter Thirteen: The Creativity Ethernet

Austin, Robert, and Lee Devin. *Artful Making: What Managers Need to Know About How Artists Work*. Upper Saddle River, N.J.: Financial Times/Prentice Hall, 2003.

Blohowiak, Donald W. *Mavericks: How to Lead Your Staff to Think Like Einstein, Create Like Da Vinci, and Invent Like Edison*. New York: McGraw-Hill, 1992.

Brooks, Frederick P. *The Mythical Man-Month: Essays on Software Engineering*. (2nd ed.) Boston: Addison-Wesley, 1995.

Demarco, Tom, and Timothy Lister. *Peopleware: Productive Projects and Teams*. (2nd ed.). New York: Dorset House, 1999.

Gretz, Karl F., and Steven R. Drozdeck. *Empowering Innovative People: How Smart Managers Challenge and Channel Their Creative and Talented Employees*. Chicago: Probus, 1992.

Poundstone, William. *How Would You Move Mount Fuji? Microsoft's Cult of the Puzzle—How the World's Smartest Company Selects the Most Creative Thinkers*. Boston: Little, Brown, 2004.

Thorne, Kaye. *Managing the Mavericks: Nurturing Creative Talent*. Newbury, U.K.: Spiro Press, 2004.

Chapter Fourteen: Digging Deeper Daily

Blau, Peter M. *Exchange and Power in Social Life*. London, U.K.: Transaction, 1986.

Bolman, Lee G., and Terrence E. Deal. *Reframing Organizations: Artistry, Choice, and Leadership*. San Francisco: Jossey-Bass, 1991.

Bray, John N., Linda L. Smith, Joyce Lee, and Lyle Yorks. *Collaborative Inquiry in Practice: Action, Reflection, and Making Meaning*. Thousand Oaks, Calif.: Sage, 2000.

Fetterman, David M. *Ethnography: Step-by-Step*. Thousand Oaks, Calif.: Sage, 1998.

Heron, John. *Co-Operative Inquiry: Research into the Human Condition*. Thousand Oaks, Calif.: Sage, 1996.

Rubin, Irene, and Herbert J. Rubin. *Qualitative Interviewing: The Art of Hearing Data*. Thousand Oaks, Calif.: Sage, 1995.

Chapter Fifteen: I Think About What I Think, Therefore I Am

Arendt, Hannah. *The Life of the Mind: Thinking*. New York & Orlando: Harcourt Brace, 1972.

Browne, M. Neil, and Stuart M. Keeley. *Asking the Right Questions: A Guide to Critical Thinking*. (6th ed.) Upper Saddle River, N.J.: Prentice Hall, 2003.

Fisher, Alec. *Critical Thinking*. Cambridge, Mass.: Cambridge University Press, 2001.

Kanter, Rosabeth Moss. *Challenge of Organizational Change*. New York: Free Press, 1992.

Kanter, Rosabeth Moss. "Creating the Culture for Innovation." Edoc from amazon.com.

Romain, Dianne Elise. *Thinking Things Through: Critical Thinking for Decisions You Can Live With*. Mountain View, Calif.: Mayfield, 1997.

INDEX

Pfeiffer Publications Guide

This guide is designed to familiarize you with the various types of Pfeiffer publications. The formats section describes the various types of products that we publish; the methodologies section describes the many different ways that content might be provided within a product. We also provide a list of the topic areas in which we publish.

FORMATS

In addition to its extensive book-publishing program, Pfeiffer offers content in an array of formats, from fieldbooks for the practitioner to complete, ready-to-use training packages that support group learning.

FIELDBOOK Designed to provide information and guidance to practitioners in the midst of action. Most fieldbooks are companions to another, sometimes earlier, work, from which its ideas are derived; the fieldbook makes practical what was theoretical in the original text. Fieldbooks can certainly be read from cover to cover. More likely, though, you'll find yourself bouncing around following a particular theme, or dipping in as the mood, and the situation, dictate.

HANDBOOK A contributed volume of work on a single topic, comprising an eclectic mix of ideas, case studies, and best practices sourced by practitioners and experts in the field.

An editor or team of editors usually is appointed to seek out contributors and to evaluate content for relevance to the topic. Think of a handbook not as a ready-to-eat meal, but as a cookbook of ingredients that enables you to create the most fitting experience for the occasion.

RESOURCE Materials designed to support group learning. They come in many forms: a complete, ready-to-use exercise (such as a game); a comprehensive resource on one topic (such as conflict management) containing a variety of methods and approaches; or a collection of like-minded activities (such as icebreakers) on multiple subjects and situations.

TRAINING PACKAGE An entire, ready-to-use learning program that focuses on a particular topic or skill. All packages comprise a guide for the facilitator/trainer and a workbook for the participants. Some packages are supported with additional media—such as video—or learning aids, instruments, or other devices to help participants understand concepts or practice and develop skills.

- *Facilitator/trainer's guide* Contains an introduction to the program, advice on how to organize and facilitate the learning event, and step-by-step instructor notes. The guide also contains copies of presentation materials—handouts, presentations, and overhead designs, for example—used in the program.

- *Participant's workbook* Contains exercises and reading materials that support the learning goal and serves as a valuable reference and support guide for participants in the weeks and months that follow the learning event. Typically, each participant will require his or her own workbook.

ELECTRONIC CD-ROMs and web-based products transform static Pfeiffer content into dynamic, interactive experiences. Designed to take advantage of the searchability, automation, and ease-of-use that technology provides, our e-products bring convenience and immediate accessibility to your workspace.

METHODOLOGIES

CASE STUDY A presentation, in narrative form, of an actual event that has occurred inside an organization. Case studies are not prescriptive, nor are they used to prove a point; they are designed to develop critical analysis and decision-making skills. A case study has a specific time frame, specifies a sequence of events, is narrative in structure, and contains a plot structure— an issue (what should be/have been done?). Use case studies when the goal is to enable participants to apply previously learned theories to the circumstances in the case, decide what is pertinent, identify the real issues, decide what should have been done, and develop a plan of action.

ENERGIZER A short activity that develops readiness for the next session or learning event. Energizers are most commonly used after a break or lunch to stimulate or refocus the group. Many involve some form of physical activity, so they are a useful way to counter post-lunch lethargy. Other uses include transitioning from one topic to another, where "mental" distancing is important.

EXPERIENTIAL LEARNING ACTIVITY (ELA) A facilitator-led intervention that moves participants through the learning cycle from experience to application (also known as a Structured Experience). ELAs are carefully thought-out designs in which there is a definite learning purpose and intended outcome. Each step—everything that participants do during the activity— facilitates the accomplishment of the stated goal. Each ELA includes complete instructions for facilitating the intervention and a clear statement of goals, suggested group size and timing, materials required, an explanation of the process, and, where appropriate, possible variations to the activity. (For more detail on Experiential Learning Activities, see the Introduction to the *Reference Guide to Handbooks and Annuals*, 1999 edition, Pfeiffer, San Francisco.)

GAME A group activity that has the purpose of fostering team spirit and togetherness in addition to the achievement of a pre-stated goal. Usually contrived—undertaking a desert expedition, for example—this type of learning method offers an engaging means for participants to demonstrate and practice business and interpersonal skills. Games are effective for team building and personal development mainly because the goal is subordinate to the process—the means through which participants reach decisions, collaborate, communicate, and generate trust and understanding. Games often engage teams in "friendly" competition.

ICEBREAKER A (usually) short activity designed to help participants overcome initial anxiety in a training session and/or to acquaint the participants with one another. An icebreaker can be a fun activity or can be tied to specific topics or training goals. While a useful tool in itself, the icebreaker comes into its own in situations where tension or resistance exists within a group.

INSTRUMENT A device used to assess, appraise, evaluate, describe, classify, and summarize various aspects of human behavior. The term used to describe an instrument depends primarily on its format and purpose. These terms include survey, questionnaire, inventory, diagnostic, survey, and poll. Some uses of instruments include providing instrumental feedback to group members, studying here-and-now processes or functioning within a group, manipulating group composition, and evaluating outcomes of training and other interventions.

Instruments are popular in the training and HR field because, in general, more growth can occur if an individual is provided with a method for focusing specifically on his or her own behavior. Instruments also are used to obtain information that will serve as a basis for change and to assist in workforce planning efforts.

Paper-and-pencil tests still dominate the instrument landscape with a typical package comprising a facilitator's guide, which offers advice on administering the instrument and interpreting the collected data, and an initial set of instruments. Additional instruments are available separately. Pfeiffer, though, is investing heavily in e-instruments. Electronic instrumentation provides effortless distribution and, for larger groups particularly, offers advantages over paper-and-pencil tests in the time it takes to analyze data and provide feedback.

LECTURETTE A short talk that provides an explanation of a principle, model, or process that is pertinent to the participants' current learning needs. A lecturette is intended to establish a common language bond between the trainer and the participants by providing a mutual frame of reference. Use a lecturette as an introduction to a group activity or event, as an interjection during an event, or as a handout.

MODEL A graphic depiction of a system or process and the relationship among its elements. Models provide a frame of reference and something more tangible, and more easily remembered, than a verbal explanation. They also give participants something to "go on," enabling them to track their own progress as they experience the dynamics, processes, and relationships being depicted in the model.

ROLE PLAY A technique in which people assume a role in a situation/scenario: a customer service rep in an angry-customer exchange, for example. The way in which the role is approached is then discussed and feedback is offered. The role play is often repeated using a different approach and/or incorporating changes made based on feedback received. In other words, role playing is a spontaneous interaction involving realistic behavior under artificial (and safe) conditions.

SIMULATION A methodology for understanding the interrelationships among components of a system or process. Simulations differ from games in that they test or use a model that depicts or mirrors some aspect of reality in form, if not necessarily in content. Learning occurs by studying the effects of change on one or more factors of the model. Simulations are commonly used to test hypotheses about what happens in a system—often referred to as "what if?" analysis—or to examine best-case/worst-case scenarios.

THEORY A presentation of an idea from a conjectural perspective. Theories are useful because they encourage us to examine behavior and phenomena through a different lens.

TOPICS

The twin goals of providing effective and practical solutions for workforce training and organization development and meeting the educational needs of training and human resource professionals shape Pfeiffer's publishing program. Core topics include the following:

Leadership & Management

Communication & Presentation

Coaching & Mentoring

Training & Development

E-Learning

Teams & Collaboration

OD & Strategic Planning

Human Resources

Consulting

What will you find on pfeiffer.com?

- The best in workplace performance solutions for training and HR professionals

- Downloadable training tools, exercises, and content

- Web-exclusive offers

- Training tips, articles, and news

- Seamless on-line ordering

- Author guidelines, information on becoming a Pfeiffer Affiliate, and much more

Discover more at www.pfeiffer.com

Customer Care

Have a question, comment, or suggestion? Contact us! We value your feedback and we want to hear from you.

For questions about this or other Pfeiffer products, you may contact us by:

E-mail: **customer@wiley.com**

Mail: **Customer Care Wiley/Pfeiffer**
10475 Crosspoint Blvd.
Indianapolis, IN 46256

Phone: **(US) 800-274-4434** (Outside the US: 317-572-3985)

Fax: **(US) 800-569-0443** (Outside the US: 317-572-4002)

To order additional copies of this title or to browse other Pfeiffer products, visit us online at **www.pfeiffer.com**.

For **Technical Support** questions call **(800) 274-4434.**

For authors guidelines, log on to www.pfeiffer.com and click on "Resources for Authors."

If you are . . .

A **college bookstore, a professor, an instructor, or work in higher education** and you'd like to place an order or request an exam copy, please contact jbreview@wiley.com.

A **general retail bookseller** and you'd like to establish an account or speak to a local sales representative, contact Melissa Grecco at 201-748-6267 or mgrecco@wiley.com.

An **exclusively on-line bookseller**, contact Amy Blanchard at 530-756-9456 or ablanchard @wiley.com or Jennifer Johnson at 206-568-3883 or jjohnson@wiley.com, both of our Online Sales department.

A **librarian or library representative**, contact John Chambers in our Library Sales department at 201-748-6291 or jchamber@wiley.com.

A **reseller, training company/consultant, or corporate trainer**, contact Charles Regan in our Special Sales department at 201-748-6553 or cregan@wiley.com.

A **specialty retail distributor** (includes specialty gift stores, museum shops, and corporate bulk sales), contact Kim Hendrickson in our Special Sales department at 201-748-6037 or khendric@wiley.com.

Purchasing for the **Federal government**, contact Ron Cunningham in our Special Sales department at 317-572-3053 or rcunning@wiley.com.

Purchasing for a **State or Local government**, contact Charles Regan in our Special Sales department at 201-748-6553 or cregan@wiley.com.

DATE DUE